Russia

A SHORT HISTORY

Russia

A SHORT HISTORY

HELEN GAY PRATT
AND
HARRIET L. MOORE

Illustrated

ISSUED UNDER THE AUSPICES OF
AMERICAN COUNCIL, INSTITUTE
OF PACIFIC RELATIONS

THE JOHN DAY COMPANY

New York

This book is a revised and enlarged edition of
Russia: From Tsarist Empire to Socialism, by Helen
Pratt, published in 1937 by the American Council,
Institute of Pacific Relations. The last two and a
half chapters are by Harriet L. Moore. The Institute
is an unofficial, nonpolitical organization, founded
in 1925, to facilitate the scientific study of the peoples of the Pacific area. It does not advocate policies
or doctrines, and is precluded from expressing opinions on public affairs. Responsibility for all expressions of opinion in this book rests solely with the
authors.

The present book is published on the same day in
the Dominion of Canada by Longmans, Green and
Company, Toronto.

CONTENTS

v

ILLUSTRATIONS

Plates

A section of illustrations from photographs and old prints will be found following page 122

Maps

(All of the maps are by Mary Lee Johansen except for those on pages 34-35 and 200-201.)

Russia

A SHORT HISTORY

RUSSIAN PANORAMA

RUSSIA—what pictures and impressions the name suggests! Old Russia—"holy" Russia, the land of churches—city churches with domes of gold and pillars of lapis—pageantry of ceremonial—magnificent singing—omnipresent village churches dominating the landscape—homes with lighted shrines and holy icons. Vast Russia, the land of plains—slowly moving rivers—the boundless horizon of the steppe—limitless forests—great distances buried in winter snows. Asiatic Russia, the land of "Oriental" despotism—Cossack troops with their whips riding down defenseless groups—diverse peoples—backward cultures. Autocratic Russia, the land of repression—secret police—rigid press censorship—exiles sent to Siberian wastes—political suspects snatched from their homes and sent to unknown destinations. Revolutionary Russia, the land of conspiracy—anarchists—nihilists—secret agitation—assassinations—violence—death. Imperial Russia, the land of contrasts—great estates—grand dukes and princes—palaces—a cultured life of elegance, luxury, and pleasure—a cosmopolitan society at home in every capital of Europe—music—the imperial ballet—the theater. Bearded peasants in embroidered blouses or sheepskin coats—the "dark" people—villages with tiny comfortless houses—poverty—cold—superstition—ignorance—vodka—balalaikas—peasant dances—harvests—famine. The tsar, the center and head of this diverse Russia—"holy," huge, "Asiatic," revolutionary, autocratic, cosmopolitan and cultured, poverty-stricken, ignorant and oppressed, Russia. Soviet Russia—"Red" Russia, the land of Bolsheviks and Communism—workmen living

3

in old palaces—churches converted into museums—"Red" corners instead of shrines—the Five-Year Plan—dictatorship—tractors on the great plains—factories in Siberia—new schools everywhere—technical training. Russia at war—the scorched earth—Leningrad under siege—guerrillas—thousands of tanks—women snipers—Stalingrad, turning point of victory.

Associated with these scattered fragmentary pictures are a few names picked out of the centuries. Genghis Khan—the Mongols—Kiev—the Golden Horde. Moscow, the city of churches—the Kremlin, the walled citadel of the tsars—Ivan the Terrible whose name alone suggests the means by which he strengthened his power. Peter the Great, ordering the erection of St. Petersburg on the northern swamps—Catherine the Great—the Winter Palace—Tchaikovsky—Tolstoy—Chekhov—Gorky. The Red Square—the Red Army—Lenin—Stalin. Each name conveys a picture, perhaps more or less indefinite, but certainly with a suggestion of something different—strange—romantic—cultured—violent—parts of the diverse impressions which make up our fragmentary idea of Russia. Each of these scattered impressions has its significance which can, however, be determined only through building up a more detailed picture in which the different aspects of Russian life may be seen in relation to each other.

In the vast country to which we still refer as "Russia," but whose official name is the Union of Soviet Socialist Republics, the most radical attempt to build a new social and economic order which the world has ever known is now in process. Conditions which existed for centuries in the empire, and which culminated finally in revolutions overthrowing everything of the old which could be cast out, lie behind the developments taking place in the Soviet Union today.

Throughout the history of the Russian empire, social contrasts were marked. Society was divided into the privileged and the unprivileged, and the people of the different levels of Russian life, for all intents and purposes, lived in different worlds. Distinctions still exist in the Soviet Union, but the people enjoying privileges are not the ones who possessed special rights under the empire, and the basis of distinction is different. Among the different worlds in which the people of the empire lived, the peasant world has been chosen for the most detailed treatment here. Although the peasants were largely inarticulate, although they had little to do with the actions of tsars and governments whose policies and deeds form so large a part of the history of Russia as it is usually written, yet they were by far the largest part of the population; they were the broad basis upon which the superstructure of the Russian state rested; from them came a considerable part of the revenues of the state; by them was produced much of the goods consumed in the country; through their labors the more privileged were maintained; from the peasants, the proletarian workers (the propertyless class possessing no means of support except the sale of their labor power), were recruited. The peasants were the only group which survived the revolutions relatively unchanged. Many of the clergy, all of the grand dukes, the princes, the wealthy private merchants, the great landowners are gone; the tsar and the court, with their palaces and estates, are gone. The proletariat, which was very small in 1917, has increased tenfold in numbers, and the conditions of labor, as well as the position of the workers, are so different from what they were under the empire that even the name "proletariat" has lost most of its significance. To the Communist party has gone more power than ever was wielded by the tsar. The peasant class is in process of transformation, but it has been responsible for one of the greatest problems the Soviet Union has had to meet.

The background for the changing conditions of life in

Russia is the geographical setting which underlies and at least partially explains Russian life, ideas, and institutions. Plains, rivers, and forests exerted their influence; long winters, short summers, drought, and rainfall affected the life of the people; isolation from Europe and contacts with Asia and the Near East led to the development of a unique culture. To understand the social and economic conditions of the past, which, in turn, help to explain present-day life in the Soviet Union, it is necessary first to have some idea of this geographical setting.

1. THE RUSSIAN LAND

SOMETHING in the quality of the vast Russian land inspired the whole people with a love for Russia. Even the most oppressed peasant felt this love. "Great is Mother Russia," he said, raising his eyes to the fields he did not own. A peasant poet writes:

> O native country, how beauteous thou art!
> How adorable are
> Thy rye steppes, thy rye people,
> Thy rye sun. Even thy songs
> Smell of soil and rye.

Or again:

> I love thee, native land,
> I adore thy gloomy face,
> Thy fields, thy pine groves,
> And the dense forests in the summer heat.
>
> Beloved country! All that is thine
> Is close and dear to me.
> The forgotten tombs of the fathers,
> The deep silence of the cemeteries . . .
>
> And I, thy son, pursued by fate,
> Am always anxious and grieved,
> For thee alone, country beloved,
> All my life I pray.[1]

Turgenev, the novelist, writes:

Oh, the content, the quiet, the plenty of the Russian open country! Oh, the deep peace and well-being! And the thought

7

comes to me: what is it to all of us here, the cross on the cupola of St. Sophia in Constantinople and all the rest that we are struggling for, we men of the town? [2]

The first and most conspicuous characteristic of the country which inspired such devotion is its size, embracing nearly one sixth of the land of the whole world. By far the largest part of this great area is a plain unbroken by high mountains, lying in general relatively far to the north, extending from the Baltic Sea on the west to the highlands of eastern Siberia, and from the Arctic Ocean on the north to the highlands of central Asia on the south. The low Ural Mountains scarcely break this plain. The chief mountains in the country are in the south—the Caucasus region in the southwest, the Pamirs on the Indian border. The vast plain is divided into belts running from east to west, which differ in climate and in significance to man. In the far north, on the border of the Arctic Ocean, we find the tundra. South of the tundra is the wide forest belt which covers northern Russia and most of Siberia, and south of the forest belt are the steppes, which continue into the plains of Poland and Hungary on the west, and whose unbroken expanse reaches east to Lake Baikal. The fertile steppe finally merges into the deserts of the south. The belts of tundra, forest, and steppe are traversed by rivers which flow north into the Arctic or south into the inland seas, the Black and the Caspian.

The frozen swamps of the inhospitable tundra lie so far to the north that the growing season is but six to eight weeks long, and even in this warmest season of the year the ground is never completely unfrozen. Because of the rigors of the climate, the resources of the tundra have been largely unexplored. Such forms of human life as the tundra has supported have been simple and primitive, the types that subsist upon the reindeer and upon hunting and fishing. The scattered hunters of the tundra have lived outside the framework of Russian civilization; they have been little affected by it and have not influenced it. Under the Soviets the first attempts to conquer the north and to bring the people of the region into the life of the state have been made.

South of the tundra lies the forest belt, in the European portion of which the early people of Russia lived. They erected homes in small clearings, hunted the numerous wild animals of the forests, collected honey and wax, and engaged in very primitive agriculture in the immediate neighborhood of their homes. Later they cleared the southern portions of the European forest and turned to agriculture to support life. When this happened, the forests lost some of their earlier significance in the life of the people, but forest resources continued to be important in the Russian economy. Animals of the forest were hunted for their furs. The forests supplied the building materials—for centuries Russian houses were made of wood, and only a few monasteries, the city churches, and the Kremlin were built of stone or brick. Peasants' huts were crudely made of logs. Most of these primitive structures still exist, and it was only after the November revolution of 1917 that any extensive attempt to house the peasants differently was made. Until the eighteenth century the landowner's manor house was but a larger variation of the peasant's hut. The forests supplied not only the commonly used building materials, but also the fuel so essential to comfort during the long cold Russian winters. Control and utilization of forest resources were important matters affecting the life and welfare of the people, and not infrequently involving conflicting demands of landowner, peasant, and state.

Many of the great writers of Russia have described the beauty of the forests. Gorky interprets their influence feelingly and shows the effect of their peaceful solitude upon people who had little in their lives. For example:

The woods came to meet us like a dark army; the fir-trees spread out their wings like large birds; the birches looked like maidens. The acrid smell of the marshes flowed over the fields. My dog ran beside me with his pink tongue hanging out, often halting and snuffing the air, and shaking his fox-like head, as if in perplexity. Grandfather, in grandmother's short coat and an old peakless cap, blinking and smiling at something or other, walked as cautiously as if he were bent on stealing. Grandmother, wearing a blue blouse, a black skirt, and a white handkerchief about her head, waddled comfortably. It was difficult to hurry when walking behind her.

The nearer we came to the forest, the more animated grandfather became. Walking with his nose in the air and muttering, he began to speak, at first disjointedly and inarticulately, and afterward happily and beautifully, almost as if he had been drinking.

"The forests are the Lord's gardens. No one planted them save the word of God and the holy breath of His mouth. When I was working on the boats in my youth I went to Jegoulya. Oh, Lexei, you will never have the experiences I have had! There are forests on the Volga, too, stretching as far as the Urals. Yes; it is all so boundless and wonderful." . . .

The forest called up a feeling of peace and solace in my heart, and in that feeling all my griefs were swallowed up, and all that was unpleasant was obliterated. During that time also my senses acquired a peculiar keenness, my hearing and sight became more acute, my memory more retentive, my storehouse of impressions widened.[3]

East of the European Russian forests lay the Siberian forest, a land originally very sparsely inhabited by hunting people, a land whose extent and boundaries were long unknown, a land which seemed to belong to no one in particular. Hunters and adventurers from Russia began to penetrate this region as early as the eleventh century. In the sixteenth century the tsar first styled himself the ruler of Siberia, but his control was more a matter of statement than of fact. Government officers were sent into this region, but the penetration of the Siberian forest con-

tinued to be largely a matter of private initiative. Early in
the seventeenth century, Russians had advanced across
Siberia to the Pacific. Because of the nature and location
of the forest belt, and the types of life it could support,
eastward expansion across the forests was different from
southern and eastward movements into the steppe. One of
the chief effects of this eastward northern movement upon
Russian life as a whole is the fact that it eventually involved Russia in Far Eastern disputes and imperialist
aggression which had violent repercussions in Russia itself. But Siberia alone was of relatively little significance
in the lives of the Russian people. It was the property of
the state. Portions of it were granted to private individuals
who exploited the regions under their control, but peasant
colonization of Siberia was not encouraged until late in
the nineteenth century. Siberia was for years the land to
which political exiles and criminals were sent to work in
the mines or to live in distant isolated villages.

South of the forest belt lies the steppe, the great fertile
plain open to the far east, the natural highway along
which countless hordes of nomads swept westward from
Asia. In the fifth century A.D. the Huns under Attila swept
far into Europe, threatening even Rome. At that time the
Russian state did not exist to check the westward movements of the invaders from the steppe. Later, when ancient
Russia was developing as a nation, the nomadic peoples
were still there, a constant threat on its borders; these
tribes pressed in from time to time until, in the eleventh
century, they cut off the city of Kiev on the Dnieper from its
southern route to Constantinople. Then in the thirteenth
century came the last and best-known invasion, that of the
Mongols, who crossed Poland and were finally checked at
the gates of Vienna. They conquered Russia and succeeded
in holding it under very loose control for more than two
hundred years. Not until the fifteenth century did the tide
actually turn. Then the prince of Moscow refused any

longer to submit to Mongol rule, and Russia gradually
pressed first southward into the more fertile lands of the
open plains, and then eastward. The early significance of
the steppe was the fact that it provided an open highway
along which the nomadic peoples of Asia swept in from
time to time, threatening and sometimes overwhelming
everything in their path. The Mongols who came in this
fashion remained long enough to modify Russian life and
institutions. Thus the steppes extending far into Asia were
partially responsible for the "Asiatic" influences which
helped to shape Russian life.

The steppe country is not all alike but is divided into
horizontal belts of varying degrees of fertility. One by one
these belts—until the most southern merges into the desert
—are progressively more fertile than the cleared forest
lands in which Russian agriculture began. The black soil
belt which extends from the Black Sea to Lake Baikal is
very wide, and its deep soils are among the most fertile in
the world. As the economic pressure upon the peasant
cultivator in the north increased, he desired to leave the
poor fields from which he could scarcely wring the payments demanded of him and to move into these richer
lands to the south. Many peasants escaped to these lands—
it was an escape, for they were so bound by debt and obligations that they were not free to move openly. The privileged landowners and the government were unwilling to
allow the peasant to make a new life for himself; steps
were taken to prevent free migrations, to bind the peasant
to the soil, and to create such conditions that the peasant
who settled in the new lands found himself under new
obligations which in turn held him in the same bondage
he had experienced elsewhere. The frontier of servile
agriculture was constantly being extended, but beyond
the borders of the cultivated lands lay some sort of freer
life in the unconquered or partially subdued steppe, a fact
not without its significance in the history of Russia. More

than one social and political uprising had its beginnings in these regions of southern Russia, and attracted, before it was suppressed, the oppressed and discontented peasantry of adjoining lands.

Gogol's description gives the tremendous appeal of the boundless steppe.

The farther they penetrated the steppe, the more beautiful it became. Then all the South, all that region which now constitutes New Russia, even as far as the Black Sea, was a green, virgin wilderness. No plough had ever passed over the immeasurable waves of wild growth; horses alone, hidden in it as in a forest, trod it down. Nothing in nature could be finer. The whole surface resembled a golden-green ocean, upon which were sprinkled millions of different flowers. Through the tall, slender stems of the grass peeped light-blue, dark-blue, and lilac star-thistles; the yellow broom thrust up its pyramidal hand; the parasol-shaped white flower of the false flax shimmered on high. A wheat-ear, brought God knows whence, was filled out to ripening. Amongst the roots of this luxuriant vegetation ran partridges with outstretched necks. The air was filled with the notes of a thousand different birds. On high hovered the hawks, their wings outspread, and their eyes fixed intently on the grass. The cries of a flock of wild ducks, ascending from one side, were echoed from God knows what distant lake. From the grass arose, with measured sweep, a gull, and skimmed wantonly through blue waves of air. And now she has vanished on high, and appears only as a black dot; now she has turned her wings and shines in the sunlight. Oh steppes, how beautiful you are! [4]

South of the steppe lies the desert region, which did not invite Russian settlement, and which was not brought under Russian control until the nineteenth century. The increasing industrialization of the late nineteenth and early twentieth centuries brought a demand for cotton, which the irrigated desert could supply. This development, however, came late in Russian history. Compared with the great mass of the Russian plain, the tropical desert portions are relatively small, though they are economically important.

West of Russia lie the plains of Poland. Between Russia and Poland an almost continual struggle went on for many years for the possession of the southern steppe, which was just as inviting to the people of Poland as to the Russians. Not only did Poland desire the same territory which Russia coveted, but Russia wished control of the Baltic coast so that unrestricted contact with European countries would be possible, and this meant war with the nations controlling the Baltic region. In addition to these reasons for conflict and hostility, the countries to the west adopted Roman Catholicism and developed cultures, institutions, and customs different from those of Greek Orthodox Russia. These countries were both hostile to Russia and alien to it. They acted as a barrier which for years successfully cut Russia from extended contact with Europe, and which forced the country—always exposed to Asiatic influences—to develop in isolation from Europe. The hostile barrier on the west was pierced early in the eighteenth century, when Peter the Great finally gained control of the Baltic coast region. At the end of the same century Poland was divided among Austria, Prussia, and Russia. The expansion on the west and northwest brought bitterly hostile peoples into the Russian empire. Poland particularly resented foreign rule. Out of the centuries of struggle on the accessible plains were born hatreds which showed themselves over and over again in Russian history. The continual fighting resulting from the fact that hostile countries occupied adjacent portions of the open plains was one cause, moreover, for the enserfment of the Russian people.

Over the vast Russian plain, stretching southward from the Arctic to the highlands of central Asia, there is of necessity a variety of climatic conditions, but the greater part of the country lies in relatively cold regions. Leningrad—formerly St. Petersburg, then Petrograd, and once the capital—is directly on the sixtieth parallel of north latitude, a little farther north than Juneau, Alaska. Over most of Russia the winters are long and cold, the summers short and hot. The differences between winter and summer temperatures are, in certain regions in Siberia, the greatest known in the world; at one place winter temperatures of more than 90 degrees below zero and summer temperatures over 90 above have been recorded.

Because of the length of the winters and the comparative shortness of the summers, agricultural workers were for months shut within the narrow walls of their huts. They turned to various handicraft industries which might occupy them during the winter and also provide them with some additional income. Thus the conditions of village life in the long winters were a factor in the development of handicraft manufacture, which was important to the producer and to the country in general, for peasant handicraft industry supplied most of the consumption goods of the Russian empire.

In general the rainfall over the continental plain is slight and irregular. Heavy rains are unknown except in the region near the Black Sea. Agriculture in the fertile steppe was hazardous and uncertain; drought, with all that it meant in terms of famine and suffering, occurred frequently. These facts all helped to make the peasant fatalistic, accepting any misfortune as unavoidable and unescapable. They also strengthened the influence of religion in his life. Religious processions passed through the fields every year; the peasant prayed for rain and for a good harvest, and left the outcome to God, who alone, it seemed, could control the natural elements so important in the life of the people. Recurring drought and famines had other effects—political and economic. At times the peasant was driven to desperation, for in his slender economy there was small margin to support him when the harvest failed. It is significant that many of the chief peasant uprisings and disorders of Russian history have occurred at times of prolonged drought and famine. Drought and famine were important factors leading the Soviet Union, in 1921, to modify its whole economic policy.

The great rivers flowing south across the Russian plain into the Black Sea are very long, and together with their tributaries they provide natural highways for a large part of European Russia. By way of these river highways flowing south the freebooting traders of early Russia found their way to the great city of Constantinople, a more than adequate market for their honey, wax, furs, and slaves. Trade flourished, and the numerous contacts of the Russian merchants and princes with the Byzantine civilization led to their adoption of the Greek Orthodox religion. The Orthodox church brought Byzantine art, architecture, and religious pageantry; it supported Byzantine ideas of autocratic rule, court ceremonial, and the seclusion of the women of the upper classes. It created a separation between Russia and Catholic Europe and thus affected the whole course of developments in Russia. The Greek Orthodox church was one of the most important factors affecting Russian life and institutions, and the fact that it gained its dominant position in the country may be attributed, at least in part, to the simple geographical fact that the Dnieper flows south into the Black Sea. The Volga farther east, over 2,300 miles long, was an internal highway of importance; but since it flows into the inland Caspian Sea, it provided an outlet only for Asiatic trade. The huge rivers of Siberia flow north into the icebound Arctic, and while they were useful highways for the Siberian pioneers and explorers, they did not afford access to foreign countries.

Russia has exceedingly few means of access to the open sea. Its whole northern boundary is formed by the Arctic Ocean, but though most of its ports are icebound for months, Murmansk, warmed by the Gulf Stream, remains open the year round. On the west lies the Baltic, a portion of whose coast line was won for Russia in the eighteenth century. This was taken from Russia at the conclusion of World War I but was regained during World War II. Leningrad remains its greatest port on the west. On the south the Black Sea narrows to the Dardanelles, straits which never have been controlled by Russia. Russia's access to the ocean, by way of the Black Sea and the Mediterranean, is therefore an uncertain affair, depending upon the attitude of the nation controlling the narrow straits through which ships must pass. Far away on the east lies the Pacific, not reached by Russians until the seventeenth century. The port of Vladivostok did not come under Russian control until after the middle of the nineteenth century, and between the centers of production and this distant port lay the unindustrialized area of vast Siberia. The Trans-Siberian railway, begun at the very end of the nineteenth century, made Vladivostok less remote in time; the industrialization of Siberia and the far eastern region under the Soviets makes a Pacific port of more immediate significance. The scarcity of useful ports throughout the greater part of Russia's history helped to isolate the country.

Geographical influences are not, of course, constant throughout the centuries. They change as man gains control over his environment. Soviet scientific expeditions are surveying the resources of the far north; Soviet icebreakers are attempting to conquer the frozen Arctic; new irrigation devices are reducing the danger of recurring drought and are bringing desert areas under cultivation. But the framework of the geographical situation is still the same, and the main factors of this Russian framework are the vastness and the fertility of the steppe area, whose productivity is conditioned by the uncertainty of the rainfall; the relatively northern location of the land mass; the position of the rivers and the direction in which they flow, and the scarcity of useful ports.

2. LIFE UNDER THE EARLY PRINCES, THE MONGOL CONQUERORS, AND THE MUSCOVITE TSARS (9th-17th centuries)

WE KNOW that in 1917 the Russian people rose in revolution, killing their tsar and all the members of his immediate family, as well as many princes, grand dukes, army officers, landowners, and government officials. We have perhaps read descriptions of imperial days and know something of the luxury of those vanished times. In contrast, we realize that the mass of the people lived in wretched huts, that the labor of the "dark" and ignorant millions supported the few who were more fortunately placed. How had these contrasts arisen? The story of the miseries and oppressions endured by the people goes back a thousand years, and the revolutions of 1917 were fed by the accumulated discontents of centuries. To appreciate fully the force and the nature of these discontents, we need to know something of the changing life of the centuries which saw, first, the establishment in Russia of a ruling class possessing all the land and controlling the people on the land; next, the submergence of the country by the Mongol conquerors, whose influence gave a new direction to government; and then, the emergence of the absolute rule of the Moscow tsars and the final enserfment of the mass of the people.

The people who were to be known as Russians lived originally in scattered communities in clearings in the forests which covered most of the region west of the Urals and stretched from the Arctic to the plains north of the Black Sea. These people lived a communal life and maintained themselves by hunting, fishing, bee culture, and very primitive agriculture. They offered no resistance to the Norse invaders of the ninth century who became their rulers. The Norse adventurers traveled down the water roads to the Black Sea and came to the great city of Constantinople, which would buy all the slaves they could bring, and which desired the furs, the wax, and the honey obtainable in the Russian forests. To supply this trade, the adventurers of old Russia went farther on their marauding expeditions, out into the steppe and back into the forest hinterland. Although the princes plundered the rural communities or seized the inhabitants to be sold as slaves, they established no regular form of agricultural overlordship.

Portions of the southern forests were gradually cleared, and the people turned more and more to agriculture to support life. Trading towns, of which Novgorod and Kiev were the greatest, grew up along the rivers. Each town was ruled by a prince who depended upon the armed merchants surrounding him to enable him to maintain his control and to extend the sphere of his trading and freebooting activities. Some of the petty kings succeeded in making their authority recognized over the whole of ancient Russia. Any centralized control of turbulent ancient Russia was, however, short-lived, and the wars between the princes were numerous. The flavor of these wars is given in a twelfth-century folk song called *The Word of Igor's Armament*. For example:

Igor leads his soldiers to the Don: the birds in the thicket forbode his misfortune; the wolves bristle up and howl a storm in the mountain clefts; the eagles screech and call the beasts to a feast of bones; the foxes bark for the crimson shields. O Russian land, you are already beyond the mound! Night is long and murky; the dawn withholds the light; mist covers the fields; the nightingale's song is silent; the cawing of the crows is heard. The Russians bar the long fields with their crimson shields, seeking honour for themselves and glory for the Prince.[1]

In the tenth century "holy" Russia was set on its path when the pagan princes of Russia adopted Greek Orthodoxy. The story of the way the choice of religion was made was not recorded until the twelfth century, when the first Russian historical record, known as Nestor's Chronicle, was compiled by clerical writers. The account may not be regarded as accurate, but it gives an idea of the influence of the pageantry of the Orthodox church upon the Russian people. The chronicler recounts that the ruler Vladimir sent ten men to Bulgaria, to Germany, and to Constantinople, to examine the religion in each country and to report to him. In Constantinople, "the emperor went with them to church, and they were placed in a prominent place where they could see the beauty of the Church, hear the singing and archiepiscopal ministration, and watch the attendance of the deacons in the divine service. They were surprised and marvelled and praised their service." [2] When the envoys returned, they told Vladimir of their other visits, and then of their stay in Constantinople:

"They took us where they worship their God, and we do not know whether we were in heaven or upon earth, for there is not upon earth such sight or beauty. We were perplexed, but this much we know that there God lives among men, and their service is better than in any other country. We cannot forget that beauty, for every man that has partaken of sweetness will not afterwards accept bitterness, and thus we can no longer remain in our former condition." [3]

The church which was chosen by Vladimir was a church of form and ceremony, a church with profound emotional appeal. The bishops appointed from Constantinople

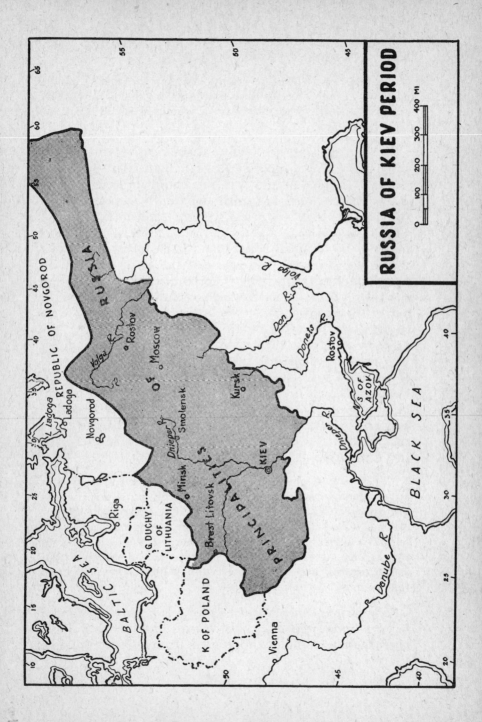

RUSSIA OF KIEV PERIOD

0 100 200 300 400 MI

brought with them those cultural influences which had direct connection with the Orthodox church—the church architecture, the religious painting; they brought church law, and the Roman law necessary for the secular control they exercised, but they brought very little else in the Byzantine cultural heritage and little of the Greek or Roman learning.

The newly converted princes of Russia hastened to show their loyalty to their religion by making grants of land to the clergy, who had control of church matters and of the punishment of offenses not covered by the very slender Russian law of the time. Thus in its earliest days the Russian church was given a position of security, authority, and wealth. Later, when the first well-organized serf-worked estates developed, they were owned by church establishments. As the years went on, the influence of the church penetrated the life of all classes of the people. The church eventually became one mainstay of the autocratic rule of the tsar established in the fifteenth century. Church festivals and fasts marked the passing years, church pageantry supplied beauty otherwise lacking in the lives of so many of the people, and church teaching encouraged the simple faith which helped the oppressed to accept their lot.

While the clergy were beginning to live settled lives on church estates, the princes of Russia continued to depend upon raiding and trading expeditions and to live in their city strongholds until the eleventh century. Then invaders came in from the steppe, occupied the region north of the Black Sea, and prevented Russia from easily reaching Constantinople. Trade with this great city was reduced, and the economic basis of Russian life was undermined. The princes, who had always considered the land they controlled as their own private property, turned to the land for revenue and began to settle down when their trading activities were restricted. They employed slave labor, and also demanded some regular services from the free peasants in return for permission to cultivate some lands for themselves. The free people were made increasingly aware that they lived upon land belonging to an overlord.

By the thirteenth century the principle that the rulers owned the land was well established. The Orthodox church, one of the chief influences which separated Russia from Europe, had attained a position of security and power. Then, in the thirteenth century, the Mongols swept in and overwhelmed Russia, cutting all the country except the northern territory of Novgorod from Europe for over two hundred years. Novgorod was not conquered; it was a member of the Hansa league, and by way of Novgorod, trade goods from Europe reached the regions under Mongol rule; but extensive contacts between Russia and Europe were not maintained.

Who were these Mongols? They were nomadic people from the plains of northeast Asia. Under Genghis Khan and his sons and grandsons they conquered a large portion of the Asiatic continent, including the empire of China. They moved west, seeking to establish a world empire. They were not looking for temporary plunder but for new and permanent sources of revenue. With a technique which they had mastered when they went against the walled cities of China, they laid siege to the Russian towns, the strongest centers of the country and the only places which could offer any organized resistance. Novgorod alone was not captured and destroyed.

After they had reduced Russia to submission, the Mongols proceeded to administer the conquered territory after the manner they had developed in the steppe and modified through contact with the bureaucracy of China. They divided the southern steppe among Mongol leaders, but they permitted Russian princes to remain in possession of their cleared and forest lands. Each prince had to be in-

vested with his authority by the Great Khan himself, who
at this period controlled the whole Mongol empire as a
unit and ruled first from his capital at Karakorum and
later from Cambaluc (on the site of Peiping). When the
portions of the great empire drew apart, Russia was held
under the kingdom of the Golden Horde, which had its
capital at Saray on the Volga.

Since the Mongols desired revenue from their conquered territory, they levied regular taxes, a tax on each
household. At first Mongol officials collected these, but
later the prince of Moscow was permitted to be responsible for the collection and transmission of the taxes. The
Mongols were accustomed to dealing with an organized
hierarchy of officials, not to handling numbers of more or
less independent princes tied together by no recognized
lines of authority. When they observed that the prince of
Moscow was in a position of headship in a certain portion
of Russia, that he was not too powerful, and that he was
entirely subservient to the khan, they chose him to be the
head of the Mongol administrative system in Russia and
thus greatly contributed to the rising power of Moscow.

Between Russians and Mongols there were few contacts.
This was particularly true because the Mongols did not,
to any extent, settle in the regions occupied by Russians,
but lived outside their borders. The Mongols were uncon-
verted pagans, and to the Orthodox Russian a pagan was
a being from another world, with whom there could be
little in common. The Mongols on their part were satisfied with forcing the submission of the princes and re-
quiring the payment of taxes; in all other respects their
rule was lax, and it did not reach into the lives of the
people and interfere with details.

Under these circumstances and conditions Russian
households continued to cultivate their holdings much as
before. Several households might be united in communes
in which the elders exercised various important functions,

planning for the use of meadows and forests, and for raising the taxes and payments which were regarded as a
communal responsibility. Individual landowners made
their own arrangements with the peasant households, de-
ciding what payments should be rendered for the use of
the land. Peasants who met their obligations and were not
in debt to the landowner were free to move about. As the
years passed, the changes which took place in the life of
the people were due not so much to Mongol rule as to the
relations existing between peasant and Russian landowner.

The Mongol rule permitted the consolidation and the
strengthening of the church, already a strong influence in
Russia. The Mongols were liberal and enlightened pagans;
they conducted no campaign against any religion, and in
Russia they conferred special privileges upon the church,
exempting it from obligations and giving it authority not
only in the field of religion but in certain secular matters
as well. The power of the church over the people was
recognized by the practical Mongols, who were willing to
grant the Russian church concessions in the hope of gaining its friendly support. Having no religious prejudices of
their own, the Mongols were unaware of the pious hatred
of the church for the pagan. As a result of the Mongol
policy toward it the church became very powerful.

When we view the period of Mongol domination as a
whole, we see that it was responsible for important changes
in Russian life and thought. Mongol rule introduced and
enforced for two hundred years the idea of a state controlled by one prince who obtained his authority from a
single outside power—in this case, the Mongol khan. It
remained only to restate the Byzantine idea of the divinity
of rulers—to transfer the source of the prince's authority
from the khan to God and reinforce his power with that of
the church—to create the special prestige of the ruler
which was to underlie the new Moscow state. During the
period of Mongol rule the revenues of the state were ob-

tained through a regular system of taxation, a new practice in Russia, where the robber princes had held sway so long and had gained their revenues through plundering and slave trading. Both people and rulers became habituated to these new ideas and practices. The influence of the Mongol administrative system and devices went deep. Throughout the two hundred years of Mongol rule Russia was severed from direct contact with Europe. It knew almost nothing of the culture and learning of medieval Europe; its chief contacts were with Asia.

In the middle of the thirteenth century, when Mongol domination had been established, Moscow was a tiny principality. In 1480, when the prince of Moscow refused longer to submit to the Mongols and styled himself the first tsar of Russia, the Muscovite state extended from the Arctic Ocean south to the steppe, and included the head-waters of the Don and the upper curve of the Dnieper. From there the southern boundary slanted upward, crossing the Ural Mountains on the east about midway. On the west, a curving line drawn from the Gulf of Finland met the Dnieper River on the south. This change in the Muscovite territory had come about gradually, and through various means. The northern forests claimed by the city of Novgorod were penetrated by churchmen whose reputation for holiness attracted followers who settled in communities near by, and grants of land were made by the princes to these religious settlements. People under the rather rigorous rule of Novgorod moved into these communities, which were friendly to Moscow, and which were gradually absorbed by the latter. Novgorod needed the food supplies which could come only from the territory under Moscow rule, and thus Moscow possessed an effective means of subduing the northern city and of gaining the large territory it claimed. Refugees from the regions suffering from Mongol raids, particularly dispossessed and moneyless peasants, came into the Moscow state. Since they had no means of obtaining land for themselves, land-owners loaned them money or equipment in return for service and payments; thus the revenues of the landowners were increased, and they bought more land, while at the same time the peasants were bound by debt to their over-lords. The landowners needed to put themselves under the protection of a strong prince, and they attached them-selves to the ruler of Moscow. The church supported the authority of the Moscow prince and through colonization played its part in extending the Moscow territory. Armed expeditions brought some territories under Moscow rule.

Nearly all the time that this gradual expansion was going on, the prince of Moscow was subservient to the Mongol khan, offering submission and making elaborate presents to him as well as rendering the required taxes. When the Golden Horde began to be weakened by in-ternal dissensions, however, the prince of Moscow went less frequently to Saray and made briefer, less ceremonial visits. Then he dared to cut the required tax payments in half. Finally he refused to send any payments at all. We often read of the casting off of the "Tartar yoke"; this sounds very dramatic, but actually it was a slow and grad-ual process involving both the building up of the Moscow state and the disintegration of the Mongol power.

The Golden Horde was breaking up; three separate kingdoms were in process of formation, Kazan, Astrakhan, and Crimea. Faced with the refusal of the Moscow prince to make the customary submission, the khan collected an army and moved against Moscow; Ivan III (1462-1505) was so reluctant to fight that he contemplated leaving the city, but a bishop openly accused him of being a coward and a betrayer, so he joined his army. After a few skir-mishes Ivan tried to treat for peace. Suddenly the khan's army departed of its own accord, and the khan himself was murdered by Tartar enemies. The Golden Horde was too divided to attempt to move again against Moscow.

Ivan III now felt he could declare himself tsar of Russia.

It should be remembered that the Moscow tsar had been but one of the princes of Russia, though he had become the most powerful. He was surrounded by the boyars, the hereditary princely landowners who had great power over the people on their estates. Ivan III attempted to set himself apart from, and above, the boyars; to that end he adopted the elaborate ceremonial of the Byzantine court. His wife was a Byzantine princess who encouraged him to surround himself with pomp and ceremony. In addition, the church fostered the idea of the tsar's peculiar prestige and authority, derived from God himself. In spite of these devices aimed at making the tsar an autocrat who could not be questioned, the boyars did not give up their power without a struggle. The conflict came to a head under the tsar Ivan IV, known as the Terrible. Under Ivan IV (1533-1582) Russia was involved in almost continual warfare with the remnants of the Mongol kingdoms and with Poland, and for these wars huge numbers of fighting men were needed. Ivan rewarded his military men with estates, carved for the most part out of the newly conquered steppe. These new landowners held their lands directly from the tsar, in return for military service rendered; they were dependent upon the tsar and sufficiently obligated to him so that he in turn was able to seize some of the hereditary lands of the old boyars and to redistribute them among his men. At the end of Ivan's reign the power of the old boyars, as a group, was broken, and autocracy reigned supreme.

Something of the resentment felt by Ivan the Terrible's boyars at the despotism of the Tsar and the warfare in which he embroiled the country is shown in a letter written by one of his generals, who, after a defeat, feared Ivan's wrath and fled to Poland for refuge. From this secure retreat he wrote what he thought.

Why, O Tsar, have you struck down the mighty in Israel?
Why have you delivered to various deaths the generals given
to you by God, and why have you spilled their victorious,
saintly blood in the temples of the Lord, at your royal ban-
quets? Why have you stained the thresholds of the Churches
with the blood of the martyrs, and why have you contrived
persecutions and death against those who have served you
willingly and have laid down their lives for you, accusing good
Christians of treason and magic and other unseemly things,
zealously endeavouring to change light into darkness and to
call bitter what is sweet? [4]

Ivan answered in unsparing terms, justifying his numerous acts of despotism and cruelty, turning the accusation
back upon the boyars who refused to support him uncon-
ditionally.

You say that your blood has been spilled in wars with for-
eigners, and you add in your foolishness, that it cries to God
against us. That is ridiculous! If it has been spilled by the
enemy, then you have done your duty to your country; if you
had not done so, you would not have been a Christian but a
barbarian:—but that is not our affair. How much more ours,
that has been spilled by you, cries out to the Lord against you!
Not with wounds, nor drops of blood, but with much sweating
and toiling have I been burdened by you unnecessarily and
above my strength! Your many meannesses and persecutions
have caused me, instead of blood, to shed many tears, and to
utter sobs and have anguish of my soul.[5]

The old boyars resented Ivan and suffered under his
rule, but the people paid an even higher price for the
extension of the Muscovite state and the consolidation of
the tsar's autocracy. The new military landowning class
created by Ivan laid heavy obligations upon the peasants,
and the oppressed peasants of the old areas were attracted
by the fertile southern steppe. Peasants were still legally
free to move about, providing they were not in debt to the
landowner, but the payments demanded of them had so

increased that large numbers of them were hopelessly
bound by debt. In this situation, escape into the steppe
began, a type of unpermitted migration which was to go
on increasingly, in spite of efforts to curb it. The landowners who had depended upon the labors of the escaped
peasants demanded that they be returned to their villages.
When the peasants fled, the burden of obligation resting
upon those who remained grew heavier, since all payments
were a communal, not an individual responsibility. As a
result peasants in the old areas were willing to join the
hunt after fugitives, for which, at this time, five years were
allowed. If fugitives were not found and returned within
that time, they could not be sent back later.

Those peasants who succeeded in escaping into the
southern steppe were without money or equipment, and
they were obliged, if they remained, to exchange their
labor and produce for loans which would enable them to
cultivate the soil. Thus they became bound by debt to
new landowners. A few peasants fled still farther into the
unconquered steppe, where roamed bands of Cossacks—
frontier warriors, themselves originating from freedom-
loving peasants—and where the Tartars were a terrifying
threat. Life there was anything but secure; and moreover
the boundary of the cultivated lands was being continually pushed farther south and east, and servile agriculture
was absorbing the freer steppe.

A folk song recounting the exploits of the Cossack Yermak who began to conquer Siberia for Ivan the Terrible
gives an idea of Cossack independence, and also of the fear
with which Ivan was regarded. The expedition to Siberia
was Yermak's own idea, and after it was over, he had to
face Ivan with the fact of his unpermitted warfare. The
song gives Yermak's exhortation to the Cossacks before
the expedition, and recounts his interview with Ivan later.

"Ha, brothers, my brave Hetmans!
Make for yourselves boats,

Make the rowlocks of fir,
Make the oars of pine!
By the help of God we will go, brothers;
Let us pass the steep mountains,
Let us reach the infidel kingdom,—
Let us conquer the Siberian kingdom,—
That will please the Tsar, our master.
I will myself go to the White Tsar,
I shall put on a sable cloak,
I shall make my submission to the White Tsar."

.   .   .   .   .

"Oh, thou art our hope, Orthodox Tsar;
Do not order me to be executed, but bid me say my say,
Since I am Yermak, the son of Timofey!
I am the robber Hetman of the Don;
'Twas I went over the blue sea,
Over the blue sea, the Caspian;
And it was I who destroyed the ships;
And now, our hope, our Orthodox Tsar,
I bring you my traitorous head,
And with it I bring the empire of Siberia."
He spoke, the Terrible Ivan Vasilevich:
"I pardon you and your band,
I pardon you for your trusty service;
And I give you the glorious gentle Don as an inheritance." [6]

While the military commanders were being rewarded
with estates, while the Cossacks adventured in Siberia and
received "the glorious gentle Don" as an inheritance, the
peasants who cultivated the soil were being pushed further
into a condition resembling serfdom. Rewarding the "serving people" with land dispersed to the frontier regions
the more prosperous and progressive people who might
have provided a market or who might have taken part in
the extension of trade if they had remained in the towns.
As it was, they lived in distant regions, widely separated.
Each estate tended to produce what it needed and consumed. Russia became largely a collection of self-sufficient

EURASIA
AT THE HEIGHT OF
THE MONGOL DOMAIN

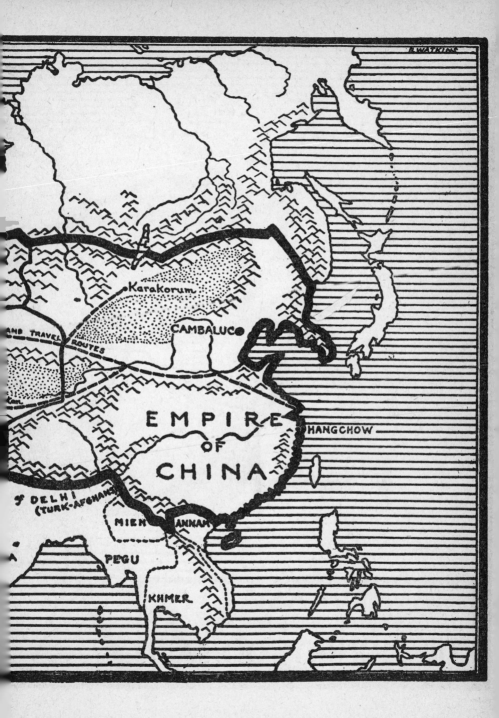

rural communities, with distinct upper and lower classes, and with a small middle class of little importance.

From 1598 to 1613 Russia went through a period of terrible disorder known as the Time of Troubles. The disintegrating influences of this period were so great and widespread that when order was finally restored, the hand of autocracy was tightened upon the people in order to prevent another such disaster in Russian life. The Time of Troubles started with conflicts over the succession; the dynasty which had organized the Moscow state died out, and ambitious and dissatisfied boyars opposed the new tsar, Boris Godunov, who had, they contended, no legitimate right to the throne. Watchful Poland on the west supported and encouraged a pretender who claimed to be Dmitry, the son of the dead tsar Ivan the Terrible, and arranged his marriage to Marina, a Polish princess. The pretender succeeded in making himself tsar; he was recognized as her son by the widow of the dead ruler, his Polish marriage was carried through—but he was attacked and killed by some boyars. The increasing disorder and violence in the capital was reflected in confusion in the country. A terrible famine increased the misery of the people, and landowners seized the opportunity to exploit the starving. A former slave, Bolotnikov, who organized a revolt aimed at seizing everything from the landowners and distributing their possessions among the people, advanced almost to the gates of Moscow. Numerous other uprisings occurred, and Cossacks joined the peasantry against the landowners. At this time, another pretender arose, claiming to be the true Dmitry; he was recognized as her son by the widow of Ivan, and as her husband by Marina! Confusion and disorder spread; in this situation it was not strange that no one knew whom to support or why.

The new pretender was assisted by Polish adventurers. One of the boyars obtained the assistance of several thousand Swedish troops. The king of Poland came to the conclusion that the time was ripe to attack Russia and obtain some of those always coveted lands adjoining Poland. The nobility were so unable to settle upon a candidate to the Russian throne that they even made overtures to the Poles, offering to accept the son of the Polish king as their ruler if he would accept the Orthodox church. King Sigismund of Poland, however, was by now determined to get Russia for himself, and on his own terms. When the Poles had gone so far as to seize and imprison the patriarch of the Church, when they had dared to order that no Russian should be armed, and when they had attacked and burned almost the whole city of Moscow, at last Russia was aroused to effective action against the invaders. A year after the Poles had entrenched themselves in the Moscow Kremlin, they were driven out. The nobility set themselves seriously to work to select a tsar who would receive the support of the country. Young Michael Romanov, indirectly related to the tsar Ivan the Terrible, was chosen.

The country was greatly impoverished. Weeds grew in the uncultivated fields; whole villages were empty. The peasants were ragged, hungry—and powerless. Many of the landowners had been killed in the civil wars, but those who remained were eager to see the peasants put back on their lands; they desired that society be rebuilt exactly as it had been. The new dynasty had no prestige; it chose to create it through meeting the demands of the landowners and thus securing their support. Between 1621 and 1646 the legal period for hunting down fugitive peasants was extended from five to ten to fifteen years, and finally it was abolished altogether so that no escaped peasant could ever be free of the threat of seizure. From 1646 on, each landowner was required to register the names of his peasants. All registered peasants, and any unregistered children of registered parents, belonged to the land and could not voluntarily leave the estate on which they were born. Peasants on private estates, on church estates, or on state lands were thus bound to the soil, and the bondage was made hereditary. They were enserfed. Many of the bonded peasants were sold apart from the land, and in 1675 this practice was confirmed by law. The bonded peasant became legally the property of his owner. Slaves settled on peasant lands were registered with the peasants, and no peasant was allowed to sell himself as a slave in order to discharge a debt or to escape the obligatory payments resting on the peasant class. The earlier distinction between slave and peasant was thus modified, and the two merged into the serf. The only peasants who escaped the net of serfdom were those who lived in the far north, on lands which as yet had not attracted the attention of landowner or state.

Folk songs give an idea of the contrasts of life at this time. For example, the lament of the daughter of Boris Godunov after her father had been killed and the family had been driven from the royal palace suggests the luxury of the "tsarian life" whose passing she mourns:

> And in Moscow the Princess weepeth
> The daughter of Boris Godunov:
> "O God, our merciful Saviour!
> Wherefore is our tsardom perished—
> Is it for father's sinning,
> Or for mother's not praying?
> And you beloved palace halls!
> Who will rule in you,
> After our tsarian life?
> Fine stuffs of drawn lace!
> Shall we wind you around the birches?
> Fine gold-worked towels!
> Shall we throw you into the woods?
> Fine earrings of hyacinth
> Shall we hang you on branches,
> After our tsarian life,
> After the reign of our Father,
> Glorious Boris Godunov?" [7]

The atmosphere of power and ceremony surrounding
the tsar is further suggested in a folk song recounting the
return of the patriarch Filaret, the father of young
Michael Romanov who had been chosen tsar at the end
of the Time of Troubles. The Patriarch had been imprisoned in Lithuania; now he was returning in honor.

> There had come together many princes, boyars, and dig-
>   nitaries,
> In the mighty tsarate of Muscovy:
> They wished to meet Filaret Nikitich
> Outside the famous stone-built Moscow.
> 'Tis not the red sun in its course,—
> 'Tis the Orthodox Tsar that has gone out,
> To meet his father dear,
> Lord Filaret Nikitich.
> With the Tsar went his uncle,
> Ivan Nikitich the boyar.—
> "The Lord grant my father be well,
> My father, Lord Filaret Nikitich."
> They went not into the palace of the Tsar,
> They went into the cathedral of the Most Holy Virgin,
> To sing an honourable mass.
> And he blessed his beloved child:
> "God grant the Orthodox Tsar be well,
> Grand Duke Mikhail Fedorovich!
> And for him to rule the tsarate of Muscovy
> And the holy Russian land." [8]

The attitude of the despoiled people, the spirit of resig-
nation which was fostered in them to make them accept
their lot, is given in this folk song:

"Whither art Thou fleeing?" they spoke in tears to Christ.
"For whom art thou leaving us? Who will without Thee give
us to drink and eat, will clothe us and protect us against dark
night?"

"Weep not, poor people," replied Christ; "Weep not, men-
dicants and homeless and small orphans! I will leave you a

golden mountain, will give you a honeyed river, will give you vineyards, will give you heavenly manna. Only know how to manage that golden mountain, and to divide it among your- selves; and you will be fed and given drink; you will be clothed and covered up in dark nights."

Then John the Theologue retorted: "Hail to Thee, real Christ, King of Heaven! Permit me to tell Thee a few words, and take not ill my words! Give them not a golden mountain, nor a honeyed river, and vineyards. Give them not heavenly manna! They will not know how to manage that mountain; it will be beyond their strength, and they will not taste the manna. Princes and noblemen, pastors, officials and merchants will hear of that mountain, and they will take away from them the golden mountain and honeyed river; the vineyards and heavenly manna; they will divide up the golden mountain among themselves according to their ranks, but the poor peo- ple will not be admitted, and there will be much murder, and much spilling of blood. The poor will have nothing to live on, nothing to wear, and nothing to protect themselves with against dark night; the poor will die of starvation, will freeze to death in cold winter. Give them rather Thy holy name and word of Christ; and the poor will go all over the earth, will glorify Thee, and the Orthodox will give them alms; the poor will be fed and given drink, will be clothed and protected against cold night."

"Thank you, John the Theologue!" replied Christ the Heavenly King. "You have said a sensible word, and have dis- cussed well,—you have taken good care of the poor." [9]

Not all of the people were so meekly submissive as this folk song suggests. Peasant flights and uprisings occurred. In 1670 a Cossack, Stenka Razin, collected a great band of Cossacks and fugitive slaves and serfs and sailed up the Volga, looting, killing landowners, and preaching class war. He was captured and taken to Moscow, where he was publicly executed in the great square before the Kremlin; but the disorders in the Volga region continued for some time after this. To prevent such uprisings in the future, the government increased the authority and power of the landowner over the serf.

During the two centuries in which the Moscow state was consolidated and extended, it will be recalled, a large class of landowners who held their lands in return for military service was created. This class gradually became hereditary, though the hereditary rights of the landowners had never been confirmed by law, and though in principle the members of this class held their lands, serfs, and privileges at the will of the tsar. The church was immensely wealthy and powerful; its great estates allied its interests with those of the other landholders. Its crusading spirit had disappeared—a great change had taken place since the days when holy men penetrating the northern forests were followed by bands of the devout and pious. The mass of the people had been progressively enserfed until they had become the personal property of private landowners, or of the state if they lived upon crown lands. Chiefly upon the serfs rested the burdens of the state. Their labor cultivated the land, their payments supported the landowner, their taxes maintained the state. "The bulk of the Russian people," one writer puts it, "descended into a kind of abyss, of which there is no history." [10]

In such a social structure there was no legal check upon the power of the tsar, who had become an autocrat dispensing privilege and commanding service. The end of the Muscovite period saw the full flowering of "holy," "autocratic," "Asiatic" Russia.

Several of the Muscovite tsars, however, were conscious of the fact that European culture was different from the Russian, and that European techniques were superior to those of Russia. More than one tsar tried to break through the cultural barrier to the west. Ivan the Terrible carried on a lengthy correspondence with Queen Elizabeth of England and tried to persuade that astute and evasive ruler to consent to a Russian alliance. He even attempted to negotiate a marriage with Lady Mary Hastings. Italian and German ambassadors, physicians, engineers, and architects came to Russia—the Moscow Kremlin was built under the direction of Italians. Some trade had been carried on by way of Archangel. But the European contacts of these years were, in general, superficial and fleeting. The western nations were unwilling to enter into close relations with Russia, so vast, so different, and with so inexhaustible a supply of fighting men. They felt safer to remain behind the cultural and diplomatic barrier which kept them free from entanglements with Russia. Russia, however, had reached the point where the western barrier must be forced. Finally Peter the Great (1682-1721) succeeded in accomplishing this, and with his reign the Muscovite period came to an end.

3. SOCIAL CHANGES FROM THE EIGHTEENTH CENTURY TO THE EMANCIPATION OF THE SERFS

WE KNOW that today the Soviet Union is one of the three greatest world powers, possessing the giant industrial establishment that modern nations must have. We have heard that American engineers acted as advisers and directors in the erection of its first huge factories, dams, electrical works, and steel plants. But now the Soviets' own engineers are in charge of the great projects for postwar building. The backward agricultural people of twenty-five years ago has been transformed into an industrial one. This is not the first time in Russian history that the transformation of the country has been attempted. In the eighteenth century Peter the Great determined that the backward "Asiatic" culture of Russia should be Europeanized. The eighteenth and nineteenth centuries witnessed this process, while at the same time the autocracy of the tsar continued unchecked in principle, and until 1861 the mass of the people remained serfs. Europeanization, expansion of Russia to the ocean, autocracy, serfdom—all of these intensified the existing social discrepancies, economic problems, and social unrest. Pressure accumulated in the vast boiler of the country, and no adequate outlets were provided because the government, and the social structure, remained rigid.

Peter the Great's chief concern was to Europeanize Russia—to build an army on European models, to gain unobstructed access to ports from which trade with Europe could pass, to create a navy, to introduce European industrial methods and techniques. He broke every tradition as to how the tsar should live and act. He never lived in the great citadel of the Kremlin. As he moved about over Russia investigating local resources and laying plans for using them to his ends, any hut might be his headquarters. He traveled abroad; on his first visit he went incognito and worked in shipyards as a common laborer that he might best learn the techniques which he wished to bring to Russia. In spite of the informality of his method of life, Peter the Great was no informal ruler—he was an autocrat who knew the extent of his power and used it to the utmost. He forced change upon a reluctant and unwilling Russia.

Though Peter was interested in the people—he was probably the only tsar who ever had any friendly informal contacts with the peasants—the changes which he inaugurated worked out to make the peasants immediately more wretched and to separate the upper classes from the lower classes by new distinctions.

When, for example, Peter determined to create an army trained and equipped in European style, so that he might break through the hostile western barrier, he introduced a system of conscription under which every province had to draft, clothe, equip, and feed the men levied from that district. The new army was a crushing obligation added to the already heavy burden of taxation and service resting upon the population—but after twenty-one years of fighting, Peter won his doorway to Europe. Again, when Peter needed officers for his new army, and government officials for the elaborate administrative system which he copied from various countries of Europe, he gave rank to the men in the new offices regardless of their birth, demanded from them the service of the best years of their lives, and forced their sons to be trained for the same service. In return, while exacting all this, he recompensed the state officers with crown lands and the peasants living on these lands, or with newly enserfed previously free people from the far north. He increased the autocratic power of the landowner by permitting him to take serfs from the land and use them as household servants. When Peter tried to break the power of the church by secularizing church lands, he converted the church estates into state properties which, together with the serfs on these lands, could be transferred to private owners. When Peter wished to encourage the development of industry, he not only granted government subsidies to members of the nobility who would undertake to manage industrial enterprises, but he transferred state serfs from the land and gave them to factories. These wretched people came to be known as "possessional serfs"; they were owned in heredity, to be exploited in industrial work. When Peter needed new revenues for his undertakings, he levied a poll tax, which replaced the previous tax on land, and in order that this new obligation might not be evaded he caused a rigorous census to be taken. Peasant life soon became so unbearable that, in spite of the laws binding them to the soil, thousands of the peasants attempted to escape. Peter then made escape more difficult by forbidding any peasant to leave his owner's land without a passport issued only to heads of households. No other member of the family could move from the estate except in the company of the head of the household bearing a passport. Anyone without a passport was considered a fugitive and a criminal and was treated as such. Thus Peter's changes fell heavily upon the people.

When Peter insisted that the Muscovite nobility copy European styles of dress and manners, the change appeared a superficial one. In addition he demanded, however, that the gentry be educated along European lines, and he took education from the sole control of the church. As the upper class, trained in secular schools, came more and more in contact with European thought, the distinction between privileged and unprivileged was intensified by a difference in culture, as well as in other aspects of life, since no secular schools were available for the masses for more than a century after Peter's death. When Peter changed the system of control of the church by abolishing the patriarchate, the ancient religious office which ruled the church, and substituting for it the Holy Synod appointed by the tsar and of which the most influential member was the procurator, a layman responsible only to the tsar, he made the church a department of the state. The upper clergy under these conditions could be no more than an instrument of the state. The church service continued to offer the pageantry, beauty, and emotional appeal which had so great an influence upon the people, but the church organization necessarily became the tool of the autocracy. Thus when intellectuals, as a result of their contacts with European thought, began to question autocracy, they questioned the church as well. In the villages, on the other hand, the relations between the lower clergy and their parishioners were but little affected by the change in the church organization. The peasants continued to be humbly religious; their faith was a part of their lives. The village clergy taught the people "tsarism" and inculcated devotion to the ruler; this was their function in the state-controlled organization, and their teaching on this matter, as on others, was not questioned by the devout peasants. Thus some of Peter's changes eventually further separated the nobility from the lower classes.

When Peter died, the bishop of Novgorod said in his eulogy, "O Russia, seeing what a great man has left you, see also how great he has left you!" Whether or not Russia was "great" at Peter's death, certainly in the following years the tendencies he had set in motion gathered momentum and Russia was definitely changed. Peter's efforts to Europeanize the upper classes had not, in his lifetime, produced any very profound change in the life, tastes, and outlook of this group. But by the middle of the eighteenth century the nobility were freed from compulsory state service and were at liberty to enjoy life. They were increasingly attracted by European culture. They built city and country residences copied after the palatial homes of European nobility. They began to be interested in the theater of Europe, a form of art and entertainment hitherto undeveloped in Russia. They learned European languages, especially French, and often ceased to speak Russian in their homes. Particularly in the time of Catherine the Great (1762-1796), who was herself a German in touch with European thought, the privileged class became interested in the intellectual speculations which permeated eighteenth century Europe. Such speculations were very stimulating to Russians who had never before pondered such matters as the function of the state in an ideal society, the place of the church, the rights of man, and the meaning of freedom. Under the stimulus of European thought, some of the nobility became increasingly skeptical in outlook; their allegiance to the church became more a polite formality than the expression of sincere belief. The wealthier nobility left their estates for long periods and spent much time in the cities, where they could enjoy the society of others interested in the same things. The separation of the upper classes from the mass of the people had become cultural as well as economic. The nobility enjoyed what has been called their "Golden Age."

When, in the nineteenth century, the great writers of Russia began to picture Russian life, some described the cultured Russian in satirical terms. Turgenev (1816-1883) —a nobleman who spent much of his life abroad—suggests in one sentence the preoccupation with European culture:

Litvinoff immediately recognized them for Russians, although they were all talking in French . . . because they were all talking in French.[1]

He describes the cultured young man of Petersburg society:

The young Vladimir Nikolaevich spoke excellent French, good English, and bad German. That is just as it should be. Properly brought up people should of course be ashamed to speak German really well, but to throw out a German word now and then, and generally on facetious topics—that is allowable: "c'est même très chic," as the Petersburg Parisians say. Moreover, by the time Vladimir Nikolaevich was fifteen, he already knew how to enter any drawing room whatsoever without becoming nervous, how to move about in an agreeable manner, and how to take his leave exactly at the right moment. . . . He was cordially received everywhere, for he was very good looking, easy in manner, amusing, always in good health, and ready for anything. . . . Where he was obliged, he was respectful; where he could, he was overbearing. Altogether an excellent companion, *un charmant garçon*. The Promised Land lay before him.[2]

The elaborate governmental organization devised by Peter became more complicated; it evolved into a bureaucracy with large numbers of officials of all grades. At the top were powerful officers of the state with authority over their subordinates, and so on down the scale until the last minor clerk was reached. The subservience to superiors which permeated the Russian bureaucracy was delineated most successfully in the play *The Inspector General* by Gogol (1809-1852). In this play the officials of a distant town hear that an inspector general from Petersburg is coming, and they are terrified. One of them remarks, "It makes me tremble just to be in the room with a man one grade above my rank." The mayor says, "Until now, praise God, they have prowled around other provinces. Now our time has come. God, what a moment!"

As the play goes on, an impecunious youth staying in the village inn is taken for the inspector general, and all the officials and townspeople hasten to offer him bribes and subservience to gain his favor. The mayor takes him to his home; great dinners are given for him. One landowner approaches him with this request:

When you go back to Petersburg, say to all those great gentlemen that you know so intimately, those Senators and Admirals and Ambassadors—please say to them, "Do you know, Your Excellency" or "Your Highness," as the case may be—"in such and such a town there lives a man called Bobchinsky." Just say that. "There lives a man called Bobchinsky." I would like to know I have been mentioned to those great people.

Everyone bribes the supposed inspector general, even though the mayor earlier had reproached the judge for taking bribes.

Judge: I admit I take bribes, but what sort of bribes? Puppy dogs, that's all. Now there's no sin in taking puppies.
Mayor: It's the same thing. The sin is in the bribe, not in the puppy.[3]

The restricted life of the minor clerks who filled the offices of the bureaucratic government is presented in Gogol's short story *The Cloak*. Discomfort, ridicule, privation make little difference to the clerk who is described, but the cold St. Petersburg winter finally forces him to purchase a new cloak to replace his thin, patched, ancient one. For months he deprives himself of food and warmth to secure the necessary sum for the cloak, and finally he succeeds in obtaining the new garment. He wears it to the office where it attracts a great deal of comment, and it is proposed to have a celebration in honor of the new cloak. The little clerk goes out into a strange world that night, and as he returns home late, his cloak is stolen. The treasure of his life has disappeared; he tells of his loss at the office, he informs the police, but he gets no attention and no sympathy. Finally he is taken suddenly ill and dies.

And St. Petersburg is left without Akaky Akakiyevich, as though he had never lived there. A being disappeared, who was protected by none, dear to none, interesting to none, . . . A being who bore meekly the jibes of the department, and went to his grave without having done one unusual deed, but to whom, nevertheless, at the close of his life, appeared a bright visitant in the form of a cloak, which momentarily cheered his poor life, and upon him, thereafter, an intolerable misfortune descended, just as it descends upon the heads of the mighty of this world.[4]

The type of society which flourished upon serfdom is satirized in Gogol's greatest work, the novel *Dead Souls*. In this story an enterprising young man decides to travel about Russia, buying up the "dead souls"—those registered peasants who have died since the last census, and who are thus technically still among the living. He, in turn, plans to borrow money on these fictitious possessions and accumulate funds to buy some serfs of his own. He is obliged to develop a technique for dealing with the minor officials of the countryside, and here again we are given a picture of the Russian officialdom. For example:

The newcomer set off to make calls upon all the dignitaries of the town. He paid his respects to the governor. . . . Then he went to the deputy governor's, then visited the public prosecutor, the president of the court of justice, the police-master, the spirit tax contractor, the superintendent of the government factories. . . . He even called to show his regard for the inspector of the medical board and the town architect. . . . In conversation with these potentates he very skilfully managed to flatter every one of them. To the governor he hinted, as it were casually, that one travelled in his province as in Paradise, that the roads were everywhere like velvet, and that governments which appointed wise rulers were worthy of the greatest praise. To the police-master he said something very flattering about the town police; while in conversation with the deputy-governor and the president of the court . . . he twice said by mistake, "Your Excellency," which greatly gratified them.[5]

In the years following the reign of Peter the Great, the changes which he initiated were reflected not only in the Europeanization of the upper classes and the crystallization of the government bureaucracy but also in other matters as well. The opening up of Russia to Europe, with the consequent development of trade and industry, led inevitably to foreign wars. With an agricultural system backward not only as regards technique but also as regards the serfdom on which it was based, Russia had to look for new lands in order to increase agricultural produce for the export trade. Also, in a country of serfs, the home market was small, and Russian industry, backward though it was, developed faster than the market. Russia must therefore have new lands to exploit. Each attempt at territorial expansion meant a war. Russia became more involved in European politics and its desire for political and strategic territorial gains increased. The internal unrest of the country was intensified as war followed war. Finally Russia was led inevitably to participation in the First World War, and to the final explosion which blew the lid off that long-suffering country.

Meanwhile, in 1733 fifty thousand Russian troops were sent to Poland; in 1735 Russia, Austria, and Persia made war on Turkey; from 1757 to 1762 Russian troops were fighting in Prussia; in 1772-1773 Prussia, Austria, and Russia divided a portion of Poland; in 1773 Russia was at war in Turkey, and the territory under Russian control was extended to the Caucasus; in 1787 another war began with Turkey, to continue until 1791. This time, Russia had gained the Crimea. In 1791 the scene of war shifted again to Poland, and a second partition of Polish territory followed; in 1794 the Poles who resisted the seizure of their lands were defeated and the third partition erased Poland from the map; it had been absorbed by Russia, Austria, and Prussia. After the French Revolution and the rise of Napoleon, Russia joined Austria and England against the Napoleonic armies. Russians fought on many of the battlefields of the Napoleonic wars; Russia itself was invaded in 1812, when Napoleon reached Moscow, saw the city fired before his eyes, and set out on his historic and disastrous retreat. In 1827 Russia, England, and France were at war with Turkey, and the following year Russia alone opposed Turkey. In 1849 a Russian army forced the Hungarians to accept the rule of the Hapsburg emperor of Austria. In 1854 Russians fought the British, French, Sardinians, and Turks in the Crimean War, which proved most disastrous to Russia. Russia's doorway to Europe proved an open sesame to international wars and inevitable conflicts.

Expansion eastward reached across the Pacific into Alaska in Peter's time. In 1859 the Amur and Ussuri valleys, including the port of Vladivostok, were obtained from China through a treaty. The only portion of Asia yet to be added to the Russian empire was central Asia, though the Russian influence was later to be extended in territory belonging to the Chinese empire, notably Manchuria. By the middle of the nineteenth century imperial Russia had, with these exceptions, reached its greatest extent, and many explosive forces had gathered strength.

Because the Russian empire was geographically a unit, it is sometimes forgotten that this empire included within it numbers of different races and nationalities, and regions which were at first regarded as dependencies and administered as such. The government was interested in securing revenue from its new territories. It permitted the colonial dependencies to retain their native customs, languages, and institutions, and even allowed them a measure of self-government so long as they met the financial and military demands of Russia. Not until the end of the nineteenth century did the government modify this policy and attempt forcibly to Russianize the different peoples, races, and nationalities included in the outlying portions of the empire.

The industrial enterprises stimulated by Peter, through the granting of subsidies and serfs to the managers of the establishments, had a somewhat checkered career in the years following Peter's reign. The government did not pursue a consistent policy with regard to subsidies and labor; sometimes it placed restrictions upon the use and acquisition of possessional serfs, and sometimes it removed them. It tended to demand that those factories using the labor of possessional serfs supply the government with the cloth needed for military uniforms, or with other materials they manufactured, and to fix the price to be paid the factory owner. Under these paternalistic and artificial conditions industry did not develop naturally.

Industrial establishments which employed "free" labor increased in number. Such "free" labor was not free, but it was recruited from among those peasants who were allowed to leave estates and to work in factories provided they remitted a portion of their earnings to their owners. "Free" workers of this type could not be regularly depended upon since they might be recalled to the estate at any time. Merchants, who were seldom permitted to acquire possessional serfs, who owned no field serfs since they were not members of the nobility, and who were largely dependent upon such "free" workers as they could secure, could gain but a slight foothold in large industrial enterprise. Since the market for manufactured goods was slender and the mass of the people could afford to buy only the less costly articles produced by means of handicraft industry, merchants turned to the encouragement of handicraft manufacture. They supplied the peasants in the villages with raw materials and paid them for their labor. The goods manufactured under these conditions proved a successful competitor to articles made in the factories, and the merchants became prosperous. Because of

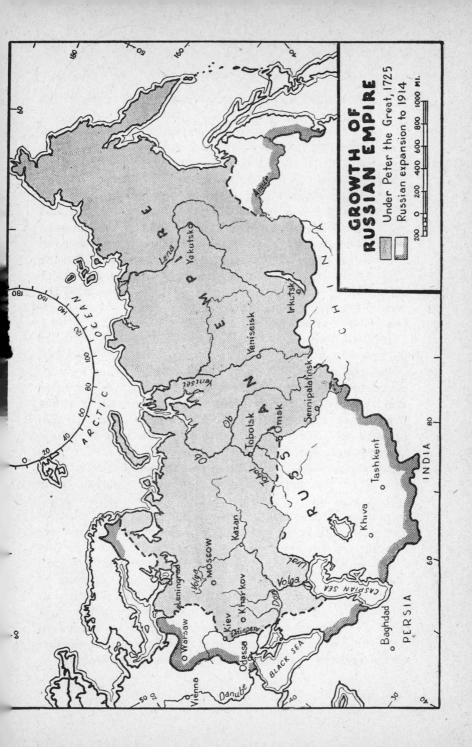

GROWTH OF
RUSSIAN EMPIRE

Under Peter the Great, 1725
Russian expansion to 1914

200 0 200 400 600 800 1000 MI.

all these conditions, and because serf labor in factories was always unwilling and comparatively inefficient, Russian factory industry did not develop to any great degree until after the emancipation.

While the nobility were enjoying their golden age and the merchants were becoming prosperous and living comfortable lives in their own social circle, the people were having exactly opposite experiences. General edicts were passed from time to time announcing that the serf should not be treated with undue cruelty; but at the same time, no serf was permitted to complain of harsh or cruel treatment which he had received. When serfdom reached its climax in the seventeenth and eighteenth centuries, custom—even law in some cases—permitted the landowner to change and reduce the allotments of land cultivated by the peasants for themselves; to order the serf beaten; to take him from the land and put him into household service; to seize any possessions the serf had accumulated; to restrict him from earning money through refusing him permission to leave the estate to engage in any kind of wage labor elsewhere; to sell him apart from the land and apart from his family; to dictate the serf's marriage; to increase the money dues or labor payments which the serf paid; to require him to work continually in the manorial fields during planting and harvest, leaving him no time to cultivate his own holding; to force him to work in the mines or factories. State serfs were a little better off than privately owned serfs in that they were not subjected to as much personal interference; but they were more frequently sent to the government mines and industrial establishments, or transferred entirely into the possession of a factory.

Such conditions of misery and oppression led to the greatest peasant uprising of Russian history. At the end of the eighteenth century, Pugachev, a Cossack, gathered a force of Cossacks and of serfs from the mines of the Urals, and defeated the troops first sent against him. Many of these troops, peasants themselves, deserted to his side, and numerous peasants from estates along the Volga joined him. The important city of Kazan was captured and burned. The uprising was then directed against the land-lords of all eastern Russia; Pugachev encouraged his fol-lowers to seize the landlords and kill them, and to take the land. The uprising developed into a revolt against the intolerable oppression of the landowning class and was marked by great violence and cruelty.

The famous writer Pushkin (1799-1837) wrote a short novel, *The Captain's Daughter,* based on this rebellion. It may not be regarded as historically accurate, but even a few lines from this give the spirit of the uprising. For ex-ample, Pushkin recounts that when Pugachev's men were gathered in an inn, their leader asked them to sing his favorite song. They sang:

> Four in number were my comrades bold:
> My first trusty comrade was the dark night,
> And my second true comrade—my knife of steel,
> And my third was my faithful steed,
> And the fourth one was my stout bow,
> And my messengers were my arrows sharp.
> Then our Christian Tsar will thus speak to me:
> Well done, good lad, thou peasant's son!
> Thou knowest how to rob and to answer for it,
> And a fine reward is in store for thee—
> A mansion high in the open plain,
> Two pillars and a cross beam I grant to thee.[6]

Pushkin describes the end of the rebellion, and ana-lyzes what such uprisings must mean in Russia:

I will not describe our campaign and the end of the Pugat-chev war. We passed through villages pillaged by Pugatchev and could not help taking from the poor inhabitants what the rebels had left them.

The people did not know whom to obey. There was no law-ful authority. The landowners were hiding in the forests.

Bands of brigands were ransacking the country. The chiefs of separate detachments sent in pursuit of Pugatchev who was by then retreating towards Astrakhan, arbitrarily punished the guilty and the innocent. The provinces where the conflagration had raged were in a terrible state. God save us from seeing a Russian revolt, meaningless and merciless! Those who are plotting impossible violent changes in Russia are either young and do not know our people, or are hard-hearted men who do not care a straw about their own lives or those of other people.[7]

Revolt, however "meaningless and merciless," was nevertheless inevitable in a country in which, as one writer says, about "nineteen and one-half millions of persons stood bondaged to the landlords in 1797, while the state peasantry numbered about fourteen and one-half millions—some thirty-four millions altogether, in a total population of thirty-six. The peasant millions were hardly likely to forget the 'Golden Age of the Russian Nobility'— but they would perhaps remember it by some other name."[8]

In the years just preceding the emancipation, serf poets expressed two different types of reaction: hatred of bondage and of the conditions of the life they were forced to lead; or endurance of their fate—even joy in the life of the land. For example, the poet Shevchenko (1814-1861), who spent the greater part of his life in bondage or in prison, wrote:

> Bondage is hateful, drear, and bad
> To live free and asleep, more hateful still.
> My youth of toil, tears, silent pain
> Long past, before me reappears! . . .
> My youth comes back—then I despair![9] . . .

In contrast, Koltsov (1808-1842) expressed the simple faith of the agricultural peasant, his joy in the beauties of the land:

> With a silent prayer
> Will I plough and sow.

Bring me, O Lord,
Bread, my riches!
Like God's guest, on all sides,
Smiles the glad sun;
The light breeze passes o'er the fields,
Rustling the golden corn
In a shining pathway.[10] . . .

The peasant lived in a world apart. He was suspicious of everyone, even of his own neighbors, and he regarded members of other classes as beings with whom he had nothing in common. Dostoievsky (1822-1881), the great novelist, expressed this clearly in *The House of the Dead,* the story of his own experiences as a political prisoner. Though he worked side by side with the peasant prisoners, though he wore the same fetters, ate the same food, slept on the same boards, endured the same privations, restrictions, and regulations, he was not accepted by the peasant prisoner as a comrade. After an attempt to get better food from the prison authorities, the peasant remarked to the political prisoner:

"But why should you make a complaint?" he asked, as though trying to understand me. "You buy your own food."

"Good heavens! But some of you who joined in it buy your own food too. We ought to have done the same—as comrades."

"But—how can you be our comrade?" he asked in perplexity.

I looked at him quickly; he did not understand me in the least, he did not know what I was driving at. But I understood him thoroughly at that instant. A thought that had been stirring vaguely within me and haunting me for a long time had at last become clear to me, and I suddenly understood what I had only imperfectly realized. I understood that they would never accept me as a comrade, however much I might be a convict, not if I were in for life. . . . But I remember most clearly Petrov's face at that minute. His question, "how can you be our comrade?" was full of such genuine simplicity, such simple-hearted perplexity. I wondered if there were any irony, any malicious mockery in the question. There was nothing of the sort; simply we were not their comrades and that was all.

You go your way, and we go ours; you have your affairs, and we have ours.[11]

It was not alone their status as serfs which set the peasants apart. They actually lived under different rules of life than the other members of Russian society. Lands were allotted to villages, not to individuals; taxes and payments to landlords were a communal responsibility. In by far the largest number of the communes, the plowland was redivided at intervals; these communes were called repartitional. The time and method of redividing were not set; they varied according to local custom. Elected village elders in these communes divided the allotted plowlands, giving each household a strip of land, or several strips, in each of the different fields, depending on the size of the household. The households in the rest of the communes held their original holdings in heredity, and there was no redivision of plowland; these communes were known as hereditary. In all types of communes, meadows, pastures, and forest were used in common by all the households, under such conditions as the village elders might determine. The elders also set the time for planting and harvesting in each field, thus virtually determining the crops to be sown by the households on their strips. The head of the household decided just what labor should be performed by the different members of his family, in somewhat the same manner, and with the same authority, as the village commune divided the fields and planned for their cultivation.

Serfdom reached its climax in the eighteenth century, and from that time the story of the classes of Russian society took a somewhat different turn. In 1861 the serfs were emancipated. Emancipation was not, however, a sudden dramatic and liberal gesture. For forty years before emancipation finally came, the government took steps in that direction. For example, in the years 1811 to 1819 the serfs in the Baltic provinces were freed, but they were freed without land, so that they became either hired agri-

cultural workers or industrial laborers. After the Baltic
serfs were freed, Russians argued about whether the serfs
should be freed, and under what conditions—should they
be allowed lands for themselves, or should they not? What
should be done to safeguard the interests of the landlords?
At this time, however, the problems were regarded as
theoretical, not as practical ones which must be faced. In
1826 the tsar Nicholas I appointed a commission to study
the question of peasant reforms. A few years later he created a new office whose business it was to attend to the
welfare of the crown peasants and to improve their conditions of life. Better officials were chosen to administer the
affairs of the crown peasants, and schools were established
for them. Some legislation was enacted which benefited
the privately owned serfs in certain localities. For example, it was made obligatory in one section of Russia for
the landlord to follow a certain set schedule of payments
in making demands upon the serfs, and no landlord in this
region could arbitrarily increase these dues. In 1797 the
sale of serfs apart from the land was forbidden in one
region. In 1833 and 1847 the sale of separate members of
a serf family was forbidden; but this law was not enforced
to any degree. In 1827 a law was enacted setting the minimum allotment of land for each male serf.

Legislation tending to improve the conditions of some
serfs was only one sign of coming emancipation. In addition there was evidence that some among the privileged of
Russia felt keenly that the conditions under which the
people lived must be improved. Not all landlords were
tyrants; many had the kindest of personal relations with
their serfs and considered their welfare. Some landlords
voluntarily freed their serfs; some established schools for
them. The growing class of intellectuals who found no
active place in Russian life, who felt frustrated by the
restrictions of the autocracy, and who, in contact with
European life, became critical of Russian institutions
found in literature an outlet which in turn had its influ-

ence upon Russian affairs. For example, one of Turgenev's early works, *A Sportsman's Sketches,* played no small part in arousing emotions which hastened the emancipation of the serfs. The sportsman, traveling about on his hunting expeditions, meets and describes different serfs, villagers, landowners; each person is described against the background of the Russian countryside; each description shows the hand of a great artist sensitive to the whole of his surroundings. In his descriptions of individuals Turgenev criticized the whole social organization. For example, there is the sketch entitled "Yermolai and the Miller's Wife." The miller's wife had been a house serf, removed from her village and made a house servant when she was fifteen years old. Her mistress, described as fat, sentimental, tearful, and spiteful, refused to employ married maids, and when Arina, after several years of faithful service, requested permission to marry, her lover was sent to the army, and her master immediately ordered that "her hair should be cut off, she should be dressed in sackcloth, and sent to the country." The miller bought her because she could read and write and would be useful to him. Arina, born a serf, must accept whatever was decided for her. The sportsman was acquainted with her previous owners and asked the peasant accompanying him on his hunting expedition:

"She doesn't seem well?" . . .
"I should think not! Tomorrow, I say, we shall have good sport. A little sleep now would do us no harm."
A flock of wild ducks swept whizzing over our heads, and we heard them drop down into the river not far from us. It was now quite dark, and it began to be cold; in the thicket sounded the melodious notes of a nightingale. We buried ourselves in the hay and fell asleep.[12]

Thus, without comment, Turgenev conveys not only the plight of the serf, but the indifference of other serfs to the sufferings which were so common.

The main cause for emancipation was, however, not sympathy but the growing conviction that servile labor was not productive enough to meet the increasing demands of the modern world. When landowners lived on their estates, and the labor of the serfs produced everything consumed by the manor, the lord of the manor was relatively well off. But when the landowner wished to live in cities, to travel abroad, to buy the manufactured products of other countries, to build palaces and to accumulate art treasures—his income proved insufficient for these demands. Many landowners became poorer and poorer; many were heavily in debt. The landlord who took over more of the manorial land for his own use and raised crops to sell found transportation inadequate for extensive and profitable marketing. The traditional methods of cultivation were so wasteful and backward that the rate of yield from Russian lands fell much below that of more advanced countries. The landowner who wished to engage in large-scale agriculture became convinced that the hiring of free labor would prove more profitable than the continuation of the servile system.

The tsar Alexander II, who followed Nicholas I, was determined on emancipation. He set his officials to work out a plan by which it might be accomplished. All the complicated questions of differing conditions and varying arrangements between landlord and serf had to be considered. Eventually, however, a plan was worked out, and in 1861 all the serfs on the private estates were declared free by Alexander II, the "Tsar Liberator," while in 1863 and 1866 legislation designed to free the majority of the state serfs was enacted.

Throughout the years we are considering, the autocracy of the tsarist government was maintained unchanged. When Russians came in contact with European thought, many of them were impressed with the liberal political institutions which were discussed, and developed, in western Europe. Revolutionary movements different in nature from the popular uprisings against oppression which had occurred earlier, and which continued in the nineteenth century, began. The first political uprising, known as the Decembrist movement, occurred in 1825 and is chiefly significant because it typifies in some ways the revolutionary movements which followed it. In the first place, it involved very few people; it was brought about through the efforts of a few idealists among the younger officers of the army who dreamed of a new Russia and thought that constitutional government might be a step in that direction. Second, the aim of the movement was not understood even by the soldiery who were used by these officers in the uprising; it is reported that the men thought that "Constitution" was the name of the wife of Constantine, whom they were trying to make tsar at the time. Third, the leaders were arrested, imprisoned, and either executed or exiled, and repression of revolutionary activities and thought followed the uprising. The political revolutionary movements of the nineteenth century all showed these characteristics: relatively few people were involved; little popular understanding was aroused; the participants were severely punished; the revolutionary movement was driven underground; repressive measures were used by the government to prevent new outbursts. These measures affected many other people, because they included the censorship of the press, the activities of the secret police, the restriction of the expression of opinion, and the strict supervision of the curricula of schools and universities.

The writer Dostoievsky, who was arrested because he was present when a revolutionary document was read, was tried and sentenced to death for this crime. His own words describe more vividly than any others can the way in which the condemned were reprieved, and sent to exile; they give an idea of the autocratic methods which were employed against so many. Dostoievsky was writing a letter of farewell to his brother.

Brother, my precious friend! All is settled! I am sentenced to four years' hard labour in the fortress (I believe of Orenburg) and after that to serve as a private. Today, the 22nd of December, we were taken to the Semionov Drill Ground. There the sentence of death was read to all of us, we were told to kiss the Cross, our swords were broken over our heads, and our last toilet was made (white shirts). Then three were tied to the pillar for execution. I was the sixth. Three at a time were called out; consequently, I was in the second batch and no more than a minute was left me to live. I remembered you, brother, and all yours; during the last minute, you, you alone, were in my mind. . . . Finally the retreat was sounded, and those tied to the pillar were led back, and it was announced to us that His Imperial Majesty granted us our lives. Then followed the present sentence. . . .

I was told, dear brother, that today or tomorrow we are to be sent off. I asked to see you. But I was told that this was impossible; I may only write you this letter; make haste and give me a reply as soon as you can. I am afraid that you may somehow have got to know our death sentence. From the windows of the prison-van, when we were taken to the Semionov Drill Ground, I saw a multitude of people; perhaps the news reached you, and you suffered for me. Brother! I have not become downhearted or low-spirited. Life is everywhere—life, life in ourselves, not in what is outside us. There will be people near me, and to be a *man* among people and remain a man forever, not to be downhearted nor to fall in whatever misfortunes may befall me—this is life; this is the task of life. I have realized this. This idea has entered into my flesh and into my blood.[13]

The new forces moving in Russia once the doorway to Europe was opened were transforming the economy of the country, making serfdom unprofitable. They were creating a revolutionary intelligentsia, who could as yet find no common cause with the people. These new forces acted within the fixed limits of the Russian social and political structure. Tremendous pressure was accumulating. Would emancipation prove sufficient to furnish an outlet for this pressure?

4. RUSSIAN SOCIETY FROM THE EMANCIPATION TO THE FIRST WORLD WAR

MANY people thought that the emancipation of the serfs would immediately usher in a new era in Russia. Just before the emancipation, most of the serfs were agricultural workers, owned by private landholders or by the crown. The relatively small proportion of serfs who had no connection with the land—household serfs and possessional serfs—were given their freedom under the emancipation act, but in most cases they were not given any rights in the land. As individuals they were free to hire themselves out wherever they could find employment. The great problems of emancipation did not arise in connection with the comparatively small group which was not attached to the land, but with the much larger agricultural group.

When the conditions under which emancipation took place were arranged by the government, the landowners who wished to keep the peasants on the land in much the same manner in which they had been held in previous centuries were the most influential element in the councils of the state, far outnumbering the industrialists who desired a regular and dependable supply of workers. Consequently the conditions laid down favored the landowner and perpetuated the old systems of communal control of the village over the household and of the household over the individual. The newly freed peasant lived under conditions different from those under which the members of other classes lived. He was tied to his commune and to his household. The expected new era did not immediately materialize, because the old aristocracy controlled the first moves in the game.

Agricultural communes were given allotments of lands. Peasants did not, as individuals, own the land they used; they did not have full title to the land, nor the unqualified right to sell or to lease. The lands to be used by the commune were determined by the landowner. It was stipulated that the peasant lands should be approximately those previously cultivated by the households of the commune for their own support, but details were left to the individual landowner. The government usually paid the landowner for the lost land and required that the peasant commune repay the state over a fifty-year period, in annual installments which were called "redemption payments." Whenever the redemption payments had been made in full, the land would become the property of the commune. The redemption payments were, in general, high; in many cases they exceeded the annual income from all the land allotted to the commune. No household in a commune could refuse to share in the communal allotment; it must accept its responsibility, including its share in the redemption payments assessed against the land.

These provisions formed the general framework of the emancipation act, but the details varied with the type of commune and with the landowner. For example, the households in hereditary communes became potential owners, in heredity, of the lands they cultivated, and a household in such a commune could obtain a consolidated holding of plowland instead of strips, provided all the households whose holdings were affected consented to the change. Households in repartitional communes did not become potential hereditary landowners, since the strips of land might be redistributed at intervals by the communes, and it was difficult to secure a consolidated holding in a repartitional commune. Other differences among the peasants arose from the facts that the amounts of land allotted, and of payments required, varied from district to district and with the various classes of serfs. Peasants belonging to the crown received in general larger allotments and were required to make smaller payments than privately owned serfs.

In many communes the lands allotted for peasant use were entirely inadequate in extent and type. On estates where the landlord had been extending his manorial fields the lands of the peasants had become progressively restricted, and the allotment of these fields alone worked a hardship upon the peasants. Sometimes the landowner refused to allow fallow fields to be included in the peasant allotment, including only those fields actually under peasant cultivation at the time of emancipation. Under the peasant system of agriculture, cultivation could not be carried on from year to year unless some lands were left fallow, so that permission to use only the fields which were not lying idle cut down the lands to a point where privation began. Under serfdom the peasants had often been permitted the use of manorial pastures, meadows, and forests; under emancipation these privileges were withdrawn. The peasant commune was very often obliged to rent or buy additional lands from the estate owner.

The emancipation provisions were such, then, that as a rule they kept the peasant household tied to the commune and under its control. In addition, the power of the head of the household over junior members was continued. No member of the household was permitted to leave the commune to seek work elsewhere without a passport which was never issued if the head of the family objected. If the head of the family desired, he could ask the government to cancel the passport and force the return of the absent member. The families of no other class of Russian society lived under such conditions as these; after emancipation, as before, the peasants were a class set apart.

The communal control perpetuated under the emancipation provisions kept peasant agriculture backward. The strip system was continued over most of agricultural Russia. This system of cultivation fastened traditional methods upon the peasants; no peasant could attempt changes or improvements in farming methods which would affect other cultivators. For example, no household could plant a little earlier, harvest a little sooner, and turn animals in for pasture on the harvested field ahead of his neighbors, for the animals would injure the crops of others. The strip system was not only a preventer of experimentation and of improvement, but it was wasteful. The little boundaries marking off the strips were uncultivated. The Russian farmers in the repartitional communes were inclined to exhaust the soil and return nothing to it. Since the cultivators in communes of this type often held their strips only temporarily, they tried to get everything they could from the soil while they held it, without enriching the land, because if they enriched the soil, another might reap the benefits. The only method of enrichment which would fall equally upon all members of the commune was the practice of allowing fields to lie fallow for a year or more, and thus land was taken out of cultivation. The backwardness of agriculture intensified the economic difficulties of the peasant and caused him to be even more conscious of his need for a larger holding. While more land might have helped him, the method of agriculture was too backward, and land rents and prices were too high, to enable the cultivation of additional fields to solve the economic problems of the peasant.

Redemption payments were, in general, excessive. Land rents and prices rapidly increased because of the peasant demand for land. The peasants paid over 99 per cent of the direct taxes, and the entire poll tax, while the indirect taxes on necessities were an additional burden. As a result of the impossible economic situation brought about by these various factors, thousands of peasants tramped over Russia seeking agricultural employment—which was wretchedly paid. Villages sent delegates on the long journey to Siberia, to find out the conditions of life there. They might be followed by fellow villagers, if the report were favorable. No peasant could, however, of his own accord leave for Siberia. He must have the consent of the commune, since taxes and other payments were a communal responsibility. Not until the last decade of the nineteenth century did the government favor peasant migrations and assist the peasants colonizing Siberia, by providing transportation and temporarily remitting taxes.

The feeling of the Russian peasant who wandered about seeking a better life, but who in the end is drawn back to "Mother Russia," is suggested in one of the stories of the great writer Chekhov (1860-1904), himself of serf descent. An old peasant attempting to comfort the young mother whose child has just died is speaking:

"Never mind," he repeated, "Yours is not the worst of sorrows. Life is long, there will be good and bad to come, there will be everything. Great is mother Russia," he said, and looked around on each side of him. "I have been all over Russia, and I have seen everything in her, and you may believe my words, my dear. There will be good and there will be bad. I went as a delegate from my village to Siberia; I worked the land there, then I was homesick for mother Russia and I came back to my native village. We came back to Russia on foot; and I remember we went on a steamer, and I was thin as thin, all in rags, barefoot, freezing with cold. . . . And when I got home, as the saying is, there was neither stick nor stall; I had a wife, but I left her behind in Siberia, she was buried there. So I am living as a day labourer. And yet I tell you; since then I have had good as well as bad. Here I do not want to die, my dear, I would be glad to live another twenty years, so there has been more of the good. And great is our mother Russia!" [1]

Through the eyes of the peasant woman leaving her village to seek employment in the city, Chekhov shows the Russian peasant:

Summer and winter there were hours and days when it seemed to her that these men lived worse than beasts, and to look at them was terrible; they were coarse, dishonest, dirty, drunken; they lived in discord; they fought eternally, because they despised, feared and suspected one another. Who kept the drink shop and dosed the muzhik with drink? The muzhik. Who squandered and spent on drink the money of the commune, of the school, of the Church? The muzhik. Who stole from his neighbor, burnt his house, perjured himself in court for a bottle of vodka? The muzhik. Who first spoke at the Zemstvo and on other boards against the muzhik? The muzhik. Yes; to live with them was torture! But despite all this, they were men, they suffered and wept as men; and in their whole lives there was not one act for which an excuse might not be found. Labour unbearable, from which the whole body ached at night, fierce winters, scanty harvests, crowding; help from nowhere, and no hope of help! The richer and the stronger gave no help because they themselves were rude, dishonest, intemperate, and foul-tongued; the pettiest official and clerk treated the muzhiks as vagabonds; even the cantonal chiefs and Church elders addressed them as "Thou," and believed they had a right thereto. Yes! And could there be help or good example from the selfish, the greedy, the dissolute, the idle, who came to these villages with but one intent; to insult, terrify, and rob? Olga remembered the piteous, humiliated faces of the old men when in winter Kiriak was brought out to be flogged! And now she was sorry for all these men and women; and on her last walk through the village she looked at every hut.[2]

Another slant on peasant life is given by Gorky (1868-1936), who was born in a town, of working-class parents.

The life of the village appears to me in all its joylessness. I have often read and heard that people in the country live a more wholesome and sincere life than those in town. But here I see the peasants living in an untiring drudgery; among them there are many who are wasted and exhausted by incessant toil, and hardly any of them are cheerful. The artisans and workmen of the town, although working no less, live more gaily and do not complain so wearily and monotonously as these sullen people. The peasant's life does not seem simple to me—it demands an intense concentration on the earth and a lot of intuitive artfulness in regard to others. And there is no cordiality in this existence, which is so poor of intellect. One perceives that all these people of the village live groping in the darkness like the blind, are incessantly afraid of something, mistrust each other; there is something of the wolf in them. . . .

I am distinctly conscious of the superiority of the town, of the thirst for happiness, of the bold inquisitiveness of its mind and the diversity of its aims and aspirations. . . .

As to the country, I do not like it and the peasants I cannot understand. . . . They are all terribly irritable, and swear at each other fiercely. On account of an earthen jug, worth twelve kopecks, three families fought one day with pikes, broke the arm of an old woman and the shoulder of a young boy. And brawls like that happen every week.[3]

In contrast to these descriptions we have those of Tolstoy, the nobleman and landowner, who made many attempts to improve the life of the peasants on his estates. He realized the misery of the peasants, but he regarded their life of toil as wholesome and worth while, and, in his later years, went out daily into his own fields to work. In *Anna Karenina* Tolstoy gives a charming description of the day the young landowner, Levin, spent mowing with the peasants. When he came out early in the morning, he heard the peasants laughing and remarking that he would never stick the day out, but he determined that he would.

The old man walked on in front with long regular strides. He swung his scythe with the same ease with which a man swings his arm when walking. It seemed as if his scythe cut of itself. . . .

The work seemed lighter to Levin during the heat of the day. His clothes were dripping wet and gave him a sense of coolness, while the sun burning his back, his head, and his arms, with the sleeves rolled up to the elbow gave him new force and energy. There were moments of complete oblivion when he lost all consciousness of what he was doing and the scythe seemed to cut of itself. These were happy moments. Still more delightful was the time when they got to the river and the old man would take up a handful of grass, wipe his scythe and dip it into the water, then fill a can and hand it to Levin.

"How do you like my kvass?" he would ask with a wink.

And really it seemed to Levin that he had never tasted anything better than that warm water in the rusty tin, with the bits of grass floating about on the top. . . .

The time flew by without his noticing it, and when it seemed to Levin that they had been working only about half an hour it was already dinner-time. The old man drew his attention to the little girls and boys, half-concealed by the tall grass, who were coming from all sides bringing the men their bread and jugs of kvass. . . .

"Well, sir, it's time for dinner," he said resolutely.

The men walked back to the river where their coats were lying and the children were waiting with their little bundles. They sat down, some under the shade of the cart, others under the lilac-bushes, where they spread some newly-mown hay. Levin sat down near them; he did not wish to go home. . . .

The old man crumbled his bread into a basin, poured some water over it, cut off some more bread, and sprinkling the whole with salt he turned to the east and said his grace.

"Have some dinner with me, sir," he said to Levin as he knelt down before his basin.

Levin found his mess so palatable that he decided not to go home to dinner. While they were eating he asked the old man many questions about his domestic affairs, and took the keenest interest in his answers. He also told him anything about his own affairs that he thought would be interesting to him. He felt more intimate with him than he had ever felt with his brother Sergei Ivanovitch, and could not help smiling at him affectionately.[4]

Each writer we have quoted saw the peasant differently; each interpretation was colored by the writer's own social origin. Meanwhile, the peasant himself could only bewail his misery.

> O my fate
> Fate of the poor.
> How hard and bitter
> How hard and joyless thou art! . . .
> O my sorrow, my bitter sorrow,
> Such must be my fate.[5] . . .

Sometimes, in the attempt to earn money to meet their obligations—to escape this "fate of the poor"—the peasants became factory workers, returning to their lands when they could; or perhaps they engaged in small scale handicraft manufacture. Finally, as power was introduced, many peasants were forced to become permanent industrial workers, though the greater per cent of them living in the cities and working in factories at the end of the nineteenth century still retained their village passports and their allotment lands. In spite of all their efforts to increase their revenue, the peasants fell steadily behind in their redemption payments. Forty years after emancipation many of the peasants were worse off, economically, than they had been as serfs.

When the peasants were emancipated, some provision had to be made for the government functions previously exercised by the serf owner. Some of these responsibilities and powers—as, for example, the maintenance of law and order, including the right to exile to Siberia for infractions of the law—were delegated to the village commune, in order to make its hold over the people as strong as possible. Local schools, roads, and medical care were given into the control of newly organized local governments called zemstvos, which managed, in the years before the First World War, to provide the rural districts with many more schools, better roads, and much more medical service than they had had before. Under the zemstvos, secular education first began to reach large numbers of the people. It was provided at first that peasant, landowner, and merchant should be represented in the zemstvo, though not equally; but later the basis of representation was so changed that landowners had the controlling vote. The power of the landowner over the peasant was economic, in so far as the landowner set allotments, redemption payments, rents for leased lands, and the wage for agricultural labor; it was political, in so far as the enactments of the zemstvos affected the people; but it was no longer the social control of the days of serfdom.

Not only was the relationship between landowner and cultivator modified by emancipation, but the nobility experienced other changes in their life and outlook. The landlords, in general, did not turn out to be successful capitalist farmers. Many landlords were already deep in debt when emancipation took place, and the redemption payments they received went to pay their debts rather than to buy machinery and improve the system of production on their lands. Under the arrangements which some landlords had had with their serfs, the serfs supplied all the animals and tools for the cultivation of the lord's land, and such landowners found themselves faced with the necessity of spending a good deal of money on equipment before they could even begin the cultivation of their estates. Landowners sometimes rented part of their estates to peasants, asking labor, produce, or money payments. They even sold land outright, to merchants, townsmen, and peasant communes. Between 1877 and 1905 the nobles in forty-seven provinces lost nearly one third of their lands. Just before the revolutions of 1917 the rented, leased, and owned land in peasant hands comprised about three fourths of the agricultural lands of Russia, whereas the lands allotted for peasant use at the time of emancipation had amounted, roughly, to one half of the cultivable area.

The longing of the old impoverished aristocracy for the days that were gone is depicted by Chekhov in his play *The Cherry Orchard*. An estate is about to be sold; the cherry orchard adjoining the garden is to be cut down, and the trees are to furnish lumber for a furniture factory owned by the purchaser. The estate owners shrink from the impending change. A young student, a friend of the family, is not unwilling to see the cherry orchard, a symbol of an unjust social order, destroyed. He says:

Think only, Anya, your grandfather, and great-grand-father, and all your ancestors were slave-owners—the owners of living souls—and from every cherry in the orchard, from every leaf, from every trunk there are human creatures looking at you. Cannot you hear their voices? Oh, it is awful! Your orchard is a fearful thing, and when in the evening or at night one walks about the orchard, the old bark on the trees glimmers dimly in the dusk, and the old cherry trees seem to be dreaming of centuries gone by and tortured by fearful visions. Yes! We are at least two hundred years behind, we have really gained nothing yet, we have no definite attitude to the past, we do nothing but theorize or complain of depression or drink vodka. It is clear that to begin to live in the present we must first expiate our past, we must break with it; and we can expiate it only by suffering, by extraordinary unceasing labour. Understand that, Anya.[6]

While some of the old aristocracy were impoverished after emancipation, many were not, and life in the cities of St. Petersburg and Moscow was marked by luxury and extravagance. Nowhere was money lavished more freely; nowhere were the contrasts of life more marked. Music, the theater, and the ballet flourished, the recreation of the privileged.

The distinguished composers Moussorgsky (1835-1881), Rimsky-Korsakov (1844-1908), and Borodin (1834-1887) lived in St. Petersburg and were the closest friends and associates. Each composed operas, symphonies, chamber music, and songs which were outstanding and which contributed greatly to the cultural life of the cities. Among the best known of Moussorgsky's works are his operas, *Boris Godunov* and *Khovantchina*. The text of *Boris Godunov* was inspired by Pushkin's drama based on those stirring times when Boris was made tsar and the pretender Dmitry rose against him. The opera is arranged in a series of short episodes, each of which gives a feeling for different aspects of the life of the period. For example, we see peasants beseeching the new tsar to relieve their troubles; life within the palace shut off from the turmoil of affairs outside; the turbulent council of boyars; peasants tormenting the boyar whom they found unaccompanied in the forest; the village inn; the monastery. Combined, these brief pictures give the life of the period, emotionally reinforced by the powerful appeal of the music. The opera *Khovantchina* is set in the time of Peter the Great, and its prologue makes particular use of national airs. Borodin began an opera, *Prince Igor,* but he did not complete it, and Rimsky-Korsakov finished it after Borodin's death. The national element is strong in Borodin's music, especially in a symphony called *In the Steppes*. The best known of Rimsky-Korsakov's works are the *Coq d'Or* and *Scheherazade*.

While Moussorgsky, Rimsky-Korsakov, and Borodin were working in St. Petersburg, Tchaikovsky (1840-1893) was composing in Moscow. Tchaikovsky is perhaps the best known of all the Russian composers; his work is performed at symphony concerts everywhere. He made much less use of Russian national airs than did the St. Petersburg group, and he was much more strongly influenced by European composers, but his music is considered very

Russian in that it expresses so strongly one side of the Russian national spirit—its melancholy. The *Sixth Symphony* is considered the outstanding example of this.

The Russian theater was as distinguished as Russian music. The best-known and most popular playwrights were the great literary men—Gogol, Turgenev, Chekhov, Gorky. Russian plays, like Russian novels and short stories, were a medium through which writers protested against the restrictions, the injustices, the oppressions, the hopeless aspects, of Russian life. Since many of the plays were written by gifted men, they are not, however, mere social documents; they are in addition dramatic, and human in their appeal. Another factor of importance was that each theater was a repertory theater, presenting not one play throughout a season or several seasons, but many different plays. The members of the company received varied experience and opportunities to develop their talents. There was no starring system; neither plays nor actors were subordinated to a "star." Directors in the state-supported theaters were freed from dependence upon box office receipts and were thus able to present plays they considered worth while. Privately supported theaters were distinguished for their experimental work. Under the great director Stanislavski, the Moscow Art Theater, founded in 1898, became the most famous in Russia.

The classical ballet which reached such perfection in Russia was introduced from France in 1735. In 1847 the great choreographer Petipa came to St. Petersburg, where he remained as director of the Imperial School of the Ballet until his death in 1910. Under his direction the classical technique was developed and modified, and the Russian Imperial Ballet became the finest in the world. The classical ballet requires years of intensive training which begins in early youth. The members of the Imperial School were the wards of the tsar, and they spent their years of training under his patronage. The ballet was thus closely connected with the court and with fashionable society.

In the years after emancipation, when Russian cultural developments reached such distinguished heights, the contrasts between the different levels of Russian society became even more pronounced than they had been. To all the older difference was added the richer culture developed in the cities, at the same time that big industry was growing and the workers coming from the rural regions were being herded into the factories and the slums. Over against this, however, must be set the influence of education, which was spreading among the people to a much greater extent than ever before.

As far as industry was concerned, emancipation did not immediately provide the labor supply which the industrialists had expected. At least ten years went by before the peasants realized that conditions of life under the emancipation provisions were unbearably hard and that their hopes of becoming economically more secure in the villages were not to be realized. During those ten years peasants left the factories to return to their villages and obtain the land they expected; but at the end of that time they began to come back to the industrial establishments, which at least offered them a wage. In the 1870's Russian industry began to develop rapidly, owing partly to the increased labor supply, partly to improved world conditions after the depression of the sixties, and partly to government measures designed to encourage industries.

The isolation of the peasant who came to the city to work is vividly suggested in Chekhov's story called *Grief*. This tale centers upon a cab driver, Iona, who waits a fare in the city streets:

The cab driver, Iona Potapov, is quite white, and looks like a phantom; he is bent double as far as human body can bend double; he is seated on his box, and never makes a move. If a whole snowdrift fell on him, it seems as if he would not find it necessary to shake it off. His little horse is also quite white, and remains motionless; its immobility, its angularity, and its straight wooden-looking legs, even close by give it the appearance of a ginger-bread horse worth a kopeck. It is, no doubt, plunged in deep thought. If you were snatched from the plough, from your usual grey surroundings, and were thrown into this slough full of monstrous lights, unceasing noise and hurrying people, you too would find it difficult not to think.[7]

Iona obtains a fare, an officer, and as he drives along he is forced to try to tell his thoughts to the officer, for he is consumed with grief at the death of his son. The officer merely asks what the young man died of and urges the driver to hasten. Iona sits motionless again waiting a fare. He tells his next passengers, a group of young men, of his son's death.

"We must all die," sighed the humpback, wiping his lips after an attack of coughing. "Now, hurry up, hurry up! Gentlemen, I really cannot go any farther like this! When will he get us there?"

"Well, just you stimulate him a little in the neck!"

"You old pest, do you hear, I'll bone your neck for you! If one treated the like of you with ceremony one would have to go on foot."

Iona hears rather than feels the blows they deal him.[8]

Iona returns to the stable and tries to tell his story to a young cab driver there, but the young man falls asleep as he speaks.

He puts on his coat, and goes to the stables to his horse; he thinks of the corn, the hay, the weather. When he is alone, he dare not think of his son; he could speak about him to anyone, but to think of him, and picture him to himself, is unbearably painful.

"Are you tucking in?" Iona asks his horse, looking at his bright eyes; "go on, tuck in, though we've not earned our corn, we can eat hay. Yes! I am too old to drive—my son could have, but not I. He was a first-rate cab driver. If only he had lived!"

Iona is silent a moment, then continues:

"That's how it is, my old horse. There's no more Kuzma Ionitch. He has left us to live, and he went off pop. Now let's say, you had a foal, you were that foal's mother, and suddenly, let's say, the foal went and left you to live after him. It would be sad, wouldn't it?"

The little horse munches, listens, and breathes over his master's hand. . . .

Iona's feelings are too much for him, and he tells the little horse the whole story.[9]

The dull and narrow horizon of the city worker is described over and over again by Gorky, who lived and worked among these people, and who knew them thoroughly. For example, he tells of life in an icon shop:

I soon realized that all the men who were engaged on this handicraft which was divided up into so many processes, disliked it, and suffered from a torturing boredom.

The evenings were free. I used to tell them stories about life on the steamer and different stories out of books, and without noticing how it came about, I soon held a peculiar position in the workshop as storyteller and reader.

I soon found out that all these people knew less than I did; almost all of them had been stuck in the narrow cage of workshop life since their childhood, and were still in it. Of all the occupants of the workshop, only Jikharev had been in Moscow, of which he spoke suggestively and frowningly:

"Moscow does not believe in tears; there they know which side their bread is buttered."

None of the rest had been farther than Shuya, or Vladimir. When mention was made of Kazan, they asked me:

"Are there many Russians there? Are there any churches?" . . .

Sometimes I thought that they were laughing at me when they declared that England was on the other side of the Atlanic, and that Bonaparte belonged by birth to a noble family of Kalonga. When I told them stories of what I had seen, they hardly believed me, but they all loved terrible tales intermingled with history. Even the men of mature years evidently preferred imagination to the truth. I could see very well that the more improbable the events, the more fantastic the story, the more attentively they listened to me. On the whole, reality did not interest them, and they all gazed dreamily into the future, not wishing to see the poverty and hideousness of the present. . . .

Later, listening to them, I found that they were discussing by night those things which other people discussed by day— God, truth, happiness, the stupidity and cunning of women, the greediness of the rich, and the fact that life is complicated and incomprehensible. . . .

Always ready to give their opinion, they were always passing judgment on others, repeating, bragging, and starting bitter quarrels about mere trifles. They were always seriously offending one another. They tried to guess what would happen to them after death; while on the threshold of the workshop where the wash-stand stood, the floor-boards had rotted away. From that damp, fetid hole rose the cold, damp smell of sour earth, and it was this that made one's feet freeze. Pavl and I stopped up this hole with straw and cloths. We often said that the boards should be renewed, but the hole grew larger and larger, and in bad weather fumes rose from it as from a pipe. Every one caught cold, and coughed. . . . There were many insignificant trifles which made our lives unbearable, which might easily have been remedied, but no one took the trouble to do anything.

They often said:

"No one has any mercy upon human creatures,—neither God nor we ourselves."

But when Pavl and I washed dying Davidov, who was eaten up with dirt and insects, a laugh was raised against us. They took off their shirts and invited us to search them, called us blockheads, and jeered at us as if we had done something shameful and very ludicrous.[10]

Gorky looked back upon the violent and unhappy scenes of his childhood, spent in the crowded slums of the towns, and made this comment:

. . . I realized that Russian people, because of the poverty and squalor of their lives, love to amuse themselves with sorrow—to play with it like children, and are seldom ashamed of being unhappy.

Amidst their endless week-days, grief makes a holiday, and a fire is an amusement—a scratch is an ornament to an empty face.[11]

Even though Gorky perceived so clearly the limitations of the outlook of the working classes, the brutalities and cruelties of their lives, he thought that the greater promise for the future lay with the city workers rather than with the peasants, whose horizon he considered even narrower than that of the workers. In this respect he was typical of the new revolutionary who was to be so influential in shaping the course of affairs in Russia.

The development of large-scale heavy industry, which was so retarded in Russia, began in the 1870's when peasants began to return to the cities, and was much accelerated in the years just preceding the First World War. In the 1870's, the government took new measures to foster industry. It placed higher tariffs upon manufactured articles imported from other countries, and thus favored Russian products; it gave railroad rebates to manufacturers shipping goods; it forbade the making of labor contracts and thus indirectly helped industrialists to secure a labor supply at their own terms. The government not only fostered industry but also took a part in it. For example, it operated an increasing mileage of the railroads, until in 1914 it controlled two thirds of the railroads of Russia. It distilled and sold liquor. Before 1914, the people of Russia were accustomed to government control of many industrial enterprises.

Between 1885 and 1900 the number of railway, mine, and factory workers in Russia doubled. Labor conditions were similar to those found elsewhere in the beginning of industrialization. In the seventies, the working day was

fifteen hours, and women and children were employed
long hours in many industries. Labor organizations were
forbidden; strikes were illegal. Nevertheless, between 1894
and 1903 there was a widespread strike movement, the
number of strikers rising from 17,000 in 1894 to 130,000
in 1899 and to 250,000 in 1903. These strikes were at first
a protest against low wages and poor working conditions.
Political strikes, accompanied by revolutionary demonstrations, and which were an expression of the growing class-
consciousness among industrial workers, began in 1902.
In 1904 working hours for men were shortened to ten and
one-half hours a day, and some raises in pay were granted.
In comparison with other European countries, labor conditions were backward; this may be attributed partly to
the fact that development of large-scale industry began so
late in Russian history, and partly to the fact that cheap
labor could be recruited from the peasantry.

The most distinctive aspects of Russian industry were,
however, the extent to which it was controlled by foreign
capital, and the concentration of industrial enterprises in
a few centers. One third of all capital invested in Russian
industry was foreign. One half of the capital invested in
the mining and metal industries, two thirds of the capital
invested in the electrical industry, were foreign. The greatest part of this capital was obtained from France, Great
Britain, and Belgium, while about one fifth came from
Germany and approximately 5 per cent from the United
States. The banks were largely under foreign control. Another distinctive and important aspect of Russian industry
was its concentration. Over 54 per cent of the factories in
Russia employed more than five hundred workers. Outside Petrograd was the Putilov steel plant, the largest in
the world, employing over forty thousand people in 1917,
and the average size of the prewar industrial establishments was larger than the average elsewhere in Europe.
The large number of workers concentrated in a few re-

gions made possible the growth of a class-conscious proletariat in a country which was industrially backward, for
wherever there were any workers, there were many who
could be reached and organized for action. In 1917 there
were half a million workers in Petrograd alone, and when
these workers obtained arms, the proletarian revolution
was possible.

After emancipation, which changed the very foundation
of Russian life, the intelligentsia—the intellectuals who
were drawn mostly from the upper classes, but whose study
and reading had made them conscious of the backwardness of the Russian social and political order—hoped and
expected that the whole governmental structure would be
modified and that all classes in the society, which now included no unfree persons, would be permitted some share
in government. When it became apparent that the old
bureaucracy would continue to manage the empire, the
intelligentsia turned their attention to the peasants. They
felt that the peasants had sufficient cause for revolt and
would support revolution. They went to the villages, lived
among the people, and tried to arouse their interest in
political revolution; but the peasants had no welcome for
these representatives from other classes. They even be-
trayed some of the young revolutionaries to the police.
The revolutionaries then turned to terrorism; if it was
impossible to educate the peasants, they felt that perhaps
acts of terrorism might arouse them to the feeling that
something was wrong with the government.

The revolutionary movements of the sixties and seventies were interpreted in a critical spirit by both Turgenev
and Dostoievsky. Turgenev was keenly aware of the weakness of revolutionary activities which could not win a
following among the people. For example:

Then cigars were lighted and the talk began, one of those
interminable, midnight, Russian talks which of the same form
and on the same scale are hardly to be found in any other

people. . . . It turned out that Solomin did not believe that a revolution was at hand in Russia; but not wishing to force his opinions on others, he did not try to prevent them from making an attempt, and looked on at them, not from a distance, but as a comrade by their side. He was very intimate with the Petersburg revolutionists, and was to a certain extent in sympathy with them, since he was himself one of the people; but he realized the instinctive aloofness from the movement of the people, without whom "you can do nothing," and who need long preparation, and that not in the manner nor by means of these men. And so he stood aside, not in a hypocritical or shifty way, but as a man of sense who doesn't care to ruin himself or others for nothing. But as for listening . . . why not listen, and learn too, if one can? [12]

In *Fathers and Children*, Turgenev analyzed the nihilist. The young convert to nihilism, Bazarov, explains to his uncle:

"A nihilist is a man who does not bow before any authority whatever, who does not accept a single principle on faith, with whatever respect that principle may be environed."

"And dost thou think that is a good thing?"—interrupted Pavel Petrovitch.

"That depends on who it is, dear uncle. It is all right for one man, and very bad for another."

"You don't say so. Well, I perceive that is not in our line. We people of the old school assume that, without principles . . . without accepted principles, as thou sayest, it is impossible to take a step, or to breathe, on faith." [13]

Dostoievsky saw the revolutionary activities of his time from another angle. He wrote *The Possessed* as an indictment of the sort of revolutionary leadership which was not sincere but which used the idealism of youth to its own ends. Dostoievsky resented the exploitation of youth by such leadership.

Small revolutionary parties—the Land and Liberty party, the People's Will party—arose, demanding redivision of all the lands and advocating terrorism as the method. The "Tsar Liberator" was assassinated by a member of the People's Will. The nobility, who controlled the zemstvos, began to form liberal organizations, advocating a national assembly and reforms which might make Russian government less autocratic and less liable to violent revolutionary attack. This group formed the basis of the party later known as the Constitutional Democrats.

The terrorist activities of the revolutionary groups caused the government to take extreme measures of repression. Thousands of young revolutionaries were exiled to Siberia, and many were imprisoned and sentenced to death. The secret police was strengthened and given great power. The press censorship was extended. Organizations of industrial workers or peasants were forbidden. The measures of repression were out of proportion to the numbers of people involved in the revolutionary movements, or to their influence, for, in spite of their self-sacrificing devotion to the cause of revolution, the revolutionaries from 1825 almost to the very end of the nineteenth century were not able to attract a large following, and they were themselves relatively unorganized.

The governmental repression spread a sort of pall over the life and thought of the Russian intellectuals. Over and over again Chekhov shows the hopeless and discouraged outlook of the members of this group, as he pictures minor officials and professional men. He knew the problems of these people, for he was himself a doctor who had tried —unsuccessfully—to build a satisfactory life, practicing his profession in the country. He describes, for example, the deputy examining magistrate in a country district:

When one dreamed of playing a leading part, of becoming a popular figure, of being, for instance, examining magistrate in particularly important cases or prosecutor in a circuit court, of being a society lion, one always thought of Moscow. To live, one must be in Moscow; here one cared for nothing, one grew easily resigned to one's insignificant position, and one only expected one thing of life—to get away quickly, quickly.[14]

The boredom and lack of interest of the professional men living in the country are more directly stated in the words of the village doctor who had once dreamed of a life of usefulness among the people:

"You ask how I am living. How do we live here? Why, not at all. We grow old, we grow stout, we grow slack. Day after day passes; life slips by without colour, without impressions, without thoughts. . . . In the daytime working for gain, and in the evening the club, the company of card-players, alcoholic, raucous-voiced gentlemen whom I can't endure. What is there nice in it?" [15]

The teacher in a small village school is pictured as living alone in a little room, without companionship of any kind, with no comforts and no feeling of confidence or security.

She was always afraid, and she would get up from her seat and not venture to sit down in the presence of a member of the Zemstvo or the school guardian. And she used formal, deferential expressions when she spoke of any of them.[16]

A government clerk who hated the dull and stupefying routine which his father designated as "intellectual," and regarded as more honorable than manual labor, speaks:

My activity in the scholastic and official sphere had required neither mental application nor talent, nor special qualifications, nor creative impulse; it was mechanical. Such intellectual work I put on a lower plane than physical toil; I despise it, and I don't think for one moment it could serve as a justification for an idle, careless life, as it is indeed nothing but a sham, one of the forms of that same idleness. Real intellectual work I have in all probability never known.[17]

The writer Tolstoy (1828-1910) rebelled in a very indi-

vidual fashion against the injustices of Russian life. Early
in his life he tried to free his serfs and give them some
land, but the serfs refused to accept his proposals; they
distrusted the sincerity of his intentions. After emancipation, Tolstoy administered his estate, the famous Yasnaya
Polyana, and wrote his greater novels, *War and Peace*—a
historical tale dealing with the period of the Napoleonic
invasion—and *Anna Karenina,* a novel of contemporary
Russian society. The latter is one of the great novels of the
world, presenting Russian life in all its forms—peasant life
as it would be known to a progressive and thoughtful
landowner, official life as it would be known to a member
of the court circle, Moscow society as it would be known
to a nobleman, country life as it would be known to the
owner of estates.

After Tolstoy had written his great novels he lost his
interest in interpreting Russian life and became increasingly absorbed in problems of social and individual ad-
justment. He went to Moscow, where for the first time
he observed life in city slums. Shocked by the conditions
he saw, he felt that philanthropical activities should be
supported. Then he went about as a census taker in the
poorer quarters of the city because this would give him
an opportunity to interview people personally. This experience convinced him that all the standards of life in
the city were wrong; that the poor as well as the rich had
false standards, and that the only solution was a return to
simple living. He felt that every person should labor with
his hands and experience the simple joys which he described when Levin worked in the fields with the peasants.
He believed that man did not live to have others work for
him, but to work for others. He wrote his doctrines of life,
and he returned to Yasnaya Polyana to attempt to conduct
his life in accordance with his beliefs. It is interesting to
see how Tolstoy reacted to the complicated problems of
the modern world; he advocated a return to simplicity

which had little to do with the changing life of his times. His philosophy was sincere and attracted followings in Russia, Holland, and England, where Tolstoyan colonies were founded and disciples attempted to carry out his teachings.

The Tolstoyan colonies were never successful. Tolstoy himself wore a peasant blouse and went out daily to work in his fields. His children and his guests and disciples joined him at times in his peasant labors, but his wife refused to allow him to renounce all his wealth and kept the great income from his published works for his family. She insisted to her children, "Counts you are, and counts you shall remain." The fact that Tolstoy dealt so openly with social problems was, however, significant; he was the first writer of Russia to succeed in speaking boldly against the existing social and political order and in escaping the heavy hand of the government.

Meanwhile, while the government was repressing revolutionary activity, while the professional intellectual class was becoming discouraged and hopeless, while the peasants were struggling along, resisting any help from distrusted members of other classes, while the proletariat was being exploited, while the old aristocracy was endeavoring to keep all of its old privileges, while the wealthy of the cities enjoyed every luxury, while Tolstoy was advocating a return to a simple life—certain definite revolutionary parties which were eventually to win a following were secretly organized. The first to be formed was the Social Democratic party, organized in 1898. Its leaders were middle-class men who depended on the proletariat to fight the cause of revolution and whose doctrines were drawn from Karl Marx. The method advocated was political education and revolution, not individual terrorism. In 1903 the party split into two groups, disagreeing over matters of organization. One group, which happened to be in the minority at the time, and which therefore came to be called Menshevik (minority), believed membership should be opened to all who sympathized with Social Democratic ideas and aims or who gave any financial support, and that there should be little party discipline. The other group, which came to be called Bolshevik (majority), believed that party membership should be rigorously selective; that the party should be composed only of professionally trained revolutionaries submitting to strict party discipline, so that the party should be able to direct and lead the proletarian revolution. There were other differences between the Mensheviks and the Bolsheviks. The Mensheviks believed that a bourgeois revolution would overthrow the tsarist government. Its leaders, opposed to autocracy, would establish a liberal democratic government such as existed in other European countries, but which would not fundamentally alter the economic setup. The Mensheviks expected the proletariat to increase in numbers, because of the growth of industry, and they expected that under the leadership of the party a proletarian revolution would sometime take place, establishing a new social and economic order. They thought it would be impossible to expect the reactionary and backward peasants to participate in any of these revolutions. Since they thought that only the proletariat could be depended upon to carry through this last revolution, they felt it would be necessary to wait a long time until this group was strong enough to control the whole country. The Bolsheviks, led by Lenin, believed that the proletariat and the peasantry had common grievances against the old regime. Therefore, they thought that while a bourgeois revolution might be the one to overthrow tsarism, nevertheless, if the peasantry and proletariat combined, they could gain control and overthrow, relatively soon, any bourgeois government which might be established. Lenin believed that the peasants, under the leadership of the proletariat, could play—indeed, must play—a part in the proletarian revolution. For one reason, the Russian army was recruited almost entirely from the peasantry, and without the help of the peasant soldiery, Lenin was convinced, no revolution could be carried through. Again, the peasants were the bulk of the population, and without the co-operation of the masses of the people, Lenin felt that no successful revolution could occur.

From the time the Social Democrat party was organized, it tried to agitate among the proletarian workers. Such agitation was a tremendously dangerous and difficult affair. Meetings of workers were forbidden; the disguised agitator might easily be detected as he went among the workers —and the punishment was exile or imprisonment.

In 1900 the Socialist Revolutionary party was organized. This was a revival of earlier parties advocating land seizure, socialism, and terrorism. The Socialist Revolutionaries believed that since the peasants were already living a partly communal life, the transition to socialism would be simple; the land should be taken from private owners, nationalized, and distributed to the peasants, who would then organize a new life along socialistic lines. Industry was to be similarly transformed, and the method for starting these changes was terrorism. Socialist Revolutionaries received, at first, no welcome in the villages. Gorky came in contact with one of the Social Revolutionaries who was living among the peasants and endeavoring to teach them. The peasants responded by opposing his influence and burning his house. Gorky was aroused to indignation, but the older revolutionary worker counseled him to have patience. He interpreted the peasant in these words:

He, the peasant, is afraid of himself, of his neighbor, and still more so of every stranger, said Romass. Thirty years have not yet passed since he has been granted freedom, and every forty-year-old peasant has been born a slave and remembers it only too well. And he thinks: it is hard to understand what is freedom. On first thought freedom seems to mean to live as one likes! But then you perceive that you are surrounded with authorities and that everybody tries to interfere with your life. The Tsar took the peasantry from the landowners—therefore the Tsar now is the sole sovereign over all the peasantry. And again—what does freedom mean, then? All of a sudden the day shall come when the Tsar will explain what it means. The peasant believes intensely in the Tsar who is the sole sovereign of the earth and all its riches. As he took the peasants from the landowners—he can in the same way seize the ships and shops from the merchants. The peasant is a tsarist—he understands that too many cooks spoil the broth. He awaits the day when the Tsar will proclaim to him the meaning of freedom. And then! Seize what you can, all of you! They all wait for that moment to come and are afraid of it at the same time, for every one of them lives on his guard anxious not to miss the decisive day of a general distribution. And he is afraid of himself, too, for he wants a lot—and there is heaps to get hold of, and how is one to do it? [18]

These different parties worked in a more organized manner than earlier revolutionary groups, but even so their influence was not particularly strong. In 1904-1905, however, Russian life was disorganized by the disasters and demands of the unpopular Russo-Japanese War, and the general discontent suddenly culminated in the disorders of the revolution of 1905, in which the parties just described participated. The disorders were widespread and involved large numbers of people, such as no other revolutionary uprising since Pugachev's rebellion had affected. There were many peasant uprisings in different parts of the country; in very few cases did the peasants actually seize land and attack and kill landowners, but in many instances, they took grain and timber and burned barns or even manors. Strike after strike occurred among the industrial workers; at one time, all the railway workers were out on strike, as well as most of the mine workers and employees in the large city factories. The total number of strikers was over three million. Some of these had the feeling that if they could only reach the Tsar, their "Little Father," and present their cause, he would help them. A large group of workers marched toward the Winter Palace to see the "Little Father." When they were in the square before the palace, the guards opened fire upon them and mowed them down; they were not even given an opportunity to state their hope and their intention of asking help from the Tsar. This ruthless act, more than any other one thing, helped to shatter the faith in the Tsar which had been so firmly built in the people.

The disorders of the revolution of 1905 were so widespread and involved so many people that the government felt forced to make gestures of compromise. Among other things, it granted the privilege of electing a national Duma (parliament) without whose consent, it promised, no law should hereafter be made. The revolution of 1905, in scope and in type, as well as in the fact that it did bring about some changes in government and in legislation, may be regarded as a forerunner of the revolutions of 1917.

Which of these different groups and parties involved in the revolution of 1905 learned the most, so that it might be more successful next time? The peasants, who demanded land and did not wish political change? The Socialist Revolutionaries, who promised the peasants land, but who asked for their participation in social and political revolution? The industrial workers, who went on political strikes? The Constitutional Democrats, who wanted Russia to have popular elections for choosing legislators who would make the laws? The Mensheviks, who wished to wait until Russia had a well-developed capitalist society with its large numbers of class-conscious proletarians before the proletarian revolution should be brought about? The Bolsheviks, who deplored the lack of political understanding which characterized the peasants, but who nevertheless felt that, in Russia, the proletariat must lead the peasants in a class war? The autocratic government, which

granted a few changes and so manipulated the new privileges that it remained in the same apparently secure position as before? Obviously, here were conflicting forces,
strong enough to make their voices heard in the revolution of 1905, determined enough to raise those voices
again—but not one yet strong enough to speak with a conviction and with an authority which would silence the
others. Even the government autocracy could not do this,
though its severe repressive measures, after 1905, did succeed in driving revolutionary movements underground,
and in sending revolutionary leaders into exile in Siberia
or forcing them to seek refuge abroad.

The revolution of 1905 was responsible for changes in
Russian life which affected all classes of society. The government wished to build up within the peasant class a
comparatively prosperous group that could be relied on to
keep the rest of the peasantry in order. To do this, it was
necessary to break the hold of the commune over the
households and of the head of the peasant household over
the members of the family, and thus to make possible the
rise of independent peasant landholders. The period between 1905, when a movement in this direction began,
and 1914, when the World War disrupted all of Russia,
was far too short to complete such a change; but the steps
taken by the government were significant in that they
modified the conditions under which the peasants lived,
and, indirectly, affected the proletariat and the upper
classes.

In 1905 all outstanding redemption payments were can-
celed, and the old regulation that junior members of the
family could not receive a passport to leave the commune
if the head of the family objected was abolished. Permission was given to sell house-and-garden plots, and laws
were passed making it easier for householders in repartitional communes to secure hereditary ownership of the
strips cultivated by the household. A later law ordered

that in repartitional communes in which there had been no general redistribution of land since 1861, the head of the household should become the owner, in perpetuity, of the strips cultivated by the household at the time. It was likewise provided that in hereditary communes the head of the household, as an individual, should own the household lands. Thus many junior members were deprived of rights in the land. It was made comparatively easy, moreover, for individuals to sell land. Steps were also taken to make the securing of a consolidated holding easier than it had been. It is obvious that the creation of even a few consolidated holdings would involve tremendous readjustments; that the difficulties of satisfying all members of the commune under these conditions might be insuperable, and that certainly the process would involve friction and dissatisfaction. Government land commissions were appointed to deal with the readjustments involved; the matter was taken out of the hands of the commune and given over to bodies which were representative, not of the peasants, but of the larger landowners and the bureaucracy. Under these conditions the creation of consolidated holdings proceeded slowly; by 1917 only perhaps one tenth of the households had received consolidated farms, and a considerable portion of these farms still shared in the use of the undivided land.

While the greater part of Russia's agriculture was still carried on under the old strip method of cultivation, the whole basis of the life of the peasantry was shaken in the years after 1905. Communal control over the household, and family control over the individual, were weakened. Traditional habits could not be suddenly effaced, but their hold over the people was lessened. Individual peasants had greater opportunity to secure land and wealth than they had hitherto possessed, since they were given more freedom to buy and to sell. The interests of the wealthier peasants were detached from those of the less prosperous and identified with those of the propertied classes. This identification was one of the chief aims of the legislation which began in 1905. One writer calls this government bid for peasant support "the wager on the strong." [19]

The loosening of traditional holds over individual peasants had its effect upon the proletariat. Workers who had no claims upon the land increased in number. Without connections with the land, they were, as proletarians, more easily made class-conscious than those workers who retained their peasant rights and obligations. Another factor affecting the workers was the social insurance scheme adopted in 1912, which gave them some voice in managing the system, and permission to meet to transact the business connected with it. Before this, workers had been forbidden to gather in large groups. Now it became comparatively easy for revolutionary agitators to make contacts with the proletariat. Revolutionary literature and newspapers circulated in secret among a more organized audience than heretofore.

A quotation taken from one of Lenin's best-known writings, *What Is To Be Done?*, helps to show something of the nature of this literature.

Social-Democrats lead the struggle of the working class not only for better terms for the sale of labour power, but also for the abolition of the social system which compels the propertyless class to sell itself to the rich. Social-Democracy represents the working class, not in its relation to a given group of employers, but in its relation to all classes in modern society, to the state as an organized political force. Hence, it . . . follows that Social-Democrats must not confine themselves entirely to the economic struggle. . . . We must actively take up the political education of the working class, and the development of its political consciousness.[20]

The purpose of the revolutionary periodicals which

Lenin advocated and later edited abroad is adequately described in Lenin's words:

In our opinion, the special task of Russian Social-Democracy is to overthrow the autocracy. Russian Social-Democracy is destined to stand in the front rank of the fight for Russian democracy; it is destined to achieve the aim which the whole social development of Russia set before it, and which it has inherited from the glorious fighters in the Russian revolutionary movement. . . . We call upon all those who are oppressed by the present political system in Russia, to all those who are striving for the emancipation of the Russian people from their slavery to support the publications which will be devoted to the work of organizing the labour movement into a revolutionary political party. We place our columns at their disposal in order that they may expose the despicability and criminality of the Russian autocracy.[21]

These quotations give the intense, determined note of the revolutionary literature; they forecast the culmination of revolutionary agitation in direct action—but they do not give the main points of Bolshevik theory. Bolsheviks believed that, after tsarism had been overthrown, under the leadership of the proletariat directed by a disciplined Bolshevik party, and with the assistance of the peasants, a new revolution would take place, and a new society would be developed, in which no private person could own the means of production. They believed that when the means of production were in the hands of private persons, other individuals were unable to make use of these unless they agreed to the terms set down by the owners. This division of the population into those who control the means of production, and those who do not control them makes what the Bolsheviks term a class society. According to Bolshevik theory, after the proletarian revolution had occurred, the new society which would develop would be classless. While all individuals would not share equally in wealth, no individual would be exploited by another, and all persons would eventually have equal opportunity to satisfy their needs. "From each according to his ability, to each according to his needs" was the ultimate goal of the new society.

The full implications of this theory were not understood by the workers of Russia among whom revolutionary literature was circulated. Party leaders were to disagree over interpretations of the theory, and over ways of achieving desired ends. Nevertheless, as a result of the circulation of revolutionary literature there were among the workers of Russia groups which were organized and politically educated to play an active part in the revolutions of 1917.

Although the proletariat was increasing and industry was expanding, Russian industry before the World War was still backward. The following tables show the nature of the prewar economy of the country.

Average annual exports, 1909–1913 (all figures in rubles)

Total 1,501,421,000

A. Agricultural Export 1,050,639,000
    Grain 625,974,000
    Other agricultural products 157,761,000
    Products of livestock, and poultry raising 250,965,000
    Products of hunting and fishing 15,939,000

B. Industrial Export 450,782,000
    Timber and products 148,820,000
    Food, alcohol, and tobacco products ... 143,910,000
    Products of mining industry 55,059,000
    Products of other branches of industry. 102,993,000

Average annual imports, 1900–1913

Total 1,140,164,000

Food, alcohol, and tobacco products 206,014,000
Animals and animal products 99,189,000
Timber products, wooden- and basketware,
    plants and seeds 42,406,000
Building materials of mineral origin and
    manufactures therefrom 20,742,000
Mineral fuel, asphalt, tar, and their products 97,439,000

Materials and products of chemical industry.	59,381,000
Ores, metals, and metal manufactures	244,448,000
Electrical and technical equipment	24,779,000
Paper products and printed matter	31,476,000
Textile materials and manufactures	297,426,000
Other goods	23,865,000

The main items of the export trade were materials either produced directly from the land or transformed by very simple industrial processes. Many of the imports were rather complex manufactured articles, scattered over a wide variety of items, indicating that Russian industry was still relatively undeveloped and the labor comparatively unskilled.

Just before the First World War, however, Russia was in the process of becoming a modern industrial nation, and the social changes which accompany industrialization were taking place. Along with the new and relatively small classes of a comparatively backward capitalist order existed the older, larger classes of the semifeudal, autocratic, agrarian state which Russia still was. Additional pressure was exerted by the great increase in the population; 67,-000,000 in 1851, it was 129,000,000 in 1897, and 175,000,-000 in 1914. What the country might have developed into under these conditions of feudal survivals, modern industrialization, and population pressure if there had been no World War—it is impossible to say. The First World War had a profound effect upon Russia; it shattered and disintegrated the country. Back of the revolutions of 1917 lay the grievances of centuries, but the disorganization which accompanied the war created the conditions under which successful revolution could be carried through by the peasants and groups of workers who rose against property owners and officials.

5. WORLD WAR I AND REVOLUTION

NOT infrequently war seems to call forth from a country a type of unified effort which is never experienced in time of peace. Sooner or later, however, the disintegrating effects of war appear. National weaknesses eventually emerge in new proportions, and forces of discontent which have been moving toward change in the state thrive upon the conditions brought about by war. In Russia the weaknesses of the state were so marked, and the forces of discontent so strong, that the country was rapidly disintegrated as it attempted to grapple with the abnormal conditions caused by the First World War. Revolution became inevitable.

The vast empire of Russia with its great population exceeding that of all the Central Powers taken together was regarded by the Allies as a country whose resources of manpower were almost unlimited. The illusion of the Russian "steam roller" was created by Allied propaganda as an aid in keeping up morale when affairs on the western front were going badly. The superstructure of the empire was so imposing that the world at large did not fully realize the internal weaknesses of the country and the forces of discontent at work there. Among these may be mentioned the backwardness of industry and transportation, the inefficiency of the government, the waning prestige of the Tsar, and all the cumulated dissatisfactions of middle-class liberals and of peasants and workers.

We have seen that before the war Russia imported manufactured goods demanding technical skill in production, and exported raw materials or simple manufactured articles. Russia did not possess large numbers of skilled technical workers, or factories which could produce the quantities of specialized materials used in modern warfare. The supplies needed by the army could not be manufactured in sufficient quantities. As a result thousands of Russian soldiers were sent unarmed into the trenches—they were, quite literally, cannon fodder. The lack of adequate railroads contributed to the shortage of supplies, for such materials as were available frequently could not reach their destination. Before the war, the whole Russian empire had but 36,800 miles of railway. Russia was isolated from her allies; between Russia and the countries producing vast amounts of war materials, lay the Central Powers and the blockade on the European side, and on the other, the whole expanse of Siberia, traversed only by the single-track Trans-Siberian railway. At the conclusion of the First World War, acres of land outside Vladivostok were covered with war supplies of all kinds—rubber, automobile parts, munitions—which had been sent across the Pacific, only to lie there for months waiting transportation to the regions where they were so sorely needed. The railroads of European Russia, especially, could do little more than move the troops and supply them with food and other necessities. Before 1917 Russia had a vast unwieldly army of over fifteen million men in active service. The entire railway system, inadequate at best, was demoralized by the demands made upon it and by the impossibility of securing replacements of rolling stock.

However backward Russian industry was, it had to attempt to meet the needs created by the war. The cities, crowded with additional factory workers, were also called upon to accommodate great detachments of troops waiting transportation to and from the front, as well as the permanent garrisons stationed there. In 1917, for example, Petrograd's garrison consisted of 160,000 men and the industrial workers of that city numbered 400,000. After the Russian retreat began, the cities were further overcrowded by the refugees from Poland and the western provinces. Everywhere the housing provisions were entirely inadequate, and there was no means of relieving the congestion. Because the railroads were devoted chiefly to military purposes, the cities suffered acute shortages of fuel and food. As far as the rural regions were concerned, much of the grain raised could not be sold because it could not reach its market. There was also an extreme shortage of consumption goods in the villages. The backwardness of Russian industrial development and of the means of transportation affected the soldiers, the city dwellers, and the people as a whole, as well as the conduct of the war.

The government was both inefficient and autocratic. Under pressure of the emergencies created by the war, all its inefficiencies stood out in high relief. They became apparent to people who had hitherto supported the autocracy, and criticism was directed at the one responsible head, the tsar. The prestige of the Tsar had been steadily diminishing. After the revolution of 1905, Nicholas II had withdrawn from the Winter Palace and from the social life of St. Petersburg, and had lived a retired existence at Tsarskoe Selo, seldom meeting anyone outside his immediate family. This withdrawal had not reacted pleasantly upon the privileged, who looked to the imperial court to set the note of gaiety for St. Petersburg society, and a barrier had arisen between the Tsar and the members of the imperial family and the court. The Empress, who had never been liked in Russia, was blamed for the Tsar's retirement. When the war began, it was remembered that the Empress was a German, and when it became apparent that she strongly influenced the decisions of the Tsar, who took her advice in preference to that of army officers and state counselors, the Tsar was distrusted, and the dislike of the Empress flamed into something much more active. The Empress was openly accused of treason, particularly after she had persuaded the Tsar to assume the high command of the army and military matters had gone from bad to worse. The widespread feeling that the government was pro-German and only halfhearted in its prosecution of the war was increased by the Tsar's attitude toward the liberal organizations—the Union of Zemstvos and the Union of Towns—which had undertaken to secure supplies and medical service for the army and which were accomplishing remarkable results under the circumstances. Nicholas, however, looked coldly on their activities and refused to listen to their pleas for a responsible ministry which would have the confidence of the country. He answered their requests by removing his best ministers and substituting individuals of whom everyone, even his own brothers, were suspicious. Many of the nobility who would ordinarily have supported the monarchy lost confidence in the Tsar.

Throughout Russian history, as we have seen, the peasants were forced to bear most of the burdens of the state. When Russia entered World War I, the peasants were called upon to furnish most of the soldiers for the vast armies placed in the field. Upon the peasant families fell the hardships of the greatest number of the personal losses of the war, in terms of men killed and injured, captured and missing; it is estimated that by 1917 the Russian army had lost over seven million men. Horses for the army were taken from the peasant cultivators, as well as grain for the army and for the cities and towns. Payment could only be made in depreciating paper currency, for the finances of the Russian government were anything but sound, and because of the shortage of industrial goods the peasant was unable to buy what he needed with the money he received. Discontent among the peasantry was tremendously increased by the conditions brought about by the war.

Among the workers, the revolutionary agitation which

had been going on for years before World War I was an important contributing cause to the large number of industrial strikes which occurred in 1914. The government, in spite of the need of skilled workers, sought a solution for industrial unrest by dispersing many of the most radical workmen to the army. These workers spread revolutionary ideas among the peasant soldiers, who thus came directly in contact with the type of agitation which had been affecting the city worker. For the first time the peasant was responsive, as to his earlier discontents were added the effects of the severe army discipline and of the hardships endured by the army in the field.

Even if the Russian offensive had been entirely successful, Russian industry and transportation would have been seriously taxed, there would have been a shortage of supplies both at the front and in the cities, and there would have been a tremendous loss of life. While one cannot be certain of the effect of victory upon the Russian people, it seems that all of these conditions would have tended to lower the morale of the people even if victory could have been obtained. But the Russian offensive was only temporarily successful, and it was followed by defeat and the retreat of the Russian armies across Poland. Populous cities and towns were evacuated and destroyed in the attempt to check the German advance; thousands of refugees choked the roads leading to Russia. Into Russia came news of defeat, and the tangible signs of it as the refugees came pouring across the frontier. With the refugees and the soldiers came typhus, a disease always common in Russia, but which now assumed epidemic proportions in certain regions. Large numbers of soldiers deserted from the army. Many army officers were critical of the high command; liberals were alienated from the government, which was obviously inadequate; and the peasants and the workers were restless.

In 1915-1917 the number of strikes, which had de-

creased immediately after the outbreak of the war in 1914,
suddenly increased—an expression of unrest among the
workers. A Soviet (or council) of Workers' and Soldiers'
Deputies was organized in Petrograd. On March 8, 1917,
almost 90,000 workers in Petrograd went on strike. When
they made a street demonstration carrying banners with
the words "Down with Autocracy," they were joined by
hundreds of women demanding bread. This was the beginning of the March Revolution, which from this time
moved with incredible and amazing swiftness. The next
day the number of strikers was about 197,000 and the
street demonstrations were more violent, though no fire-
arms were used. The following day the strike became
general throughout Petrograd, where it is estimated there
were 400,000 industrial workers. On the night of the third
day the Tsar sent a telegram ordering the Petrograd garrison to disperse the rioters by force. On the fourth day,
March 11, some troops fired upon the street crowds, but
most of the garrison showed unwillingness to act. On
March 12 mutinous troops joined the workers, bringing
guns and ammunition with them. The garrison melted
away, regiment by regiment. Four days after the first street
demonstration, Petrograd was in the hands of armed revolutionaries, who at this time had no program and who
offered no plan for a new government.

Upon the Duma, the only group in Petrograd with any
kind of governmental authority, fell the responsibility of
attempting to restore order. It had been ordered to dis-
solve, and it had formally accepted its dismissal, but it met
in spite of this and elected a temporary committee to deal
with the situation as best it might. This was in the morning of March 12, the day that the soldiers joined the
workers. By evening of the same day matters had moved
so rapidly that the Duma announced the formation of a
provisional government; it hastened to do this lest the
Petrograd soviet anticipate it and seize the power.

During these swiftly moving times, appeals were made to the Tsar—who was with the army—to announce changes in the government which might restore the confidence of the people, but Nicholas II failed to understand the seriousness of the situation, and he had no conception of the rapidity of the changes in the capital. When on March 14 he was persuaded to announce that he would permit the formation of a responsible ministry, a provisional government was already organized and functioning in Petrograd, and revolution had spread to other cities and communities. In Moscow the soldiers had mutinied and joined the revolutionaries. Sailors at Kronstadt and Helsingfors rose against their officers, killing some and imprisoning others. In general, however, these revolutionary uprisings throughout the country were not accompanied by bloodshed. On the night of March 14 the Petrograd soviet issued the famous "Order Number One" which instructed soldiers to recognize the Soviet of Workers' and Soldiers' Deputies as the body exercising supreme control over the army. All of these events indicated very clearly that the army could not be depended upon to suppress the revolution.

On March 15 the provisional government laid down some generalizations regarding the conduct of affairs. Civil rights were announced—freedom of speech, for example, and the right to organize in unions—and plans for electing a constituent assembly, which should deliberate about the form of government to be set up and about the nature of any changes in landholding, were made public. A cabinet was chosen; it included one representative from the soviet, the Socialist Revolutionary Kerensky, who was made minister of justice. This was eight days after the first street demonstration, and the Tsar did not yet comprehend what had happened. He was not the only person who failed to see the situation in its true light. More than one member of the Duma hoped to establish a constitutional monarchy with some representative of the Romanov family at its head. On the night of the fifteenth one leader of the Duma announced that such a government would be formed, but he was met with opposition and resentment. Other members of the Duma set out secretly to meet the Tsar and lay this proposal before him, but their train was delayed by revolutionaries, and they did not join the Tsar until late in the evening of the fifteenth. Nicholas, at last realizing that he could not rely upon the army to support him, had already agreed to abdicate. At first he had named his son as his successor, but a few hours later he changed his mind and named his brother, the grand duke Michael, since his son was afflicted with an incurable disease.

The signed abdication and the Tsar's recommendation for his successor were brought to Petrograd. The scheme of keeping the Romanov dynasty was received with hostility. Members of the provisional government conferred with Grand Duke Michael on March 16; some begged him to accept the throne, while Kerensky pointed out to him that if he did, his life was endangered because the people would not accept a Romanov ruler again. The Grand Duke decided to refuse.

On the same day, March 16, the provisional government planned to arrest Nicholas and the imperial family; the formal arrest was carried out five days later. The intention of the provisional government was to exile them, but the soviet intervened and prevented their departure to the proposed refuge in England. Nicholas and his family remained under arrest in Tsarskoe Selo.

In the brief time since March 8 the entire superstructure of the empire of Russia had been destroyed. Whole regiments had mutinied, the workers had risen, the Duma had been forced to admit a Soviet member to its provisional government, the people of Petrograd had refused to accept constitutional monarchy under any Romanov, the Tsar and his family had been made prisoners—all in thirteen days. The incredible swiftness of the revolutionary movement, which lacked leadership, plans, or program, is testimony to the strength of the forces of discontent in Russia. Tremendously aggravated by the war, they flamed out in an amazing manner.

It must not be imagined, however, that the provisional government had the confidence of the country or even of all the revolutionary elements. Most of its members were moderate liberals who expected that some sort of constitutional parliamentary government would be set up to replace the fallen autocracy. Such ideas were not acceptable to Socialist Revolutionaries or to any Social Democrat, Menshevik or Bolshevik. The government's proposals for the election of a constituent assembly to deliberate later upon land redistribution and related problems did not meet the desires of the great masses of the people, who demanded peace, bread, and land—at once. It was soon apparent that one group of the people had some power— the Soviet of Workers' and Soldiers' Deputies. The provisional government was unable to move against this group, since it had behind it no reliable army.

The provisional government, weak from the beginning, and powerless to enforce its will, was faced with a disturbed and disorderly country which was still fighting the Central Powers. The workers began to take over the factories, replacing experienced management with soviets of inexperienced workers, and as a result factory production was reduced. The peasants began to seize land, in some cases burning landlords' houses and killing landowners. Many peasant soldiers, hearing reports that land was being taken over, deserted that they might return to their villages and secure land for themselves. Soviets were formed in the army; officers were deposed by the soldiers' soviets; and army discipline was soon almost nonexistent. Railway and telegraph offices were seized by employees, and transportation and communication became even more chaotic than they had been. Over the country there was no clear understanding of events. No one anywhere, even in Petrograd, knew exactly what was happening. Rumors and reports were numerous and conflicting, and confusion prevailed even in the center of action. In addition to the disturbed internal conditions, pressure was exerted by the Allies, who used every inducement to persuade the provisional government to arrange that Russia continue to fight in the war.

The radical leadership which had been lacking in the first days of the revolution began to assemble in Petrograd. Stalin came from Siberia, to which he had been exiled for the fifth time. His work for the party, and his determination to continue this work within Russia in spite of arrests and imprisonments, were well known to Russian Bolsheviks, though because he had never been abroad, and used no foreign languages, he was relatively unknown outside Russia. Lenin arrived from Zurich on April 16, traveling through Germany in a sealed train allowed to pass because the Germans rightly thought that the uncompromising Bolshevik leader would lend his influence to ending Russia's participation in the war. In May, Trotsky arrived from the United States. Not a member of the Bolshevik party until after his arrival in Russia in 1917, he had lived abroad much of his life and was the revolutionist best known to the outside world. He was a brilliant orator and an able organizer. He never agreed with Lenin on certain points. He had, for example, a different attitude toward the peasants from that of Lenin. When the peasants did not fall into line, Trotsky was impatient and distrustful; he advised the use of force against them. Nevertheless, in spite of differences of opinion between them, Lenin and Trotsky worked together for the establishment of Bolshevik control in Russia. These two men were most closely linked with the revolution as reported to the outside world. Working with them, however, were a host of others in addition to Stalin, who have since become familiar:

Kalinin, Dzerzhinsky, Bukharin, Kamenev, Zinoviev, Budenny, Lunacharsky, Rykov, Krylenko, Kharakhan. Some of these are now dead; others, prominent then, have since become discredited and have been executed for seditious activities; still others continue to occupy high and important posts.

Lenin, the greatest of them all, was, in 1917, a person of whom the world at large had never heard. He had unflinching determination combined with practical common sense which guided him in crises and enabled him to make decisions which met situations adequately for the time; when the solution ceased to fit, Lenin changed his method of action, but he never modified his fundamental beliefs. Thus he was enabled to guide the troubled affairs of confused Russia, or follow wisely in the path of mass action when he could not guide. Lenin was an untiring and unselfish worker. He never sought personal power and glory, though a tremendous amount of each came to him. He had no personal hatreds such as many revolutionaries of history have shown, but he had an unwavering hatred of capitalism as a system, of exploitation of individuals as a means to personal gain, of imperialist war, of compromise with any of these as a way of bringing about change. He believed that only revolution could overthrow capitalism, which, according to his belief, was responsible for recurring wars, for human miseries and inequalities, and for the exploitation of the poor.

When he was a youth of seventeen, his much loved older brother was executed because he was implicated in a plot against the life of the tsar Alexander III, and Lenin from this time was convinced that terrorism was ineffective and costly. Imprisoned in St. Petersburg for a year, and exiled to a Siberian village for three years more, he had opportunity to reflect, write, and study, and also to come in contact with other exiled revolutionaries, as well as with Siberian peasants, from whom he gained his understanding of the peasants. In order to escape further imprisonment and exile, he lived abroad most of the time from 1900 to 1917 and devoted his time to revolutionary work —writing, editing, publishing, organizing. The failure of the revolution of 1905 provided a lesson whose value was not lost on Lenin. He returned to Russia in 1917, determined that this time the old social and economic order should be destroyed and a new one erected.

— Lenin was inflexibly opposed to the creation of any new form of government which would perpetuate private trade and private control of industry and which would permit the exploitation of the labor of the powerless and the poor. He did not favor the provisional government, which was controlled by liberals but in which the soviet had representation, since he felt that any such combination of elements would lead inevitably to the subordination of the interests of the workers.

Lenin had strong convictions, but he was not backed by a strong organization. The Bolshevik element in the soviet was weak and much outnumbered by the Social Revolutionaries and Mensheviks. Lenin's ideas were not cordially received by the great, unwieldy Soviet of Workers' and Soldiers' Deputies, which had no clear conception of what it was about, but which was tasting power. Aware of the fundamental desires of the people, and fully conscious of the significance of what was happening, Lenin advocated immediate peace and withdrawal from the war, the seizure of the factories by the workers, and the seizure of all privately owned land by the peasants. Lenin pressed the last two of these because they were already in process, and he wished to win to his party the large groups of people involved. He supported the slogan "All Power to the Soviets!" because strong soviets, he believed, could at this time quickly overthrow the provisional government. Similarly, he regarded the seizure of the land by the peasants as an essential step in breaking down the power of the privileged landholders, but he did not intend that from the peasantry should arise a new class of private landowners. He believed that only a rigorously chosen and disciplined party, working through soviets, could discharge the responsibilities of managing the country in which all means of production should be owned and controlled by the state for the benefit of the whole people. He supported the actions of the soviets and the peasants in order to attain this end.

By June certain portions of the old empire—Finland and the Ukraine—had erected virtually independent governments. Also in June was held the first Congress of Soviets, at which the conflicting points of view of the different revolutionary elements were openly discussed. The Bolshevik party was still in the minority, but it was already apparent that it was correct in its attitude toward the provisional government, since that government had taken few steps toward meeting the demands of the people and was even planning for a new offensive on the war front. This offensive took place in July; it was a failure, and desertions and mutinies increased.

Mutinous soldiers and excited workers attempted, in July, to overthrow the provisional government. They used the Bolshevik slogan—"All Power to the Soviets!"—and forced the party into accepting responsibility for a movement for which it was not prepared. At the same time, it could not refuse this responsibility, since if it was unwilling to support the movement, it would lose its hold upon the groups which were getting out of hand and upon whose assistance it had to depend. The July movement was confused and unsuccessful, violent and unorganized. An unplanned and unpreventable demonstration of sailors, soldiers, and workers, it was accompanied by shooting, destruction, looting, and violence. It gave the provisional government an excuse for attacking the Bolshevik party, which was forced to work underground for the next two months. Lenin was obliged to go into hiding in Finland, and Trotsky was placed under arrest.

The provisional government was reorganized in August. Kerensky became premier and selected his new cabinet almost entirely from among the elements supporting constitutional government rather than radical economic change. The conservatives, who wished the re-establishment of the old order, hoped that the new government could check the seizure of factories and land. They refused to support the policy of withdrawal from the war. General Kornilov accepted the command of the Russian army on condition that he be permitted to restore military discipline and that the government not interfere with the conduct of military affairs. Distrust arose between Kerensky and Kornilov, each of whom apparently thought of himself as potential dictator. The weak provisional government was split by dissensions. In September, Kornilov ordered troops to move on Petrograd. The movement was hampered by soviets in control of railways, and the whole plot came to nothing as far as Kornilov was concerned. It served, however, to infuse the revolutionaries in Petrograd with a new determination to overthrow the provisional government and to prevent, by any means, the establishment of a military dictatorship under any person as sympathetic to the old regime as a general of the old army.

It was impossible for the old privileged classes of Russia —the army officers, the landowners, the nobility—or for the conservative liberals, to imagine that any group which advocated the abolition of private property rights could actually gain control in Russia, where for centuries the private ownership of the land, and even of the people, by the few and privileged, had determined the institutions of the country. Even if they had understood the seriousness of the situation which was brewing, they lacked the means to avert it. There was still a huge force under arms, but the millions remaining in the army could not be depended upon to support the conservative and reactionary elements. The soldiers were restless, war-weary, longing to return home; they were more responsive to the offers and arguments of the Bolsheviks than they were to the exhortations of the provisional government.

The Russian setting in the weeks just before the Bolshevik revolution is described by John Reed, an American Harvard graduate, a journalist present at the time and in close touch with the revolution as it developed:

September and October are the worst months of the Russian year—especially the Petrograd year. Under dull grey skies, in the shortening days, the rain fell drenching, incessant. The mud underfoot was deep, slippery and clinging, tracked everywhere by heavy boots, and worse than usual because of the complete breakdown of the Municipal administration. Bitter damp winds rushed in from the Gulf of Finland, and the chill fog rolled through the streets. At night, for motives of economy as well as fear of Zeppelins, the street-lights were few and far between; in private dwellings and apartment houses the electricity was turned on from six o'clock until midnight, with candles forty cents apiece and little kerosene to be had. It was dark from three in the afternoon to ten in the morning. Robberies and house-breakings increased. In apartment houses the men took turns at all-night guard duty, armed with loaded rifles. This was under the Provisional Government.

Week by week food became scarcer. The daily allowance of bread fell from a pound and a half to a pound, then three-quarters, half, and a quarter-pound. Toward the end there was a week without any bread at all. Sugar one was entitled to at the rate of two pounds a month—if one could get it at all, which was seldom. A bar of chocolate or a pound of tasteless candy cost anywhere from seven to ten rubles—at least a dollar. There was milk for about half the babies in the city; most hotels and private houses never saw it for months. . . .

For milk and bread and sugar and tobacco one had to stand in *queue* long hours in the chill rain. Coming home from an all-night meeting I have seen the *kvost* (tail) beginning to form before dawn, mostly women, some with babies in their arms. . . . Think of the poorly-clad people standing on the iron-white streets of Petrograd whole days in the Russian winter! . . .

As in all such times, the petty conventional life of the city went on, ignoring the Revolution as much as possible. . . . The ladies of the minor bureaucratic set took tea with each other in the afternoon, carrying each her little gold or silver or jewelled sugar-box, and half a loaf of bread in her muff, and wished that the Tsar were back, or that the Germans would come, or anything that would solve the servant problem.

All around them great Russia was in travail, bearing a new world. The servants one used to treat like animals and pay next to nothing, were getting independent. . . . But more than that. In the new Russia every man and woman could vote; there were working-class newspapers, saying new and startling things; there were the Soviets; and there were the Unions. . . .

At the Front the soldiers fought out their fight with the officers, and learned self-government through their committees. In the factories those unique Russian organizations, the Factory-Shop Committees, gained experience and strength and a realization of their historical mission by combat with the old order. All Russia was learning to read, and *reading*—politics, economics, history—because the people wanted to know. . . . In every city, in most towns, along the Front, each political faction had its newspaper—sometimes several. Hundreds of thousands of pamphlets were distributed by thousands of organizations, and poured into the armies. The thirst for education, so long thwarted, burst with the Revolution into a frenzy of expression. From Smolny Institute alone, the first six months, went out every day tons, car-loads, train-loads of literature saturating the land. . . .

We came down to the front of the Twelfth Army, back of Riga, where gaunt and bootless men sickened in the mud of desperate trenches; and when they saw us they started up, with their pinched faces and the flesh showing blue through their torn clothing, demanding eagerly, "Did you bring anything to *read?*"

It was against this background of a whole nation in ferment

and disintegration that the pageant of the Rising of the Russian Masses unrolled. . . .[1]

Against this background, the Bolsheviks perfected their plans and their organization for a new revolution. In Petrograd, the center of activity, conferences between soviet representatives and party leaders went on continuously, day and night. The party headquarters at the Smolny Institute—a few months ago a school for the daughters of the nobility—hummed with excitement. Delegates came in scores, departed with instructions, fell asleep on the floors—forced to snatch a few minutes' rest. At last, on November 6, 1917, the Bolshevik revolution began in Petrograd, with the seizure of the railway stations, telegraph offices, bridges, the Winter Palace, and the State Bank. From that time to this day, power has remained in the hands of the Bolshevik party. The upsurge of the Bolshevik party, with all that it implied, was even more dramatic than the spontaneous demonstrations which had overthrown the tsar. It was comparatively simple to seize power; it was another matter to hold it and to erect a new society. This was the problem facing the Bolshevik party, which found it easy to overthrow the provisional government, but which had to struggle for years to consolidate its power and to extend its influence.

There was very little bloodshed in Petrograd, and by November 8 the provisional government was declared overthrown. The Congress of Soviets set up a Council of People's Commissars. Lenin was the president of this council, in which Trotsky was commissar for foreign affairs. On the same day the Congress of Soviets declared its intention of making immediate peace, and announced that all private property in land was abolished without compensation for the previous owners. Land was to be taken and used by those who cultivated it themselves; the hiring of agricultural labor was forbidden. The peasants interpreted this to mean that at last they were to own the lands they had so long coveted; but Bolshevik leaders interpreted the situation otherwise. Private property in land, whether in the hands of the wealthy or the poor, was not permissible in a Bolshevik society.

The revolution begun in Petrograd spread rapidly over the country. A serious conflict occurred in Moscow, where there was a week of fighting and the historic Kremlin was bombarded before the Bolsheviks gained control of the city. The Bolshevik dead were publicly buried in the great square before the Kremlin, the Red Square which had for centuries witnessed so many demonstrations, royal processions, religious ceremonies, and executions.

The new government was faced with the most difficult situation. An army largely officered by men of the old regime was still in the field. Russia was still at war. Outside of Russia the Bolsheviks had no friends; the Allies were making every effort to prevent Russia from making peace with Germany, and the Central Powers threatened Russia on the west, the north, and the south. In Russia the Bolsheviks were opposed by all the old privileged interests, by all the liberal parties, and by all the other revolutionary elements except the extreme left wing of the Socialist Revolutionary party, which at this time joined the Bolsheviks and was represented in the new government. Industry was disrupted; transportation and communication were demoralized; disorder was common throughout the country, where the peasants were violently seizing land and property; food was lacking in the cities. To all of these was to be added civil war. Elements hostile to the new government were to gather armies, and within a few months Russia was to be literally ringed around with enemies. Counterrevolution, foreign intervention, struggles of White and Red armies were to combine with the earlier forces of disintegration to create conditions which would appear to be insuperably difficult.

At the same time the revolutionary spirit was growing.

Peasant poets, who before the revolution had written in tones of hopelessness and depression, now expressed a new spirit of hope and determination:

> Yesterday's slaves break the chains,
> Yesterday's pariahs forge the swords.

> Friends, our day is hot and red,
> Our world is tempestuous ocean.

> To the fight rises the peasant
> The giant of work and thought.

> For land and freedom, for earned bread
> We march in arms to meet our foes!
> Upon us enough they did tread!
> Rush on to fight, to blows!

> The peasants with fiery ensigns
> March in file through the villages.
> Land and freedom are finer than gold,
> Land and freedom is our motto.[2]

Proletarian poets exulted in the revolution and in its violence:

> Today
> The last ladders
> And the bridges of the past are burnt.
> Today
> The weakest
> Is the power in a free land.

> Today, workmen, the Earth, all the Earth
> Crimsoning on the streets and paths,
> Discards the black blouse of night,
> And echoing with our songs now rings.[3]

These spontaneous outbursts, the result of fierce hatreds and of exultation at trampling Yesterday "under boots shod with anger," give the feeling of the revolutionary days when the peasant thought at last he would have bread and freedom, and the worker saw power and plenty coming into his hands. It remained, however, for a famous lyric poet, Alexander Blok, to write the great poem of the revolution—*The Twelve*—for this sensitive poet perceived some of the undertones of which neither peasant nor proletarian verse maker was conscious:

> The wind is whirling, the snowflakes dance.
> In the night twelve men advance.
>
> Black, narrow, rifle-straps,
> Cigarettes, tilted caps.
>
> A convict's stripes would fit their backs.
> Fires mark their nightly tracks.
> Freedom, ekh, freedom—
> Unhallowed, unblessed!
> Trah—tah—tah!
>
> .   .   .   .   .
>
> Fires blaze upon their track.
> Their rifle-straps are gleaming black.
>
> March to the revolution's pace;
> We've a fierce enemy to face.
>
> More daring, friends, take aim, the lot!
> At Holy Russia let's fire a shot.
>
> .   .   .   .   .
>
> And the twelve, unblessed, uncaring,
> Still go marching on,
> Ripe for death and daring,
> Pitying none.
> On, with rifles lifted
> At the hidden enemy.
> Through deep alleys where the snow has sifted;
> Where the lonely tempest tosses free.
> Onward, where the snow has drifted
> Clutching at the marcher's knee.
>
> The red flag,
> Flaunts in their faces.

Steady beat
Their sounding paces.

Grimly followed
Are their traces.

Ruthlessly the storm-wind smites
Days and nights.

Forward, forward, the thundering beat
Of the workers' marching feet! [4]

It was this revolutionary spirit, so ruthless, so determined, aroused by years of oppression, which was to be at
least partly responsible for the efforts that were to enable
the Bolsheviks to meet the difficult problems of the next
few years.

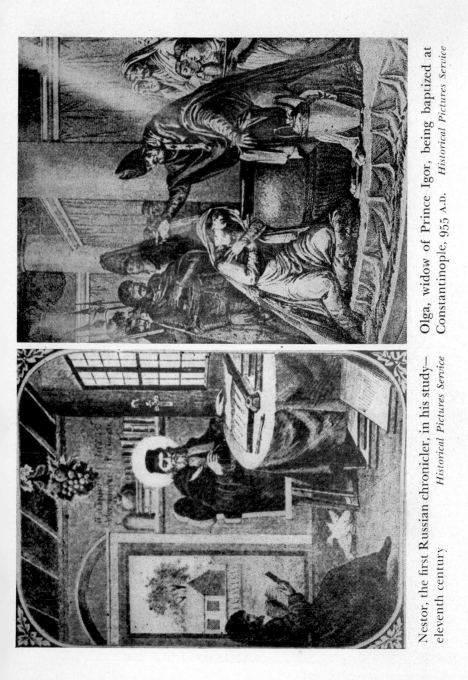

Nestor, the first Russian chronicler, in his study—
eleventh century   *Historical Pictures Service*

Olga, widow of Prince Igor, being baptized at
Constantinople, 955 A.D.   *Historical Pictures Service*

As one of his reforms, Peter the Great forced his subjects to cut
their beards
Historical Pictures Service

The Kremlin in the thirteenth century
Sovfoto

Exploring the Pacific—Bering on his expedition which resulted in
the discovery of Alaska for the Tsar *Historical Pictures Service*

The coronation of the first Romanov *Historical Pictures Service*

Moscow was burned by Napoleon in 1812   *Historical Pictures Service*

Tolstoy tilling the soil   *Sovfoto*

In periods of famine starving peasants surged toward the cities in search of food

Historical Pictures Service

Lenin addressing a meeting of the Moscow Soviet in 1922   *Sovfoto*

A group of Moscow children and their mothers on the first day of
school   *Sovfoto*

A village school   *Sovfoto*

A group of Tadzhiks in the passenger plane which provides regular service between the Tadzhik Socialist Soviet Republic "on the roof of the world," high in the Pamir mountains, and the lowlands of central Asia   *Sovfoto*

Scene of wartime destruction in the city of Kiev. Here, as elsewhere, the Germans destroyed the richest industrial sections of the Soviet Union   *Sovfoto*

Threshing grain on a collective farm

A shop of the Birobidjan spinning mill under construction as part of the new Five-Year Plan

6. THE YEARS OF CONFUSION
(1918-1921)

CIVIL war, foreign intervention, and foreign blockade, together with the policies adopted by the Soviet government to enable it to establish a socialized economy and to fight the hostile forces gathered against it, created a situation marked by confusion, suffering, violence, and privation. The Russian Socialist Federal Soviet Republic was invaded from all sides, while at the same time it struggled with counterrevolution and grappled with the problems of defending itself, averting starvation, and establishing socialism. An iron determination sustained the people who fought against such tremendous odds. "I am ready to give another year of starvation to our revolution," said a half-fed youth to the special agent sent by President Wilson to Russia in 1919, and these words reveal the spirit which enabled the Soviets to carry on their desperate fight.

The situation was, however, so complicated that not all the people were welded together by this spirit. The November revolution had been but the beginning of the Bolshevik struggle for power. Now the Bolsheviks had to grapple with counterrevolution, as well as deal with the people who were ignorant of the issues involved. Over the land, into the villages, came first one army, then another. The confusion of the people in the war areas is suggested in a narrative of the civil conflict in Siberia, written a few years later. The Red Army had arrived in a village, and steps were being taken to form a village soviet.

The villagers looked somewhat mistrustful. And no wonder.

Only yesterday the Cossacks had summoned them to this very place and elected their authorities; today it was the Reds who were establishing a revolutionary committee, and tomorrow, for all they knew, the Cossacks might be back again. What were they to do? Perhaps those of the villagers who accepted leading posts would have to pay with their lives for this honour!

Nobody volunteered to work on the committee. Fear paralysed the peasants. Those who were not afraid, or who understood the present events in all their complexity, had long ago left the villages for the towns, or had enlisted in the Red Army.[1]

After the November revolution the immediate objective of the Soviet government was a general peace; but when the Allies ignored its proposals in this direction, it took steps to negotiate separately with the Central Powers. When the terms were discussed, German and Austrian troops were in control of the Baltic provinces and of Poland; they held Odessa and occupied a strong position in the Ukraine, which had erected an independent government. The Soviets were forced to pay a high price for peace with enemies so strongly entrenched. The treaty of Brest Litovsk declared that Poland, Lithuania, Estonia, Courland, and Livonia were no longer under Russian rule but under German control. It provided that Bolshevik troops should be removed from Finland, whose independence had already been recognized by the Bolsheviks. In addition the Central Powers concluded a separate peace with the Ukraine and retained their influential position there. The territories thus detached from Russia included over one fourth of the former empire's population, arable lands, and railways; in them were almost three quarters of the iron industries and fully three fourths of the coal fields, as well as one third of the manufacturing industries. The severe terms of the treaty led to bitter opposition to peace at this price, but Lenin forced the treaty through, convinced that any peace, no matter how disastrous its provisions, was better than continuing to fight at this time. Lenin expressed himself as being willing to surrender anything necessary to preserve the Communist revolution and to keep it alive in any portion of Russia.

Serious differences of opinion regarding the policy toward Germany continued to show themselves in the Soviet government after Brest Litovsk. Elements which had been opposed to the peace terms, especially the left-wing Socialist Revolutionaries who were represented in the Soviet government, advocated the reopening of hostilities against the Germans because of their actions in the Ukraine. These Socialist Revolutionaries planned and carried through the assassination of the German minister, and revolted against the Bolshevik leaders, hoping to force a new war with Germany and to overthrow the Bolsheviks. The revolt was unsuccessful, the left-wing Socialist Revolutionaries were arrested, and the Bolshevik party was left in control of the Soviet government. Under Lenin's leadership this government remained inflexibly opposed to renewing war with Germany—but on account of Allied intervention it found itself fighting an undeclared war with the Allies. Brest Litovsk ended Russia's war with Germany, but it did not bring the peace so desired by Lenin.

The Allies were brought into the situation because when Germany made peace with the Soviets, it was in a favorable position to secure badly needed foodstuffs and raw materials. If Germany obtained these, the war would be indefinitely prolonged, and it might result in the victory of the Central Powers. Two courses were open to the Allies. They might support the Soviet government so that it would be in a position to refuse German demands and to keep the Germans from advancing farther into the regions from which they could obtain supplies. Or they might, without Soviet consent, place forces in Russia to prevent the Germans from securing stores of war materials accumulated in the northern ports, food supplies from the Ukraine, or oil from Baku. They decided upon the second course. In the first place, they were hostile to Bolshevism, and their unfriendliness was increased by the mass of anti-Bolshevik propaganda sent out from Finland and adjoining regions controlled by the Whites. Then, they were not sure that the Soviets would continue in power. Also, they were alienated by the fact that it was Soviet leadership which had caused Russia to withdraw from the War. It must not be forgotten that the world situation was very tense in 1918, and the decision of the Allies was made at a time when emotions fed by years of terrible warfare were in full flood.

Foreign intervention began when a small detachment of British troops landed at Murmansk in March 1918 to prevent the war stores there from falling into German hands. When, in April, the Japanese entered Vladivostok, nominally to protect Japanese subjects in this region, a new problem complicated the situation—the question of intervening in Siberia. The Japanese, desirous of extending their influence on the continent of Asia, proposed that they place large detachments of troops in Siberia and be given the right to manage affairs there as they saw fit. The British supported this idea, but the United States refused to agree. While Siberian intervention was being discussed, 4,000 Allied troops were landed in Murmansk. By the end of 1918, the Allied forces (which included American troops) numbered 10,000 in the north, and French troops, which were to reach 12,000, had entered the Ukraine. Before this had happened, the United States had finally agreed to Siberian intervention, on the grounds of co-operating with Japanese troops to guard the Trans-Siberian railway so that the Czechs might be safely moved out of the country.

Who were the Czechs? Fifty thousand of them were in

Siberia. Coming from Czechoslovakia, a portion of the Austrian empire which longed for independence from Austria, they had been forced into the war on the side of the Central Powers. When the opportunity came, they deserted to the side of Russia to fight against the hated Austrians. Now, when the Soviets had made peace with Germany, the Czechs were stranded in Russia. They wished to return to the western front to continue their fight for independence. The only possible route was through Siberia and across the Pacific, the North American continent, and the Atlantic. For this long journey, the Czechs were promised the help of the Allies. They began their dramatic anabasis, involving a journey almost around the world. Some of them had reached the port of Vladivostok, while others were scattered through Siberia. The Soviet government placed no obstacle to their departure; but the transportation promised by the Allies did not materialize. The Czechs could not understand the delay. When local soviets in the far east ordered them to disarm because of certain clashes which had occurred in a region already disturbed, they refused. The freedom-loving Czechs found themselves fighting against the Communists (the party name was changed from Bolshevik to Communist in March 1918) on the side of White counterrevolutionaries who were attempting to restore the old regime. Not sympathetic to Communism, but even more opposed to autocratic monarchy, the Czechs were caught in the situation developing in Siberia.

The dramatic war record of the Czechs, together with their known desire to win independence for themselves, provided the final argument which was necessary to win American consent to Siberian intervention. It was agreed that the United States and Japan should each place some 7,000 men in Siberia but within a few months the Japanese had sent 70,000 troops into the country, while the American forces there numbered about 8,500.

Meanwhile, White forces were springing up everywhere to oppose the Soviets—in the Ukraine under Kornilov, then under Denikin, and finally, under Wrangel; in the Baltic region under Yudenich; and in Siberia under Kolchak, Semenov, Rozanov, Kalmykov. Public opinion in the Allied countries, aroused by anti-Bolshevik propaganda, supported the idea that Allied troops should give active assistance to the Whites. Diplomats urged this; conflicting instructions were sent to the commanders of Allied troops in Siberia and elsewhere. Kolchak's men were, to a great extent, armed and equipped by the Allies; Denikin's Cossacks wore British uniforms and used British guns; Wrangel's forces were equipped by France; the Japanese openly supported Semenov—who was, in the words of General Graves, the American commander, one of the "worst criminals" in Siberia.

Allied forces placed in Siberia to safeguard the return of the Czechs to the western front remained in Siberia over a year after the armistice with Germany had been signed. Japanese troops were not removed from Siberia until after the Washington Conference of 1922, and they were in North Sakhalin until late in 1925. In November 1919 the Czechs were still in Siberia, trying to co-operate with the Allied forces and carry out the tasks assigned them, at the time when the Whites controlled that region. Their feeling is best described in the words of one of their leaders, for they reflect not only the position of the Czechs but the Siberian situation as a whole:

The intolerable position in which our Army is placed, forces us to address ourselves to the Allied powers to ask them for counsel as to how the Czech Army can be assured of its own security and of a free return to its own Country, which was decided with the assent of all the Allied Powers.

The Army was ready to protect the railway in the sector which was assigned to it and it has fulfilled its task conscientiously. But now the presence of our Army on the railway to protect it has become impossible because the activities of the Army are contrary to its aspirations in the cause of humanity and justice.

In protecting the railway and maintaining order in the country, our Army is forced to act contrary to its convictions when it supports and maintains an arbitrary, absolute power which at present rules.

The burning of villages, the murder of peaceable Russian inhabitants by the hundreds, and the shooting without reason, of democratic men solely because they are suspected of holding political views are daily facts; and the responsibility for them, before the Courts of Nations of the entire world, will fall upon us because being an armed force, we have not prevented these injustices. This passiveness is the direct result of our neutrality and non-intervention in Russian internal affairs, and, thanks to our being loyal to this idea, we have become, in spite of ourselves, accomplices to a crime.

In communicating this fact to the representatives of the Allied Powers to whom the Czech Nation has been and will be a faithful Ally, we deem it necessary to take every measure to inform the nations of the whole world in what a moral and tragic position the Czech Army is placed and what are the causes of it.

As to ourselves, we see no other way out of this situation than to evacuate immediately the sector which was given us to guard, or else to obtain the right to prevent the injustices and crimes cited above.[2]

With respect to the actions of Whites and Reds in Siberia, General Graves says: "There were horrible murders committed, but they were not committed by the Bolsheviks as the world believes. I am well on the side of safety when I say that the anti-Bolsheviks killed one hundred people in eastern Siberia for every one killed by the Bolsheviks." Why did the Allies give such aid and encouragement to the Whites that civil war in Russia was prolonged and its bitterness and violence were intensified? The words of the leaders who met in Paris early in 1919 to discuss the situation in Russia shed some light on this question. In conference Lloyd George said:

Firstly, the real facts are not known.
Secondly, it is impossible to get the facts. . . .
Thirdly, conditions in Russia are very bad; there is general misgovernment and starvation. It is not known who is obtaining the upper hand, but the hope that the Bolshevik Government would collapse had not been realized.[3]

President Wilson asked to be permitted to urge one aspect of the case. As M. Sonnino had implied, they were all repelled by Bolshevism, and for that reason they had placed armed men in opposition to them. . . .
M. Clemenceau said that, in principle, he did not favour conversation with the Bolshevists; not because they were criminals, but because we would be raising them to our level by saying that they were worthy of entering into conversation with us. . . .[4]

The hostility of the Allies to the Soviets was further shown in the rigorous blockade which was enforced against them. Neutral nations were asked to agree not to trade with the Soviets; British and French warships patrolled the seas to prevent any neutral ship from entering Soviet ports. The United States refused to join the naval blockade, but it placed an embargo on Soviet trade.

In 1919 a new pressure came in from the southwest when Polish forces advanced as far as Kiev. The Red Army conducted an offensive which reached to the gates of Warsaw; but it was unable to follow up its victories, and the Soviet government was forced to conclude an unfavorable peace in order that this division of the Red Army might be freed to move against other forces. Thereupon the Soviets reduced their activity in this direction and turned their attention to the east.

It might be thought that the White forces in control of Siberia and the Ukraine and threatening the Soviets from two sides should have been able to unite and to overcome the Red Army. There was, however, little unity among the Whites. Each leader was fighting for himself, and each was depending upon foreign assistance which never officially materialized, and which was itself divided. French, British, Japanese, and American diplomats were at loggerheads over Siberian intervention, and foreign army leaders in Siberia and elsewhere in Russia failed to agree. White leaders did not secure much support from the peasants, whom they treated with cruelty. Peasants were forced into the armies, their grain was seized, their homes were burned. They refused to support the Whites, who represented the old landlords, and were inclined to welcome the Red Army when it arrived with its promises of bread and land, even though it also made demands upon them.

Eventually the Red Army overcame the various White forces which in 1918-1919 had been successful, and which had pressed in on the small nucleus of the Soviet state and had advanced close to Moscow and Petrograd before they were pushed back and defeated. Civil war came to an end, and most of the foreign troops were withdrawn. The highly important Ukraine, with its grain fields and coal mines, though remaining for a time an independent state, became pro-Soviet. Counterrevolution was not a thing of the past—any act designed to weaken the Soviet regime is still considered counterrevolutionary—but the organized armies marching against the Soviets were defeated in 1920.

How was the Red Army created, equipped, and officered? How were army supplies and food secured? What measures were taken to crush the counterrevolutionary activities which did not take the form of civil war?

The Red Army was not formed out of the old army, because it was realized that the peasant soldiers could not be prevented from going back to the country. The Red Guards, the first military reliance of the Soviets, were recruited from among the city workers; any man presenting a card from his factory organization was admitted to the Red Guards. Though these men needed training, they refused to accept any sort of military discipline; they intended to run affairs through their own soviets. It was soon apparent that such an organization could not meet the disciplined forces of the counterrevolutionists. Trotsky, placed in charge of military affairs, built up the Red Army, and through his untiring energy and his ability to inspire and encourage, he maintained its morale. For months Trotsky literally lived in trains, dashing from one front to another, stimulating the Red Army to extraordinary effort under the most difficult conditions. If the Russian empire had been unable to feed, clothe, and equip its soldiers at the front, it may be imagined what the situation of the Red Army must have been, when industry was far less productive and transportation far more demoralized than either had been under the empire. The Red Army was in rags, it lacked proper equipment of all types, it was recruited from a country already tired of war —but it was created through the efforts of Trotsky and of such leaders as Budenny, the great cavalry commander. The emergence, however, of any army capable of fighting against such tremendous odds, from a country demoralized by war, can only be explained by the fact that the Red forces as a whole must have felt that they were fighting for the revolution which they had helped to make.

Conditions in the Red Army are suggested in this description:

It is dark as pitch in the cattle trucks. No candles, kerosene lamps, no lanterns. On bare boards, caked with mud from the tread of bast shoes and heavy boots, slimy with spittle, slops of cabbage soup and tea, littered with butts of homemade cigarettes, lie the Red Army men. The nights are long and it is wearisome to lie in the cold and dark, with a ragged coat for blanket and a tarpaulin knapsack for a pillow. . . .

After many days of travel and untold discomfort, boring halts, brawls and now and then scuffles and shots, the destina-

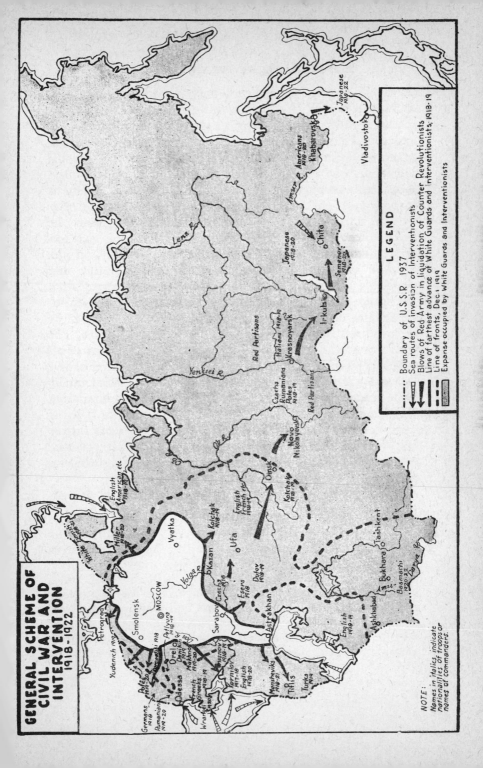

GENERAL SCHEME OF CIVIL WAR AND INTERVENTION
1918-1922

LEGEND

Boundary of U.S.S.R. 1937
Sea routes of invasion of Interventionists
Blows of Red Army in liquidation of Counter Revolutionists
Line of farthest advance of White Guards and Interventionists, 1918-19
Line of fronts, Dec. 1 1919
Expanse occupied by White Guards and Interventionists

NOTE:
Names in italics indicate
nationalities of troops or
names of commanders.

tion is reached at last. The sliding doors of the cattle trucks are pushed open and the trucks hastily unloaded. The baggage, such as it is, is thrown into a heap, and two Red Army men are set to guard it with fixed bayonets. . . .

The unloaded train takes on an abandoned air. . . There is a period of shouting and scolding, confusion and disorder, meaningless commands that nobody thinks of taking seriously. And then suddenly the order rings out:

"Fall in!"

And all at once everybody is on the run, all hurrying to find their respective sections, platoons, and companies. . . . The compact bodies of men step out in even ranks, followed by the rumbling, rattling carts, neighing and snorting horses and clanking guns. Now and then a random shot is fired. During the first versts the ranks keep straight and regular, the footsteps eager and firm; the men's voices, strong and vibrant, are lifted in song. But as the march continues, some begin to straggle. Tired, worn out and fevered men are hoisted on to the carts; the ranks become ragged, and no more songs are heard; each and all yearns for a halt. . . . At last the halt comes, and in less than a minute most of them are snoring like tired giants; others, whose defiant vitality cannot let them rest, break into song again, play the accordions or dance, squatting and flinging out one leg and then the other, hooting, shouting, full of inextinguishable mirth and fire.

And so they march from halt to halt till at last they come to the trenches.[5]

The Red Army was raised by conscription among workers and peasants who did not employ any hired labor. No other person was admitted to its ranks, throughout which Communist party members were scattered to stiffen the morale. People living on invested income, priests, traders, and businessmen of the old regime were required to assist in performing disagreeable dirty work which did not involve fighting and for which individuals did not need to be armed. The hardships involved in this requirement were a source of bitterness and suffering among those sub-

jected to them, but they were also a means of increasing
the prestige of the Red Army among those conscripted for
service.

Trotsky was determined to secure qualified leaders, and
he turned to army officers—both commissioned and non-
commissioned—of the old regime. These men, always
under strict supervision, were required to drill and train
the recruits. Sometimes the situation was made easy for
them, and sometimes it was most difficult; but always any
attempt to desert, or to injure the Red Army, was met
with punishment, not only of the man himself, but of his
whole family. Under these conditions most of the old
army officers in the Red Army served it well. Party commissars were attached to every army unit; they had the
power of veto over any proposed move, and they reported
any suspicious matters to the political department, which
was under the direction of the Cheka, the Soviet secret
police modeled on the secret police of old Russia.

While the chief function of the party commissars was to
control the officers, they were also responsible for organizing propaganda in the villages occupied by the Red
Army, and for arranging for the political education of the
troops. The way in which these activities were carried on
is described in *Chapayev:*

And thus the political education not only of the army units
but even of the population in the war zone was taken care of
more or less successfully. Villages and hamlets were visited by
workers on horseback and on foot, toured by "Red carts" with
Communist agitators, who told the people the aims and ob-
jectives of the Red Army, why it had been formed, what was
being done in Soviet Russia and what was happening beyond
its borders. Often these men did not know much themselves—
for where could they learn from?—often they could not explain
things coherently, but for all that they always communicated
what was most vital; they were torchbearers, mouthpieces,
teachers. . . . And then they would stage plays, give magic

lantern shows, display pictures, all of which, you can imagine, was a source of great wonder in a poor out-of-the-way village where the half-Tatar population had never been more than thirty or forty versts from home.

With the Red Army men it was easier to carry on work. Always under arms, ready to listen, well organized, they were head and shoulders above the rural population in political development. Even when there was no political department to supervise things, the Red Army men had their own Party nuclei carrying on constant work among them. All the nuclei needed from the political department was material aid and fresh instruction from time to time; often enough they were able to cope with their work unaided.

As regards work in the regiment, this varied according to where the regiment was and what it was doing. It was one thing when the regiment was behind the lines, resting. Here work could be carried on systematically, here the illiterate could be taught to read and write, classes and lectures could be organized, though not, of course, on a grand scale; much, in short, could be done, and was done. But it was another matter when the troops were on the march or in the fighting line. At such times newspapers would not reach the regiments for weeks on end. No time for lectures or meetings—the men were in battle, under fire! And during the hours of respite the first thought was to get a wink of sleep, to rest yourself, patch up your boots or mend your torn clothes, to recuperate and get ready for next day's marching or fighting.[6]

The Red Army was organized and put into the field under incredible conditions. In the latter part of 1918, when there were between half and three-quarters of a million men under arms, ammunition had practically given out and the counterrevolutionary activities had only just begun. Two things were essential—supplies and food for the army, and food for the city dwellers who were on the edge of starvation and who alone could produce the needed war materials. At this point the Soviets resorted to the policy known as War Communism. Its main features were government control of all agriculture and industry, and government distribution of all manufactured goods and food.

As far as agriculture and food supplies were concerned, the Soviet government created a food commissariat to attend to the securing and distributing of food. Members of this committee went out to obtain grain in the country districts, but they were met with opposition, particularly since they offered no payment which was satisfactory to the peasants. Then the "committees of the poor" were organized. These were committees of poorer peasants who were supposed to force the richer among them to deliver their surplus grain to the government. The activities of the food commissariat and of the committees of the poor led to the bitterest conflicts in the villages; peasant was set against peasant, city against country, state against peasant. When peasants realized that their surplus stocks of grain would be requisitioned, they hid the grain they had, refusing to give it up. They also reduced the area under cultivation.

While food supplies were decreasing, industrial production was steadily declining. In June 1918 the government decreed that all large industry was nationalized. Raw materials were lacking; there was an absence of efficient management, and a shortage of equipment. Workers' soviets had proved unable to manage factories. Many of the foreign and Russian managers had fled when the Bolshevik revolution took place. Any expert industrialists remaining in the country were, in general, hostile to the Soviets. Factory equipment, most of which had been imported, wore out and could not be replaced because of the foreign blockade. Workers deserted the factories because of the food shortage in the cities, and in addition many of the most efficient workers were in the Red Army. In 1917 industrial production had been three quarters of what it had been in 1913, but by 1920 it was only one fifth of the production of 1913.

One of the chief factors causing the disintegration of industry was the food shortage in the cities, and for this both government and peasants were responsible. The government did not have the organization and transportation facilities necessary to distribute food in the quantities needed, even if it had been able to obtain them; and it could not secure them. The peasants stubbornly resisted giving up their surplus grain in return for doubtful currency or promises of goods. They refused to plant and harvest crops which were the property of the state.

The scanty food supplies of the city were rationed, and ration cards were issued only to workers. Patient householders stood in line for hours, only too frequently to find that the food was gone when their turn came. Members of the suspect classes who could not find employment—the clergy, officials of the old regime, the bourgeoisie, the formerly well-to-do—and to whom ration cards were not issued, could obtain food only by selling, piece by piece, such treasures as they possessed—jewels, gold, silver, clothing—in return for something to eat. At this time there was a steady movement of the personal treasures of old Russia into the country, where these articles were illegally exchanged for food.

When peasant poets looked back on these years, they ceased to sing about the revolution; they were depressed by the continued strife and hostile to the pressure exerted upon the villages by the cities. Their poetry reflected the peasant desire for peace, and also the growing division between rural region and city:

> A voice entreats us and teaches us
> To think and comprehend.
> We have not come into the world to destroy,
> But to love and to trust.[7]

To change the ways
Of dark olden days,
We must work together
For our country dear.

Let disappear forever
The bitter enmity,
Let us unite together
For common work.[8]

We are from the land of rye and oats,
Of chintz and rusticity;
You—from that of iron and concrete
Of splendor and electricity.

We are fire, water, pastures,
Sun and bread, and winter corn,
You can tell us no mysteries
Of the fragrant garden.

Your songs are the groans of the hammer;
Their tune is dross and tin;
Your tree of life is a broken limb,
It bears no fruit but heads.[9]

On the other hand, a proletarian poet described the villages and the factory in these words:

Huts that stand like plaited baskets.
Birds. Green forest. Space. And heat.
Cobwebs in the dark soul's corners.
Thought's slow whisper. Peace. Retreat.

Dirt and soot. Thick sweaty odors.
Crisp steel shavings. Whistles. Noise.
Straight bold thinking. Heavy labor.
Life's pulse throbbing like a boy's.[10]

Another cause of the division between city and country was the antireligious activities of the Soviets, generally accepted by the proletariat, but more often resented by the peasants. For example, a peasant poet writes:

> Shattered Ikon,—
> Lacerated Russia mine!
> My heart is broken,
> I pray for thee.[11]

Instead of writing sadly of the "shattered ikon," the proletarian says:

We love life, and its intoxicating boisterous ecstasy,
Our spirit is tempered with a terrible struggle and agony.
We are all, we are in all, we are the conquering fire and light,
We are to ourselves God, Judge, and Law.[12]

The Soviet attitude toward religion was caused partly by the counterrevolutionary activities of the Orthodox church, partly by the way in which the church had held the people in ignorance and in submission to tsarism, and partly by the definite atheism of Bolshevism. After the November revolution, with its threat to privilege and property, the church took a very antagonistic attitude toward the Bolsheviks, attacking all their policies of abolishing private property in land, secularizing education, and changing marriage laws. In one meeting of the clerical group controlling church affairs a member is reported to have said, "The only salvation of the Russian people is a wise Orthodox tsar." The church organized mass demonstrations against the Communists; it excommunicated Communists and revolutionaries, and it gave aid to White forces during the counterrevolution. The government meanwhile had issued a decree allowing freedom of worship, but it had excluded all religious observances from state functions and had forbidden the teaching of religion in any school. Church lands had, of course, been confiscated along with all privately owned estates.

Another factor contributing to the emotional tension

was the assassination, on August 30, 1918, of Uritsky, the head of the Cheka, and the attempt to kill Lenin. These events—as so often before in Russia in similar cases—ushered in a period of extreme repression, of terror and violence. The "Red Terror" began. Over five hundred persons of the suspect classes were immediately seized and put to death in Petrograd alone as a measure of reprisal. The Commissar for Foreign Affairs issued to all soviets orders which included the following directions:

There must be an end of laxity and weakness. All Right Socialist Revolutionaries known to local Soviets must be immediately arrested. A considerable number of hostages must be taken from among the bourgeoisie and the officers. Mass shooting must be applied upon the least attempts at resistance or the least movement in the midst of the White Guards. Local Provincial Executive Committees must show special initiative in this respect. . . .

Last of all, the rear of our armies must be finally cleared of all White Guardism and all scoundrelly conspirators against the power of the working class and the poorest peasants. Not the least wavering, not the least indecision in the application of mass terror.[13]

No one knows the total loss of life in the Red Terror, and there are no authentic accounts by unbiased observers. The Red Terror was entrusted to the Cheka, which seized, tried, and sentenced its victims in secret. The peculiar nature of the Red Terror may be attributed, in part at least, to the inheritance from the empire of secret violence as a device of government, and to the fact that the Soviets were, at this time, in a most desperate situation. Terroristic methods applied by a powerful authorized secret police carrying out the will of the Communist party continued to be officially used after the Red Terror had come to an end. It changed in intensity from time to time, depending upon the situation of the country and upon the nature and scope of the activities it was trying to repress or to punish.

In these difficult years, when the Soviets were menaced on all sides and were utterly insecure, the government went ahead formulating on paper the most elaborate plans for the reconstruction of the country. For example, in 1917 the government announced its plans for social insurance. All persons who were working for hire were included in the social insurance scheme, which covered all types of loss of ability or opportunity to work and hence to earn— illness, injury, invalidism, old age, maternity, widowhood, orphanhood, unemployment. All expenses of the system were to be borne by the employers—state, organization, or private person, as the case might be—and none of the cost was to be met by contributions from workers. In case of loss of ability to work, or to find employment, the compensation was to amount to the full wage previously earned. The entire system was to be managed and controlled by those who were to be benefited; that is, the employees. Of course the government was unable to carry through this scheme during the period of civil war, foreign intervention, and the complete disruption of all resources and order; but the formulation of such a plan, and similar ones in other fields, served to indicate the intentions of the new government and to create in some quarters, at least, a determined support for the regime which contemplated such legislation.

During these hard years the entire social structure of old Russia was overturned. The former tsar, his immediate family, and many of his relatives were killed, while others had escaped from the country. The nobility lost their landed property, their palaces, and their homes. Many were killed; others were in exile or living precarious lives not knowing when their turn was to come. Clergy, private businessmen, people who were living on unearned income or who were employing others for profit, agents and employees of the tsar's police and secret service were disfranchised. People who had possessed property had lost it; they were suspect and lived under a constant threat. Thousands of refugees from these classes of the people could be found in Constantinople, Manchuria, China, western Europe—often penniless. Others, recruited into the service of the Soviets, were held there through the threat to their families, who were practically held as hostages. The workers had seized the power, and those high in the Communist ranks were exercising power. The labor of the masses of the workers was conscripted by the Soviet government, which could not even manage to feed the proletariat. The peasants had been allowed to seize private estates, but their grain was requisitioned by the government, which could offer them no satisfactory payments. The backward peasantry favored the Bolsheviks when they permitted them to seize land, but were politically too uneducated to understand the emergencies faced by the Communists and to co-operate willingly when they were asked to give up their grain. Economic differences between classes, and within classes, practically disappeared. To the leveling influences of the seizure of private property and the distribution of land among the peasants was added the great equalizer—starvation. Suffering among the people was as acute as it had ever been under the tsars.

In 1921 the misery of the people was increased by a great famine caused in part by the refusal of the peasants to cultivate all the land, and intensified by the failure of the harvest because of drought in the Volga regions, the Ukraine, and the Crimea. Suffering was so widespread that it attracted the attention of the world. The American Quakers began to provide relief; special relief from America was administered under Herbert Hoover; the Soviet government also raised funds. With famine came another epidemic of typhus. These conditions gave the final blow to War Communism. In 1921 the New Economic Policy was announced, a return to private trade, marking a change in the policy of the Soviet government.

There have been many arguments over War Communism. Did it fail entirely because of the circumstances under which it was tried? Did it represent a sincere effort immediately to create a communist state with no intermediate stage, or was it merely a policy forced on the Soviet government at this time because of the situation in which it found itself, as a result of civil war, foreign intervention, and foreign blockade? It appeared to the world at large that communism had been tried and that even the Communist party had come to realize that it was unworkable.

One factor bringing about this change in economic policy was the Soviet tendency to opportunism—that is, doing at one time what seems to be dictated by the circumstances of that time. When circumstances have changed, the Soviet government has modified its tactics. When people have reached the last extremity of endurance, the Soviet government loosens the belt, as it were, and permits the people a breathing space, a time in which to recover themselves and to gather resources which may be called upon later. In 1921, the first of these breathing spaces was initiated when the New Economic Policy was adopted.

7. LIFE UNDER THE NEW ECONOMIC POLICY (1921-1928)

AT THE end of the "years of confusion" the encouraging aspect of life in Russia was the fact that civil war had been ended; the Soviets had not been conquered by counterrevolutionists or foreign interventionists. For this victory, a terrific price had been paid. In a country stripped of food the people of the cities were existing on starvation rations. Industry was at a standstill; transport had practically ceased to exist; the peasants were discouraged and far from enthusiastic over the new regime. War Communism had failed; in order to put the country on its feet and get it to the place where it could hope to build socialism, Lenin insisted that War Communism must be abandoned and that there must be, for the time being, what he called a "retreat on the economic front." He advocated a return to private trade and enterprise, for a time, and within limits. The policy now adopted to bring about the rehabilitation of the exhausted country was known as the New Economic Policy.

During this period of economic reconstruction were developed the means and the methods of educating and training people in new ideas and habits of living, so that they would be more or less prepared for a reversal of the NEP when it had served its purpose. The Soviet Union was organized. Various differences within the Communist party were fought out, and the newly organized leadership necessary after Lenin's death emerged. As the country got on its feet, foreign nations began to resume relations with it. The Soviets, a few years earlier an outlaw, now became a slightly tolerated member of the community of nations. Economic rehabilitation, education and social change, extension of the influence of the Soviets, partial division and then reconsolidation of the Communist party, and modification of foreign relations—these, then, marked the NEP period.

In 1921 the first need of the people was food. In order to encourage grain production, the War Communism policy of seizing and distributing surplus grain was abandoned. Peasants were required to pay a tax in grain and were permitted to sell any surplus on the private market. This arrangement provided the peasants with an incentive to sow and to cultivate their fields, lacking under War Communism. The cities had bread, and some grain was exported. Party leaders watched the situation developing in the villages with some anxiety; it was evident to them that as 80 per cent of the people produced as individuals and sold their grain on the private market, they would become more strongly nonsocialist in outlook. To break up this tendency, the government encouraged the formation of co-operatives to handle marketing, and of agricultural collectives to manage production.

Two main types of socialized farms had already emerged since the November revolution—the sovkhoz and the kolkhoz. The sovkhoz was a state grain factory, owned and administered by the government, which employed the agricultural workers just as it hired factory workers for the state-controlled industries. The kolkhoz was a collective farm into which peasants joining put their animals, tools, and land, and in whose profits members shared. The peasants were reluctant to join collectives; they preferred to farm their fields themselves. They had supported the Communist party because it had promised them land. They had not expected to surrender these lands and their small personal possessions and to be obliged to transform their lives. As a result of the unwillingness of the peasants to change their ways of living and working, the degree of collectivization was small. By October 1928, 10,262,000 acres of sown land were included in collectives of the kolkhoz type, 5,616,000 acres were under cultivation in state farms, while 275,700,000 acres were uncollectivized. The mass of the peasants remained outside the collective society desired by the Communist party. Throughout the second half of the NEP period, party leaders were divided over the amount of pressure which should be brought to bear at this time to force collectivization.

As a result of the way the NEP worked out in the rural regions, peasants were freed from the pressure of earlier years, and some peasants began to accumulate more wealth than others. Production, however, was not brought to the prewar level, partly because the large estates had been divided among the people who used primitive and backward methods of cultivation, and who could not therefore produce from the same area the amounts of grain previously raised. State farms and collectives could use machinery, but there was not enough farm machinery to supply even the relatively small proportion of the land under large-scale cultivation. As far as agriculture was concerned, the NEP was effective only within limits, and it permitted the development of economic differences in the villages which were considered dangerous by the Communist party.

If food was the first need of the country in 1921, manufactured goods was the second. Factory production had been steadily declining for years, and there was practically a famine of all types of goods—clothing, building materials, household equipment, tools, machinery, paper. The first essential for reopening the prewar factories was labor. The workers had returned to the villages in the hope of getting food, and now, given preferential treatment, they were attracted back to the factories. Workers had been given heavier representation in the soviets than the peasants—in the cities, one representative was elected for every 25,000 voters, while in the rural regions there was one representative for every 125,000 inhabitants. Workers' children were given special opportunities for education; crèches in which small children were cared for while their parents were at work were first established in connection with factories; medical care was first provided for workers; social insurance benefits applied only to those working for hire, thus excluding all peasants farming their own lands. All of these advantages had their appeal, and workers came back to the cities. Besides workers, managers were needed. Private control and management of small factories was again permitted, and private trade in manufactured goods was allowed, though the government continued to manage large industry and foreign trade. As a result of the provisions of the NEP, industrial production, which at the beginning of the period had been but one fifth of that of 1913, by 1927 exceeded that of prewar Russia.

By 1925 the country was sufficiently rehabilitated so that the government felt it was safe to take measures to discourage the private traders, or nepmen, in order to check the growth of capitalism within this group. To do this, the government put all its weight behind the co-operative marketing system, and increased the taxes and disabilities imposed upon private trade. Co-operatives obtained their goods from state industries; they were permitted to use government railways at lower rates than private merchants; they were given state credits to enable them to finance their enterprises, and they were almost wholly exempted from taxation. Membership in co-operatives was encouraged by the trade unions; problems of co-operatives were taken up in party congresses. The trend of trade during the second half of the NEP period shows the effect of these measures:

	Wholesale trade		Retail trade	
	1924–1925	1927–1928	1924–1925	1927–1928
State	56.6%	43.4%	16.2%	13.5%
Co-op.	35.2%	43.4%	37.9%	62.4%
Private	8.2%	1.4%	45.9%	24.1%

One reason why private trade was able to continue at all was the fact that there was a shortage of goods. If the private trader could manage to get hold of materials to sell, he could obtain a high price for them and thus keep his business going in spite of the conditions under which he had to carry it on.

In the cities, where most individuals were working for hire, the spread in wage levels was small. All hired labor, from the unskilled to the most technical, was divided into categories. Those at the top of the lower list, which included unskilled and skilled work, were paid about three times as much as those at the bottom. The highest paid in the upper list, which included foremen, engineers, and managers, received one and two-thirds as much as the best paid in the lower list. Thus, for example, the factory manager could not receive more than five times as much as the street cleaner, a difference which was relatively small. While not all types of hired labor were paid equally, the tendency at this time was to keep the inequality very small.

In spite of the incentive which the NEP gave to industry and agriculture, rehabilitation would have been difficult if the currency had not been stabilized. During the years 1918-1921 money had lost value as a result of the inflation which had occurred. The inflated currency was called in and a new and more stable ruble was issued. All foreign purchases continued to be paid for in gold.

As the country gradually got on its feet, the government was able to begin to carry out plans which had been formulated earlier on paper, but which could not be carried out before because of the disorder, distress, and pressing problems of the counterrevolutionary years. For example, as the number of people working for hire increased, social insurance funds and benefits steadily became larger. The total income available for social insurance purposes, 474,-200,000 rubles in 1924-1926, was 1,050,100,000 rubles in 1927-1928, and with the increase in resources came additional benefits and extended activities. By 1925-1926, money was available for the construction of workers' homes and sanatoria, and within two years the amount spent for this purpose had increased fourfold. The sums paid out for disability, invalidism, medical care, and the construction of hospitals greatly increased in the same years.

Comprehensive plans for education had been outlined. These not only included reducing adult illiteracy and providing schools, but they also dealt with ways and means of educating the people to a fuller understanding of the new society in which the Communist party believed. Many agencies were drawn into this scheme—factories, the Red Army, the theater, youth organizations, even the courts and prisons. Adult illiteracy was reduced through organized work arranged in connection with the army, the factories, and campaigns in the villages. It is estimated that during these years seven million adults learned to read and write.

As far as the schools were concerned, the Soviet government wished to make them a means of building a new generation which had not been exposed to traditional discipline or curriculum content. To attain this end, types of experimentation for which both teachers and pupils were unprepared were encouraged. School discipline was turned over to the pupils; teachers were supposed to be advisers, but they were forbidden to take the lead and were never permitted to interfere in matters of discipline. Inexperienced and immature schoolboys and -girls were expected to manage school affairs.

The Diary of a Communist Schoolboy, for example, gives an idea of the situation created in the schools by the introduction of experimental methods:

September 27th

The Dalton Plan is being introduced at our school. It's a system under which the skworkers (teachers) do nothing and the pupils have to find out everything for themselves. At least, that's what it looks like to me. There will be no more classes, and the pupils will merely be given "tasks." These will be handed out a month in advance, and may be prepared either at home or in school, and when your "task" is finished you get examined at the lab. . . .

October 1st

The Dalton Plan has begun. All the desks have been crammed into one room, which will be the lecture hall. Instead of desks we'll have long benches and tables. Vanka Petukov and I loafed all day about these labs, and I felt silly. Even the skworkers don't seem very clear how to go about this Dalton business. . . .

October 3rd

The Dalton thing is a wash-out. No one can understand a thing, not even the skworkers. The skworkers discuss it every evening amongst themselves. The only novelty so far is that we have to sit on benches and have no place to put our books. . . .

The boys say that this plan was invented by some Lord Dalton, of bourgeois stock. Now I wonder what the devil we need this bourgeois plan for? . . . [1]

After describing a silly schoolboy argument with a teacher, the diarist shows some of the background which explains the Soviet school of these years.

In the old school the skworkers used to torment the boys any way they liked: but we shan't allow that now. I remember Nikpetosh reading us passages from *Stories of the Seminary,* in which even grown-up fellows were flogged right in the classroom at the door; and I have read also how boys were made to swot, and how they were given all kinds of nicknames. But in those days the boys had no idea of the times through which we have had to live. For we've known famine and cold and anarchy: we've had to feed the whole family, and have travelled a thousand miles in search of bread, and some of us have been through the civil war. It isn't three years yet since the war ended.[2]

Theoretically, the government intended to provide education for all; but there were not enough schools to go around, and not enough trained teachers. Consequently preference was given to the children of the proletariat; peasant children came next, and higher education was entirely denied to the children of the disfranchised. This restriction was partly the result of the lack of schools and trained teachers, and partly caused by the fact that the Soviet government was unwilling at this time to educate the youth who, because of the influence of their social background, might later destroy what it was trying to build.

The factory began to emerge as a center of educational work of different types. When babies were placed in factory crèches, they were given, as far as possible, excellent care; mothers were thus indirectly, or even directly, instructed in the correct care of infants. Doctors hired by factories gave instruction in health and sanitation, and various simple rules of hygiene were emphasized in workers' meetings and papers. Factories provided reading rooms for adult workers, also the classrooms of the workers' universities, to which only the proletarian of at least three years' experience was admitted and the clubrooms in which various groups might meet. On the factory walls were posted the "newspapers" which were composed and edited by the workers. Every factory had its party "cell," or group of party members. Workers, particularly party members, took active part in the management of the different educational enterprises centered in the factory.

The Red Army was used as a training ground not only for military service but also for life in the new society. Recruits were given a program of physical education, health instruction, and training in Communist theory, as well as other education. It was considered a privilege to be allowed to enter the Red Army, from which members of the disfranchised classes were barred, and in which young men were educated and comparatively well fed and clothed. The Red Army allowed no social differentiation between officers and men, and the authority of the officer was confined to army activities. In the party cells organized in the Red Army, officer and private sat as equals; or the soldier might be the superior in the party organization. This system helped to erase from the minds of Russian youth the hatred of conscription which had always been felt under the empire. The Red Army was able to influence the recruits, who frequently became convinced Communists, ready to work in village or factory and trained to work effectively for the Soviets.

Youth organizations were an important educational agency whose influence was extended during the NEP years. The class principle was emphasized here, as in the Red Army and in the schools. The Young Communists, or Komsomols, were first organized during the counter-revolutionary years. They included young people between the ages of fourteen and twenty-three whose parents were workers or poorer peasants. The exciting days of the civil war gave the Komsomols many opportunities for showing their devotion to the Bolshevik cause. Their third congress met in 1920, representing a membership of over 400,000. Since the days of war were over, Lenin talked to them about how necessary it now was for them to set about the sober business of learning, so that they might be able to assist in the hard work of building a new order. This idea did not, however, appeal to them at the time, and some of their first enthusiasm died. By 1922 the membership had decreased to less than 250,000. When, in that year, plans were made for the employment of youth in factories, for the establishment of factory schools, and for promoting an association of younger people to be called the Young Pioneers, a new interest in the organization was stimulated. After Lenin's death in 1924 the Young Communists swore never to lower the banner of Lenin. They engaged enthusiastically in the literacy campaign, sending thousands of volunteers throughout the whole union to instruct the masses. Not all the Komsomols were literate at this time, and their enthusiasm was often misdirected, but their activities were nevertheless important. The Young Communist aspires to become a party member, though not all may join the party. The organization is a training ground for party membership, just as the less selective Young Pioneers is a preparation for membership in the Komsomols.

Even the courts and prisons served the cause of education. When cases were brought before Soviet courts, people were frequently given opportunity to discuss the new laws, and they were instructed as to their meaning and purpose. When sentence was given, it was often after full explanation of the issues involved. People confined in prisons were organized much as the factory workers were. They were given opportunity to work in factories attached to the prisons; they were paid for their work, at perhaps half the rate paid outside; they were allowed to manage some of their own affairs, edit their own wall newspaper, organize classes and obtain instruction. They were even permitted two weeks' vacation! The aim of this setup was to train people in prisons so that they might take part in life outside after their sentences had been completed. There is another side to this picture, however. Many people considered dangerous to the state never saw a court or a prison; they were seized, examined, and sentenced in secret by the GPU, the secret police organization which succeeded the Cheka. Court sentences were based on class distinctions, as well as upon the nature of the crime for which the person was accused. For example, a party member might receive a heavier sentence than a non-party member, for the same offense, because the party member was considered more responsible. On the other hand, a member of the disfranchised class might be more severely punished than a worker, on the ground that he was, by birth, a non–co-operative member of society. Soviet justice presented a mixture of liberalism and repression; it was based on an open recognition of class distinctions.

The theater, taken over by the Soviets after the revolution and placed under the department of education, began to take its unique place in Soviet life. Once the recreation of the few, it now became the possession of the people. The theaters were expected to identify themselves with the ideas and the aims of the new society which was being built, and to educate the people to a new understanding of Communist principles. When the director had satisfied these requirements, he was free to experiment with techniques.

The most significant aspect of the Soviet theater was not, however, the advanced and spectacular techniques employed by certain directors but its organization. Today several of the theaters of Moscow have their own schools for training actors, and the graduates of these schools are absorbed into the permanent companies which remain at each theater. In addition to these special training schools directly connected with certain theaters, there is a state training school in Moscow, and out in the factories and on the collectives there are amateur companies from which many candidates for further training are selected. This setup implies a wide participation in dramatic performance; such participation and interest does exist, but it was at first deliberately fostered because of its influence not only on the ideas of the people but also on their use of leisure. It offered many possibilities for enlarging the interests of the Russian people, who have a marked ability for the interpretative arts. It also provided opportunity for the different national groups to make their distinctive contribution and to express their legends, customs, and national histories in dramatic form. To get this work going, companies went out to tour the rural regions. Workers' clubs organized dramatic sections which presented plays of their own; the members of these organizations were particularly interested in the work done in the professional theater, and the discussions beginning in the dramatic sections contributed to the growing interests of larger groups. Late in 1927 the workers' theaters were described as follows:

A group of artists in the Grand Opera have just made an interesting innovation by accepting the "kultsheftsvo," or art patronage, of one of the largest factories in Moscow. They have promised to give performances at the factory club's theatre and to supervise the workers' dramatic section. Most important of all, they will encourage other theatres to follow their example in other factories.

In point of fact, the dramatic movement in workers' and other clubs is one of the most successful experiments of the Soviet regime. There the innate Russian talent for the drama and decoration finds freer play than in the orthodox theatre, which is still largely under the spell of prerevolutionary culture despite two or three notable exceptions.

The pieces presented in the club theatres are mainly satirical and they mirror contemporary life with a sharpness and an accuracy that atone for any lack of technique.[3]

The development of workers' theaters, together with the fact that performances in the professional theater were presented for the people as a whole, gave the Soviet theater a particularly interested audience. New plays were discussed in workers' clubs and factory organizations, and these groups sent their reactions and suggestions to directors. In the schools for the training of actors one of the subjects of study was Communist theory. Thus the theater was drawn into a consideration of the problems of contemporary life; it was not an institution set apart.

While the professional and nonprofessional theaters contributed to the education of the people and called upon their fundamental talents, the cinema performed a similar role. The themes were, to a large extent, based upon the exciting events of the years just past. Scenes of the revolution were filmed in the very spots where they had occurred; the people themselves shared in the action which, on the screen, duplicated events as they had happened. Thus the confused memories of confused times were given emphasis and were pointed toward a definite end—the education of the people.

The ballet, whose training was so exacting that it absorbed the thoughts and interests of its members, had been but slightly interrupted by the revolution.

"Oh, yes, the revolution was terrible—it interrupted the work of the ballet school three whole weeks." In these astounding words the rising star of the ballet, the twenty-year old Abramova, gave her impression of one of the greatest national convulsions history ever recorded. "There was shooting all over Moscow," she continued, "so we had to stay home, and even the big theatre was shut more than a fortnight. Yes, it was really terrible." [4]

It was difficult to arouse so absorbed a group to an interest in using their art in the cause of educating people along a particular line. Ballets based on revolutionary themes were arranged and presented, but the ballet did not rank with the theater and the cinema as an educative agency.

As, through the media of the literacy campaigns, schools, the Red Army, youth organizations, the system of justice, and the theater, new ideas were steadily brought to the people, and as they appreciated more fully the way in which ancient restrictions had been removed, social changes occurred. Marriage and divorce, for example, had been made extremely simple, and no such thing as illegitimacy was recognized by Soviet law. The whole status of women was modified by Soviet law. Under the empire, lower-class husbands had complete authority over their wives. Soviet law made an end to this situation; in addition it stipulated that women should receive the same wages as men for the same work; that no discrimination should be made against women in hiring workers, and that women should be given maternity leave with full pay before and after the birth of a child. Women were encouraged to participate in local soviets and in the management of agricultural collectives. The Russian woman of the lower classes, so long exploited and defenseless, began to see a new horizon opening before her—and with this new horizon came changes in family life. Drastic modification of family authority, changes in the way in which the members of the family lived, the breaking of old restrictions and laws introduced sudden freedoms which, in the cities particularly, were somewhat abused. Life among the young people of the towns was marked by a considerable degree of license.

Communist propaganda against religion also helped to break down old conventions. The Communist party regards religion as an undesirable influence; it calls religion, of any kind, the "opium of the people." In addition to breaking the power of the Orthodox church through the measures taken directly after the revolution to deprive it of privileges, income, property, and authority, it took steps to educate children against religion. During the NEP period, schools were required to give antireligious instruction. No party member was allowed to have any church affiliations, and this prohibition was extended to the Young Communists and other youth organizations. Many churches were converted into museums for antireligious propaganda, or put to other uses. Antireligious activities were especially marked at the time of the great church festivals of Christmas and Easter. Even the sale of Christmas trees was prohibited. Every attempt was made to destroy the influence of religion and to break its hold upon the life of the people.

The NEP period was not only a time of rehabilitation, educational activities, and social change; it was also a time of organization in government. In 1922 the Russian Socialist Federal Soviet Republic, which embraced but a portion of the old empire, was incorporated with the Ukrainian Republic, the White Russian Republic, and the Trans-Caucasian Republic, to form the Union of Soviet Socialist Republics. Later, three states in central Asia—Tadzhikistan, Uzbekistan, and Turkmenistan—joined the U.S.S.R.

When the U.S.S.R. was formed, the Soviet policy with respect to peoples of different races and nationalities was given definite expression. This policy, affecting the peoples of Asia entering the union, is very significant. Those territories which were regarded as dependencies or colonies by the empire are integral parts of the Soviet Union; there is no distinction of race, color, or creed. Instead of repressing national languages, customs, and beliefs the Soviet government encouraged national cultures. Instead of exploiting certain regions as colonies for the benefit of Great Russia, the Soviet government adopted the policy of helping these regions to develop their own resources. In the NEP period hitherto unwritten Asiatic languages were reduced to writing; national presses were established, and the publication of national literatures was encouraged. At the same time nationalistic isolation was broken down, because under the Soviet system persons from every portion of the union participated in the elections, were represented in the Congress of Soviets, and had opportunity to share in the discussions. The Soviet attitude toward these hitherto oppressed peoples of Asia had a tremendous influence upon Asiatic peoples who were not free from foreign domination or exploitation.

The basis of the system of government, as defined in the constitution which was drawn up in 1918 and modified later to take into account the new republics forming the union, was the local soviets, which elected the delegates to the All-Union Congress of Soviets. Supreme power was vested in this congress, which was to be convened once a year. The congress chose the Central Executive Committee —some two hundred in membership—which was the supreme authority in the period between the congresses. The Central Executive Committee chose the Council of People's Commissars to head the various divisions of the government—foreign affairs, war and marine, food, labor, finance, transport, posts and telegraphs, workers' and peasants' inspection, foreign trade, supreme economic council, etc. (The size of this council and the types of offices have varied from time to time.) The elaborate and indirect soviet system was a means through which the desires and opinions of the people might be transmitted to the capital. It stimulated widespread discussion. Actually, however, at this stage of development, supreme power was not exercised by the All-Union Congress, nor by any of the councils which it was instrumental in selecting, but by the Communist party. The whole process of securing and holding power was, moreover, contrary to western ideas of political freedom. For example, elections were not secret; voting was by show of hands, and candidates were usually proposed by some party member of the soviet.

Sanction for the Soviet government may not be found in ballot boxes, nor in All-Union Congresses—but it may perhaps be sought in the factories which are being built all over the land, in the great electric plants which are being erected to transform the life of the people, in the changes which are taking place from the deserts of Turkestan to the icebound harbors of the north. All these are being accomplished through the effort of the people, who, it appears, thus set their seal of approval upon the government planning these enterprises.

In connection with any discussion of Soviet government it must be remembered that the Communist party was, after 1918, the only recognized party in existence. Within the party there have been great differences of opinion. These differences began to manifest themselves particularly after the death of Lenin early in 1924. The question of who should be the party leader to succeed Lenin was of course involved, but other matters also contributed to the party controversies which marked the years 1924-1928. Should the party continue to be a sternly disciplined organization with rigorously controlled membership, or become a more liberal one? To what extent might adverse opinion be voiced after the policy to be followed—the party line—had been determined and announced? Should the gradual attempt to socialize farming be continued, or should the peasants be left out, as stubborn and backward elements, and their labor exploited for the benefit of the new society developing in the industrial centers until they could be socialized by force? Could the Soviet Union stand alone in a capitalist world, or must it depend upon proletarian revolutions elsewhere before it could hope to build a Communist state? Trotsky, who was popular, but who was not an old-line Bolshevik, advocated liberalizing the party, and not attempting to socialize the peasants; he supported the idea that world revolution was essential for the building of socialism. Stalin, the secretary of the party, thoroughly disbelieved in Trotsky's ideas and in the means he took to spread them. He was in a position to defeat Trotsky, and he did. In 1927 Trotsky was expelled from the party, and the following year he was exiled from the Soviet Union.

Under Stalin's leadership the way in which the party

line functions was made clear. The party line is the particular set of tactics determined upon by party leaders as the most effective way, under a particular situation, to enable the union to move nearer the desired goal—the communist state. Before the party line is announced, masses of evidence are brought in from all portions of the country. Local soviets, party men in the rural districts, factories, co-operative stores, collective farms, contribute to the facts and to the arguments which are evaluated by party leaders. In the light of this evidence the policy is finally determined. After the policy has been announced, it may not be criticized as a policy; but again, masses of evidence as to how it is working out are collected from all over the country and evaluated by party leaders. If it is apparent that a change is expedient, the party line is changed. The system is flexible, in that it permits policies to be modified, and to be modified quickly, on the basis of this clear-cut issue—does it work? It is rigid in so far as the policy itself may not be opposed after it has been announced.

Party discipline was tightened, the result of the defeat of the proposal to liberalize the party. The system of general party cleansings, which began in 1921 and continued from time to time after that, was described somewhat later as follows:

"Spring cleaning" is one of the leading institutions in Soviet Russia, but it is somewhat different from the annual program of the New England housewife. . . . This year they began by cleaning the Communist Party. . . . This comrade had a Christmas tree—that one let his wife go to church—a third gets drunk—a fourth sells apples for profit—a fifth voted the wrong ticket or failed to vote the right ticket—a sixth is addicted to a "right" heresy—a seventh was found reading a Trotskyist document. They sweep away these backsliders like cockroaches . . . because the party must be cleansed.[5]

Happenings in foreign countries had affected the decision that one country could build a communist society, alone in a capitalist world; and this policy, in turn, had its effect on foreign relations. A few years before this, when every nation regarded the Soviets as an outlaw, the only hope of the Bolsheviks was revolution elsewhere—but that hope had not been realized, and now conditions had changed. Before the end of the NEP period twenty-four countries, among them France, Great Britain, Germany, Italy and Japan, had recognized the Soviet Union. Trade agreements had been concluded with many countries, or with concerns in foreign countries. Since all foreign trade was controlled by the government, trade agreements— which were essential for the development of the Soviet Union—were made wherever favorable, or moderately favorable, terms could be secured. The Soviet government was bound, both by the terms of recognition, and because of trade agreements, not to interfere in the internal affairs of other countries and not to propagandize in other countries. Thus, while the Soviets continued to believe in the inevitability of proletarian revolution elsewhere, some of the abnormal pressure of the years of foreign intervention was removed, and relations were being established between a soviet state and other countries.

As early as 1919 one American observer of the Soviets gave the following interpretation of their attitude toward external peace and internal development:

They think they have carried a revolution through for once to the logical conclusion. All other revolutions have stopped when they had revolved through the political phase to political democracy. This one has turned once more clear through the economic phase to economic democracy, to self-government in the factory, shop, and on the land, and has laid a foundation for universal profit-sharing, for the universal division of food, clothes, and all goods, equally among all. And they think their civilization is working on this foundation. They want time to go on and build it higher and better. They want to spread it all over the world, but only as it works. As they told us when we reminded them that the world dreaded their propaganda:

"We are through with the old propaganda of argument. All we ask now is to be allowed to prove by the examples of things well done here in Russia, that the new system is good. We are so sure that we shall make good that we are willing to stop saying so, to stop reasoning, stop the haranguing, and all that old stuff. And especially are we sick of the propaganda by the sword. We want to stop fighting. We know that each country must evolve its own revolution out of its own conditions and in its own imagination. To force it by war is not scientific, not democratic, not socialistic. . . . We have proved that we can share misery, and sickness, and poverty; it has helped us to have these things to share, and we think we shall be able to share the wealth of Russia as we gradually develop it. But we are not so sure of that; the world is not so sure. Let us Russians pay the price of the experiment; do the hard, hard work of it; make the sacrifice—then your people can follow us, slowly, as they decide for themselves that what we have is worth having." [6]

Some may disagree with this interpretation, raising the question of why, then, there was a controversy with Trotsky about whether socialism can be built in one country. Others may raise the question of how Soviet participation in Chinese revolutionary activities fitted into this picture. But of the great desire of the Soviets for peace, both then and now, few doubts are entertained.

As we know, the Soviet Union was obliged to continue to fight after 1919, but the hope expressed in 1919 had now to an extent been realized, and the leaders who controlled the Communist party were unwilling to surrender the peace so essential for the development of the country. They made definite moves toward supporting and insuring peace. The Soviet Union was one of the first nations to sign the Kellogg Pact; but, regarding it as not sufficient to assure world peace, it made separate peace pacts with many nations. It also renounced connection with one primary

cause of modern warfare when it gave up imperialist aggression and announced its Asiatic policy.

In spite of peace pacts, trade agreements, and foreign
recognition the Soviet Union was not regarded with any
particular cordiality, except on the continent of Asia, and
its policies in Asia increased the hostility of the great
powers toward it. We have noted that the treatment of
minor nationalities admitted to the union profoundly
affected Asiatic peoples who were exploited or dominated
by foreign nations. At the same time, the exploiting powers were naturally not pleased by the policy which
endangered their control. Then, the Soviet Union sur-
rendered all the privileges which imperial Russia had
gained in other Asiatic countries. Of these countries China
was the most important, and the privileges there were the
most extensive. Every special right the Russian empire had
secured from China was renounced by the Soviet Union,
including the principle of extraterritoriality and the right
to exploit portions of China. The Chinese Eastern Railway was retained by the Soviet Union only as a commercial
enterprise, and the management of the railway was made
a joint affair. The Soviet Union was the first important
country to treat China as an equal; the relations of other
nations with China were thus thrown into high relief—and
naturally, foreign powers did not appreciate this emphasis
on their attitude toward China.

The great Chinese revolutionary leader, Sun Yat-sen, encouraged by the Soviet attitude toward China, and needing
assistance in building a strong revolutionary party to weld
war-torn China into a unified state, obtained it from the
Soviet Union. Michael Borodin, a veteran Communist,
was permitted to go to China as an employee of the Kuomintang or National party. He and other Communists
helped to strengthen the Kuomintang—but the party fell
into the hands of Chiang Kai-shek, who used the National
army to make himself dictator. Chiang Kai-shek got his

financial assistance from the powers which still held to their special privileges in China, and the Soviet advisers returned to their own country.

The distrust of the Soviets, which resulted partly from their growing prestige in Asia and the threat to imperialism there, manifested itself in different ways. As early as 1924 Great Britain was much concerned over a letter which was supposed to have been written by Zinoviev, the head of the Communist International, instructing British Communists as to the way in which they should vote in a forthcoming election. The letter was later shown to have been a forgery; but the suspicion of Soviet interference in the affairs of other nations persisted. Three years later the Peking police raided the Soviet embassy and found papers dealing with Communist activities in China. Shortly afterward the London office of the Soviet Trade Delegation was raided by British police, who made a thorough search for incriminating documents, breaking open the safes and strongboxes. Nothing was discovered which was of a nature to disturb the British public, but the British government decided to break off diplomatic relations with the Soviet Union. These relations were not resumed for two years. An American writer puts the attitude of foreign nations to the Soviet Union in these words:

When a bourgeois nation's life interests are endangered by the activities or very existence of a proletarian regime, it matters little whether legal, formal ground exists for complaint and hostility. . . . The most consistent and conscious representatives of capitalism in Britain know that the Soviet Union is a threat and a menace even if it refrains meticulously from propaganda, espionage, and subversive measures. Every Communist still believes in World Revolution and hopes England will be one of the first countries to succumb. The Soviet Government, ruled by considerations of expedience and by the necessity of maintaining outwardly friendly relations with capitalist governments, may refrain from offensive tactics, but that the sympathy of its leaders is on the side of revolution cannot be gainsaid, nor do the Bolsheviks ever endeavour to conceal the fact—though they need not any longer shout it from the house tops.

Undoubtedly, capitalist government would be justified in boycotting and ostracizing the Soviet Union. It is an anomaly that relations exist between Moscow and bourgeois capitals. They exist because capitalist states are divided among themselves, and, more significantly, because the outside world cannot get along without Russia nor neglect her. She is a potent, realistic force to be reckoned with in practical politics. She is there. To keep her beyond the pale may be fine principle, but poor policy.[7]

These events, which were given considerable attention in the press of the world, were not reflected to any appreciable extent in the life of the people of the Soviet Union, who, by comparison with the sufferings, the privations, and the violence of the years 1918-1921, were having an easy and peaceful time. Life, however, was by no means luxurious. People living in the cities were crowded together, a family to a room, several families to a single apartment; but as far as the workers were concerned, living conditions were no more crowded than they had always been, and in addition workers were not confined to the poorer quarters of the city but might live wherever a room could be found. A humorous delineation of the problem of securing any sort of place to live is given in the following selection from a short story translated from the Russian:

I arrived in Moscow, you know. Walked along the streets with my bundles. And simply no place to go. Not only no place at which to stop, can't even leave the bundles anywhere.

For two weeks I walked the streets with my chattels—grew a beard and lost all my goods. Then kept on walking without my things. I was looking for a room.

At last, in one house, I met a man descending the stairs.

"For thirty roubles," he says, "I'll accommodate you in the bathroom. The apartment," he says, "is lordly . . . three toilets. A bathroom. You can live in the bathroom. It has no windows, of course, but it has a door. And water is handy. You can draw a whole tubful of water and dive in it all day if you wish."

I say:

"I'm no fish, comrade. I have no need," I say, "to dive. I would like to live on dry land. Reduce the price because of dampness."

He says:

"I cannot, comrade. I'd be glad to do it, but I cannot. It isn't my responsibility. It's a communal apartment. And a fixed price has been set for the bathroom."

What can I do? I say: "Alright. Snatch thirty roubles from me and let me move in quickly. For three weeks I've been tramping the sidewalks. I'm afraid," I say, "I might get tired." [8]

It must be remembered, however, that the mass of the Russian people had never lived in comfort, and that the discomforts of life in the crowded cities were felt most keenly by the few who were unused to poverty. These people, members of the suspect classes, had to live and work under conditions which they found depressing and uncongenial—even hazardous. All members of the suspect classes were regarded with suspicion and hostility. They were forbidden to communicate with relatives and friends who had escaped from the country, and they themselves were not allowed to leave the Soviet Union. For that matter, travel abroad was permitted to very few.

On the other hand, the masses were enjoying new privileges. In the cities they were free to move about hitherto forbidden districts. Private grounds which had belonged to the wealthy were open to them; they might even wander unchecked through the palaces of the tsar and of the nobility, preserved as museums belonging to the people. Workers in blouses occupied the imperial boxes in the

theaters and opera houses. Theater, opera, and ballet—
once the recreation of the privileged—were now devoted
to the interests of the people. The psychological effect of
the breaking of old taboos was tremendous; it should not
be discounted when the changes in the life of the Russian
people are summarized.

During the whole NEP period the government watched
with apprehension the reappearance of private capitalism.
The Communist party was also dissatisfied with the degree
of industrial and agricultural production attained. Conditions were greatly improved, but the Soviet Union was
still a very backward country. Party leaders were convinced
that the country must be rapidly industrialized, so that the
standard of living could be raised, and the union freed
from its dependence on foreign imports. In order to do
this, it was necessary first to build heavy industry: to erect
the factories which could make the machines which in
turn could produce the goods needed in a country with a
higher standard of living. It was decided that the whole
economic policy must be changed and that the energies of
the country should be devoted to developing heavy industry. Consequently in 1928 the NEP was discarded and
the first Five-Year Plan was announced. Life was again to
involve much hardship and self-sacrifice, and the struggle
was to lead to a bitter controversy between the peasants
and the government.

8. LIFE UNDER THE FIRST FIVE-YEAR PLAN (1928-1932)

THE period of the first Five-Year Plan, which actually lasted less than five years, from October 1928 to January 1933, was a time of amazing contradictions—of stupendous achievements, and of privation and shortage; of enthusiastic devotion, and repression and terror; of pressure, nervous strain, resistance, conflict, hope, discouragement, criticism, competition, and of changes made so rapidly that the situation varied almost from month to month.

The point of emphasis of the first Five-Year Plan, as originally laid down, was the development of heavy industry. It was considered that only on the foundations of heavy industry could a better life for all the people be built. While the resources of the country were devoted to digging these foundations, as it were, it was impossible at the same time to produce the things which would make life easier and more comfortable. Another part of the plan concerned increasing the area under collective cultivation, because it was felt that private landholding must be broken down more rapidly, and also that the yield of grain must be increased through the application of improved methods and the use of tractors and other modern machinery over the large areas formed when small private farms were combined in one collective. The yield had to be increased so that grain could be sold abroad to pay for the machinery necessary for the beginning stages of the development of heavy industry laid down by the plan. The increase of collective farming, then, had both social and economic aspects, and the emphasis on heavy industry involved achievement in one direction and privation and shortage in another. While the Russian people tightened their belts and lived on restricted diets, the government exported the foodstuffs needed in the country; and it also did not produce the manufactured goods which would have made life easier. The government held out to the people the prospect of a better life in the future, when the foundations had been completed. The keynote which was to guide the Soviet Union was sounded by Stalin when he said, "We are fifty and a hundred years behind the advanced countries. We must cover this stretch in ten years."

State planning was the basis of the industrial expansion and the transformation of agriculture. The Gosplan (the State Planning Commission, which began to function during the NEP years) consolidated and organized the data supplied by industries, trusts, co-operatives, and soviets, and issued the results in terms, first, of an estimate, and then as a plan, to be fulfilled within the limits of the years set. Details were modified in terms of changing conditions of the years which saw the world depression, and also in terms of changing local situations.

In October 1928 when the plan was inaugurated, the government felt that it could push collectivization. The movement went much faster than had been planned, and it was soon stated that the time had come to crush the kulaks, the richer peasants who were the capitalists of the rural regions. Enthusiasts were sent out to the villages to persuade the poorer peasants of the advantages of joining collectives; these included preferential rights in securing available land, special tax and long-term credit privileges, and priority in securing machines, etc. Thousands of poorer peasants entered the collectives, which were organized so rapidly that the necessary machinery for improved large-scale agriculture could not be supplied, since the tractor and agricultural machinery factories were not yet built and the government could afford only a limited supply of imported machinery. The advantages of joining collectives were not immediately apparent; and in addition, the kulaks and middle-class peasants resisted the collectivization which meant the surrender of their animals and property. Kulaks and those peasants siding with them were stripped of their belongings, sent from the villages, and often put at forced labor on some distant construction project. Villages were the scene of class warfare in which lives were lost and ruthless measures applied. Peasants resisting collectivization slaughtered their livestock rather than see it seized by the government or turned in to the collective. Estimates of the livestock loss vary. In 1929-1930, according to a foreign writer, almost half the cattle, almost two thirds of the sheep, over half the horses, and over 40 per cent of the pigs of the country were destroyed by the rebellious peasantry.[1] On the other hand, Soviet figures state the losses for 1928-1930 to be 25 per cent of the cattle, over 15 per cent of the sheep and goats, 49 per cent of the pigs, and 6 per cent of the horses.

The disturbed situation in the villages,* together with the shortage of machinery on the newly organized collectives, meant a decrease in agricultural production. The supplies of grain needed for export to buy the machinery necessary to begin the expansion of heavy industry were not forthcoming. As a result the government exported butter, cheese, and eggs, as well as flour and grain. In the latter part of 1929 almost every eatable except salt was rationed in Moscow; cream or cheese was practically unobtainable, butter was extremely scarce, and milk could only be sold on children's ration cards.[2] Three years later the majority of the peasants had no meat, sugar, cheese, butter, milk, eggs, or tea, save at rare intervals and in small quantities; smaller towns and construction camps were but

* A literary interpretation of this may be found in *Six Soviet Plays*, edited by Eugene Lyons, published by Houghton Mifflin, pp. 290-291.

little better off, but the larger industrial centers were fairly well and cheaply supplied with these foods.³ The food shortage which marked the whole period was primarily due to the way in which collectivization was handled in 1928-1930, though a contributing cause was the inadequacy of the transport system.

The hastily organized collectives of 1928-1930 were too numerous, as we have seen, to be supplied with modern machinery. In addition they were too rapidly organized to be provided with proper management. They were a sort of patchwork of small farms called collectives, but actually showing few of the characteristics and advantages of collective farming. In 1930, when there was overwhelming evidence to show that the party policy of collectivization was working badly, Stalin, as leader of the party, announced that collectivization had not been wisely managed and that the party should change its policy in the villages. It was stressed that collectivization must be voluntary and that peasants must not be hurried into collectivization of a completely communist type. The type of collective favored by the government was the artel, for which careful rules were now drawn up. Each peasant entering an artel was allowed to keep his own home and garden plot, and a few pigs and chickens—perhaps a cow— for his own family; but all work animals and tools were the property of the collective. Members were paid on the basis of quantity and quality of work performed. The government likewise proposed to aid the collective farms by increasing the number of tractor stations from which tractors could be sent out, and in 1931 collectivization forged ahead. The number of tractor stations was increased from 159 in 1930 to 1,400 in 1931 and to 2,446 in 1932.⁴

The problem in the villages was, however, far from solved. Each collective was supposed to deliver to the state, at a fixed price, all produce above its needs, and the same provision was applied to land under private cultivation.

This requisitioning policy was particularly resented in the North Caucasus region and in the Ukraine, the most fertile and the most progressive farming region of the Soviet Union. In 1932 the peasants of these districts resorted to passive resistance, letting much of the grain go unharvested. In spite of this the government proceeded to enforce its collections, and famine, which was given no official publicity and no relief, occurred thoughout these regions. This last disaster reduced those peasants who were still rebellious to submission. Late in 1932 the government gave up the policy of requisitioning grain, and substituted a tax in grain, figured on the area under cultivation, and varying with the locality. The surplus remaining after the tax had been paid was to be distributed among the members of the collective according to the number of work-days performed. Work-days were figured on the quality and amount of work. A tractor driver, for example, was credited with more work-days than an unskilled laborer working the same length of time.

The bare facts of the changes forced upon the villages in the years 1928-1932, when three fourths of the area under peasant cultivation was collectivized,[5] reveal its human cost. The Russian peasant, as we have seen before, was stubborn, backward, ignorant, and suspicious of all outside interference. He had always been exploited. He had believed that the Bolshevik revolution would bring him peace, bread, and land. He had endured the privations of the counterrevolutionary years when he had land, but no peace and no bread. Some of the peasants had prospered in the NEP years, but not all of them had. Now, during the first Five-Year Plan, the prosperity of the richer peasants was swept away and the poorer peasants were herded too rapidly into collectives. Again the peasant was asked to sell his grain to the state at a fixed price which was lower than that received under the system of private trade allowed by the NEP.

Over against these facts must be set others. The wooden plow had practically disappeared; the scythe and the sickle, used to harvest 45 per cent of the crop in 1928, were no longer in use four years later. Tractor plowing, almost unknown before, was used on one third of the cultivated area in 1932.[6] Agricultural technicians and experts were sent to the villages. They taught the peasants about such things as using clean seed, incubators, separators; they showed them how to combat pests, how to improve livestock. Electricity came to many villages; village radios were not unknown. Medical care, still insufficient, but more extensive than it had ever been in the rural regions, was available. Crèches were established in the villages; the number of places in these nurseries was over 430,000 in 1932.[7] Thousands of Communists were sent to work in the country. Sometimes a factory took a particular village under its wing, and the two groups of workers were often in touch with each other. The isolation of the peasant was broken down, and his narrow horizon was broadened a little. Life in the villages was changing; the "dark" people began to be aware of an existence which was not limited to peace, bread, and land, but which included as well new technical skills, new information, new knowledge, new ways of living. The price had been high. The government had been willing to make the peasants pay the high price, if eventually the life and habits and thoughts of the peasants might be changed, and the whole peasant class be brought into the society visioned by the Soviet leaders.

The problem of developing heavy industry also was difficult, for it involved changing an agricultural people into an industrial one, and building industry when workers were not skilled. The erection of industrial plants calls for much heavy unskilled work, but it requires, as well, the leadership of skilled technicians. There were in the Soviet Union many technical experts of the old regime, but there were not nearly enough of these; and besides, under their influence, cases of deliberate resistance and sabotage occurred. As a result the Soviet government for two years subjected the disfranchised intelligentsia—the professional men, the scientists, the engineers—to a new terror at the hands of the GPU.* Hundreds of these men were secretly seized, imprisoned, put at forced labor, exiled, or killed, and members of their families were frequently imprisoned as well. In the great Shakhti trial, publicly conducted as a lesson to the people, fifty-two coal mine technicians charged with sabotage and conspiracy were convicted and sentenced.

After more than two years of harsh repression the government relaxed its attitude toward the technical experts of the old regime. In June 1931 Stalin made a famous speech which indicated many modifications of policy. One of these referred to the technicians. "Whereas," he said, "at the height of the wrecking period our attitude to the old technical intelligentsia was chiefly expressed in the policy of smashing them, now that the intelligentsia has turned to the side of the Soviets our attitude should be to attract and assist the technical intelligentsia. . . . Our task is to change the attitude toward the engineering technical forces of the old school, to accord them the utmost attention and solicitude, to more boldly draw them into work." [8]

Because of the lack of technicians in the Soviet Union, and because of the policy of "smashing" the experts of the old regime, it had been necessary to call in many foreign advisers. Most of these were Americans; American experts were especially numerous in the steel, tractor, automobile, electrical, and coal industries, but they also were to be found advising in railroad construction, in copper mining and refining, in the meat packing industry, in irrigation work—in almost all the enterprises of this great construc-

* The play called *Fear,* in *Six Soviet Plays* (see pp. 450-452), gives a literary interpretation of this period.

tive period. The problems arising in these undertakings are vividly suggested in an interview with one of the American engineers. This engineer had been at Stalingrad (in the Volga region), where he had pushed through the construction of the great tractor factory there six months ahead of schedule. Then he had gone to Magnitogorsk (east of the Urals), where he was supervising the building of the world's largest blast furnace.

Mr. Calder is as hard and tough as the steel he handles. He will not brook control or interference, but he knows his job and the Russians trust him more than any other foreigner who has worked here because he "delivered the goods" at Stalingrad.

So the raw and brutal men who run new Russia recognize him as a kindred spirit and forgive his cursing high-placed executives, his firing of important Communist Party men and his talking roughly to high officials in Moscow, because they know this American engineer, who does not care a whoop for communism or other politics but has the same passionate drive to get things done and to get steel built as they have.

Mr. Calder returned to Moscow this week with a story which, if he could tell it or I could write it, rivals Kipling or Defoe. The story is of the building of Magnitogorsk's blast furnaces.

There were forty-eight hours when neither he nor the Soviet manager left the job for an instant while the Russians were trying to hoist immense fabrics of steel into position by methods that America would condemn as dangerous or dismiss as impossible.

"Believe me," said Mr. Calder, "I waited for something to snap—I had told them what risks they were taking—and the Russian manager, Gugol, was more nervous than I. But they did it, and we were asleep on our feet when it was done.

"They wouldn't think of taking such chances in America —with skilled labor. You have got to hand it to these Russians," he said.

Then he told in a matter of fact way what chances he took with cranes handled by the same unskilled Russians.

"The rails on which the cranes ran were under water and the foundation was just mud," he related. "That was the trouble—they had begun construction on the far side, away from the furnaces, and the nearer they got the more mud piled up. So the cranes had to clear mud twenty feet high to swing the stuff into position and they could not approach near enough because of the mud.

"They carried a six-ton load on a sixty-foot boom, and each time came the moment when it was touch or go whether the crane would tip over. American cranemen would have gone crazy, and some of these Russians—they wouldn't stand it. 'All right,' I told them, 'I will find others who will.' So they stuck to the cranes, but we were lucky and not one tipped over."

The accident rate there is amazingly low—three men have been killed and a dozen injured in the last three months.

"In America on a big steel job," said Mr. Calder, "we know at the start that some of us won't live to see the finish, but we have been lucky at Magnitogorsk—how lucky!—and we have got the furnaces built within a few days of the schedule. I tell you no engineer in America would believe such a job possible with unskilled labor.

"One time when they were hoisting forty-five tons of steel in what I considered a terribly dangerous way, their gang simply passed out on the job—utterly exhausted. I told the chief engineer, 'You must get labor somewhere—we can't leave it like this.'

"So he rushed around and got Red soldiers, firemen, the Lord knows what to man the winches, and they got the steel up. I have lost thirty-five pounds and wouldn't go through it again for a million dollars—but it's worth it.

"I fought with every one until I was nearly crazy. They waste time and money and labor and there is a terrific muddle. But they get things done and learn how as they do it." [9]

Waste of time, money, and labor—muddle, disorganization, bureaucratic slowness, terrific effort in time of emergency, unskilled labor handling difficult and delicate operations—not always successfully—two to five men doing what one skilled workman accomplished in America—but

doing it, and, "learning how as they do it"—this characterized, in part, the industrial expansion of the first Five-
Year Plan. In conditions such as those described, the
tractor factory at Stalingrad was built; the largest tractor
factory in the world was erected at Chelyabinsk (east of
the Urals); the largest electric power station in the world
was constructed at Dnepropetrovsk (on the Dnieper); the
largest automobile plant in Europe was built at Nizhni
Novgorod (now called Gorki); the world's largest vegetable canning plant was built in the North Caucasus region; the huge blast furnace at Magnitogorsk and the
agricultural machinery factory at Rostov (in the Ukraine)
were completed.

A glance at the map will show that some of the largest
plants erected were east of the Urals. The Soviet government, remembering the way in which industrial centers
were threatened during the counterrevolutionary period,
planned to establish industry in portions of the union less
accessible to European invasion. The lack of transport and
the advantages of placing factories as near the sources of
materials as possible, also affected the location of factories.* Still another factor, and a very significant one, was
the Soviet policy of assisting backward regions to develop
along modern lines, of helping the Asiatic portions of the
union to make use of their vast natural resources and to
improve their whole cultural level.

The scope of the constructive enterprises pushed
through during these years is suggested in the following:

Thanksgiving Day marked the end of one of the biggest jobs
accomplished in Soviet Russia under American supervision—
the construction of the Nijni Novgorod automobile plant and
the workers' city handled by the Austin Engineering Company of Cleveland, Ohio.

* *New Russia's Primer,* by M. Ilin, translated by George S. Counts and
Nucia P. Lodge, published by Houghton Mifflin, pp. 48-49, presents this
policy in elementary terms for the school children of the U.S.S.R.

When the Americans arrived eighteen months ago they were shown a broad expanse between the Rivers Volga and Oka covered by trees, shrubs, and a village or two and told: "Build us a plant here capable of producing 144,000 Ford cars annually and a city for 60,000 people with tenements, restaurants, kitchens, bread factories, hospitals, schools, clubs, theatres, community houses and a university, plus railroads, railroad docks, sewage and water facilities and a light, heat, and power plant."

This correspondent attended the Thanksgiving dinner at Nijni Novgorod of twenty Austin engineers. The number at the peak of the work was forty, but half of the force is on the way home, as the contract only required designing and building of the plant and supervising the building of the city according to the Soviet designs and was not concerned with the actual running of the plant, which is scheduled to begin production January 1.

A two days' visit to the plant showed it was an impressive job, which had been accomplished in the face of great difficulties, augmented by poor transport and telegraph service and shortage of materials and skilled labor. It was the scene of the utmost activity, with thousands of workers striving with every Soviet device of shock brigades, social competition and volunteer drives to have the plant fully operating on the scheduled date.[10]

The shock brigades and socialist competitions mentioned in this dispatch were important means used to encourage achievement. Shock brigades were organizations of workers who were devoted to the Communist cause and trained to work. They were sent from factory to factory to set the pace and to improve the general level of technical work. Whenever a factory fell behind or peculiar difficulties were experienced, shock brigades were sent in. In addition, there were regular shock workers in every factory. These people worked under great nervous strain, devoting themselves to achieving, even to surpassing, the goals set by the government. Shock workers were rewarded with publicity, and often with better food than other workers could buy, but their material rewards, while greater than those of ordinary workers, were relatively small in comparison with those offered skilled workers in more advanced industrial countries. Socialist competitions were competitions between factories, or between groups of workers in the same factory, organized to stimulate production over a short period of time, to keep the workers of the union always aware of their progress toward the more distant goal.

The working day was shortened: the eight-hour day proclaimed in 1917 was shortened to seven hours by June 1932. An even shorter day—four, five, or six hours—was set for hazardous industries or for workers between the ages of sixteen and eighteen. The Soviet Union is the only country which ever had a maximum seven-hour day for all industry. Under pressure of time and the frequent emergencies which arose, workers were often called upon to labor overtime, but when the seven-hour day was adopted, it was supposed to include all overtime.[11] For a period of about a year the five-day working week was tried out. Factories were kept running continuously, with different shifts of workers, but each shift worked four days and had the fifth day off. This plan was adopted to break up the tendency to observe Sunday as a holiday, to increase production by keeping the factories running all the time, and to break down traditional family life. Few members of the family, from school child to parents, were free on the same day. Some months of experimentation with this arrangement showed its defects. It increased the problem of securing efficient management, it made it impossible to place the responsibility for breakages to machines, and it did not lead to increased production because of the organizational difficulties experienced. Consequently, the six-day week was established. Different industries had different days as free days, and no factory was kept open on its free day. It was thought that this arrangement would secure the advantages of the other plan and avoid its defects. It is interesting to note that thousands of workers devoted their free days to voluntary unpaid labor on some construction project. The Moscow subway was built, in part, through such labor.

During these years of industrial expansion the proletariat doubled, reaching over 22,000,000 in 1932. Seventy-four per cent of the workers were enrolled in trade unions, which were expected to give attention to educational and cultural work under Communist leadership.[12] The trade unions were schools of Communism as well as administrative organizations. They had the responsibility of arranging classes for the technical training of the workers. The tendency of all education during this period was to provide training for specific jobs. Practically everything of general cultural value was left out of the curriculum, and special technical education was stressed. The number of students enrolled in factory schools increased from 178,300 in 1928 to 1,177,300 in 1932.[13] Besides organizing classes for the technical training of workers, trade unions arranged all sorts of excursions for the education of the adult worker. These included trips to new constructive enterprises, to historical exhibits, to fine arts galleries, to typical examples of older cultures—such as monasteries and palaces kept intact as models of what had been—to co-operative farms, to a typical home of a peasant under the old regime, to a modern laundry, to the theater, to museums which commemorated all the uprisings of the people from the time of Razin.

Provisions for the welfare of the workers did not stop at the shorter working day or in arrangements for their education. Medical stations in factories increased from 1,580 at the beginning of the period to 5,674 in 1932, while the sum expended in health protection work increased 334 per cent, and sanatorium and health resort accommodations doubled.[14] By 1932 all workers were given regular annual vacations with pay, usually for two weeks. When the accommodations were available and the quality of work performed merited special recognition, these vacations, which every worker received on pay, might be spent in some splendid palace of the old regime transformed into a rest home for the proletariat. Night sanatoria were opened in connection with factories; individuals who were in a precarious state of health might enter these for the rest and care so difficult to obtain in the crowded quarters in which they ordinarily lived. While the life of the proletariat was by no means easy, it had some compensations which helped the workers to endure the pressure of the demands made upon them by the first Five-Year Plan.

Speed was the keynote of these years. The word *tempo,* which means rate of speed, was one of the expressions on everyone's lips. It came to mean "faster, ever faster." Too much haste often proved disastrous. Expensive imported machines were frequently ruined, machinery broke down, parts could not be supplied, and expected production did not always materialize. For example, after the tractor factory at Stalingrad was completed, months went by before a usable tractor was turned out. The automobile factory at Gorki, whose completion was the occasion of so much rejoicing, was within a few months a target for bitter criticism when it failed to turn out the motors expected. There were all sorts of hitches and delays; but eventually the great plants got into operation, another illustration of learning how "as they do it."

If *speed* is the keynote, *shortage* describes the period. The food shortage has already been mentioned. In addition, there was a shortage of everything else. In Moscow, for example, where the population had increased from 1,375,000 in 1917 to around 4,000,000 in 1932, sufficient additional homes or apartments had not been built. In this city of four million, there were in 1932 but thirty thousand motor-driven vehicles, and of these, two thirds were trucks and busses, the other third office cars owned by the state and used by officials. No Russian owned an automobile. Food, clothing, and all other commodities were rationed.[15]

Under the conditions of shortage and pressure the labor turnover was tremendous. The workers wandered about from place to place, seeking better food or better living conditions. The tendency to wander about in search of something different, and presumably better, had always been a marked characteristic of the Russian worker. Now it became intensified, greatly increasing the problems of training efficient workmen. In 1930 the government ruled that the unemployed must accept whatever work was offered them regardless of preference, previous training, or qualifications; and since there was work enough to go around, all social insurance unemployment payments were discontinued. No refusal to work could be made except on the grounds of illness and with the presentation of a doctor's certificate. Refusal meant expulsion from the trade union, the loss of civil rights, and the loss of all insurance protection. Consequently there were few refusals, and unemployment ceased to exist in the Soviet Union, since many workers were needed. But the labor turnover continued. Shock workers often pledged themselves to remain on one job for a specified time, hoping to create a new attitude in the wandering workmen of the union. In his famous speech of June 1931 Stalin laid his finger on one cause of the labor turnover and proposed a remedy. He said:

In each branch of industry, in each enterprise, in each workshop, there are leading groups of more or less skilled workers who must above all be constant if we really wish to secure a constant staff of workers for our enterprises. These leading groups of workers constitute the basic link of production. To insure that they are constant part of the enterprise, is to secure the whole staff of employees, radically overcome fluctuations of labor. How can they be secured? By promoting them, by paying them higher wages, by drawing up the wage scales so as to allow the proper reward for skill. Moreover, this means also to open up prospects for unskilled workers, giving them the stimulus of prospective promotion into the ranks of the skilled. We all realize now that we need hundreds of thousands and millions of skilled workers. In order to create skilled workers it is necessary to provide a stimulus and the prospects of promotion for the unskilled workers. And the more boldly we take up this policy, the better, because it is the basic means for doing away with fluctuation of labor.[16]

Since the adoption of a more widely differentiated wage scale Soviet leaders have been careful to explain that they are, at this stage, building socialism, not communism; but the press of the world saw in this change, as it had in the NEP, a repudiation of the basic theory of communism. At any rate the new policy marked a turning point of great importance in Soviet affairs. But what could a man with money to spend buy in the Soviet Union? To meet this problem, the government opened some commercial stores where articles of necessity or luxury were on sale. The supply was limited and the prices were high, but these stores at least afforded an idea of the possible advantages of earning higher wages.

The period we are considering witnessed other achievements and changes besides the development of heavy industry and the collectivization—and partial modernization —of agriculture. Numerous scientific expeditions were organized to explore the resources of the country, particularly those of the far north. Supplies of timber, coal, oil, ores, and furs were surveyed, and plans were laid for developing these resources. A mining and chemical combine was established at Khibiny (north of the White Sea), a timber and woodworking combine at Igarka on the Yenisei, canning plants in Kamchatka. Water routes in the far north were explored by Soviet seamen. The inhospitable north was forced to contribute more than it ever had to the national economy. Life in these regions was so difficult that industrial projects there were carried on by young workers who offered themselves for this service to the state, or by state prisoners sentenced to hard labor in exile. While the north was being explored, the mountains of the south were penetrated and the southern deserts were being transformed through large irrigation projects. The area devoted to cotton growing increased from 2,400,000 acres in 1928 to 5,370,000 acres in 1932.[17] Life in large portions of central Asia was affected by the changes brought about by irrigation and the growth in cotton production. This development was in line with the Soviet policy of enabling regions to develop their own resources and thus to modify old habits and ways of living.*

Transport was improved, but the development of transportation facilities lagged behind the other accomplishments of the period. Early in 1933 a 140-mile-long ship canal connecting the Baltic and the White Sea was finished, twenty months after the start. It was one of the enterprises on which the labor of state prisoners was used. This canal formed the last link in an inland route 674 miles long connecting Leningrad with the White Sea, and affording a route less dangerous and very much shorter than the outer sea route, which is 2,840 miles long. The Turk-Sib railway, connecting the Moscow-Tashkent railway with the southern spur of the Trans-Siberian railroad, was completed and opened during these years. In general, however, transport fell behind industry, or even agriculture, in degree of development. The critical evaluation of accomplishment which was publicly applied to every Soviet undertaking was particularly harsh when it was applied to transport. One Soviet newspaper, for example, in an editorial published in 1931 said, "The results of

* See *New Russia's Primer*, pp. 18-20.

railroad work for the first half of the fiscal year cannot be described as other than shameful."

During the whole period there were drives against the moral laxity which had resulted from the changes in law and customs and the sudden relaxation of the bonds which had held the people for so long. In 1928, when it was noted that in one month there were 2,122 divorces in Moscow and only 1,976 marriages during the same time, an active campaign against a careless and unconsidered attitude toward marriage and divorce was launched. The license which had characterized life among the youth of the cities during the NEP period was frowned upon. Youth organizations particularly showed a tendency to prudishness; members subjected their slightest actions to the most critical examination. Youth became overserious; it was considered wrong to smoke, wrong to drink, wrong to dance, wrong to attempt to dress becomingly, wrong to enjoy one's self. When, in 1929, for example, Communist youth organizations followed the example of the party and held an annual "spring cleaning," members were swept out on such grounds as these:

One youth or damsel behaved in a rowdy fashion. Away with him or her. Another danced a foxtrot in public—there is no place for such in the stern Communist Youth body. A third overindulges in flirtation. The Communist Youth body wants no "vamps!" [18]

A pleasant aspect of life during this time of speed, shortage, seriousness, and pressure—to work, to learn, to build—resulted from the approval given to physical training and athletics. In prewar Russia 30,000 people were in regular training; in 1927 there were 60,000 in Moscow alone; in the R.S.F.S.R. 800,000; and in the U.S.S.R. 1,100,000, of whom 20 per cent were girls. These numbers steadily increased. In spite of the privations and hardships of life under the first Five-Year Plan, the young people of the Soviet Union were given opportunity for physical training and encouraged to engage in sports and games. Even in the hardest years there were competitive winter sports in Moscow. The ranks of young people who marched in the May Day parades or who participated in other Soviet celebrations became yearly a more impressive sight and a testimony to the effect of the new interest in sports, physical training, and games.

During this period, private trade was almost entirely replaced by socialized trade. The consumers' co-operatives of the type so strongly supported by the government during the NEP period had a membership of 24,700,000 in 1928, of 73,100,000 in January 1933.[19] Membership in co-operatives was restricted to the franchised classes. Managers were elected indirectly, as in soviet elections. Prices in co-operatives were much lower than in the commercial stores opened in the latter part of the period, and prices in the commercial stores were lower than prices on the open market. Prices varied not only with the type of store but within the co-operatives. The different types of stores, the varying scales of prices, the closing of stores to certain purchasers, combined with the shortage of things to be bought, made shopping in the Soviet Union unique. The problem was not, as elsewhere in the world, to attract the purchaser, but for the prospective buyer to secure what he desired.

Under the pressure of the first Five-Year Plan many women were needed in industry, and the number of women in industrial work doubled during these years. Women engaged in all types of heavy labor, but it must be remembered that the Russian woman was accustomed to the heaviest kind of work and was able to perform labor which women in many other countries could not attempt. The welfare of the woman worker was safeguarded by the types of legislation described earlier. In order to care for the little children whose mothers were employed, many more crèches were opened in connection with factories; and also, by 1932, 23.7 per cent of all children between the ages of three and seven were enrolled in preschool institutions.[20] To relieve women in industrial work of housekeeping responsibilities, public restaurants attached to factories were increased; this service, extended to 750,000 people in 1928, was available for 2,300,000 in 1932.[21]

All of these facilities were regarded not only as conveniences, but as important means of transforming habits of work and life. With the staggered week and the shortage of housing, home life tended to become different from anything we associate with the term. Husband and wife employed in different factories could buy their meals at their own place of work. Their free days were different. Their children, if very young, spent the day in a factory crèche; if older, they attended school and were seldom free on the same day as their parents. If still older, they were employed in some factory, where their life centered. The formative influences for Soviet youth were crèche, kindergarten, school, and youth organizations under Communist leadership. Youth was growing up without knowledge of religion, with few individual home influences, but with a host of socialized contacts and pressures designed to mold him in the direction of group life, group activities, and Communist ideals.

During the hard and repressive years of the Five-Year Plan, the government changed its attitude toward religion. In 1929 the constitution was changed; freedom of religious faith was still permitted, but any freedom of religious propaganda allowed earlier was discontinued. At the same time, antireligious propaganda in schools, the press, and all other educational agencies was actively continued.

Technicians of all types, desperately needed in the development of the country, were trained as rapidly as possible. The increased enrollment in the factory schools has been noted. In addition new institutions for technical training were opened in Siberia, in the far east, and in the republics of the national minorities. Elementary schools increased, and the number of elementary school pupils enrolled doubled, reaching 23,100,000 in 1932.

With the growth of school enrollment and literacy came an increased demand for books and papers. The newspaper circulation, 2,700,000 in prewar Russia, rose to 8,800,000 in 1928, and to 36,000,000 in 1932. Only the shortage of paper kept the figure as low as this. In 1928, 34,200 books were published; in 1932, 55,000. Books were published in 13 languages in 1913, in 55 in 1927-1928, and in 90 in 1932. Village reading rooms, 21,300 in 1928, reached 46,000 in 1932.[22]

During the period the censorship took a characteristic form. In the Russian empire, as in all countries having provisions for press censorship, rulings were made against publishing certain works. In the Soviet Union, however, press censorship was at this time interpreted not only in the familiar terms, but in addition it came to include the idea that all writers should devote their talents to furthering the plans and ideas of the Communist party. The attempt was made to mobilize every resource of the country, including the literary gifts of the writers, in the service of the state. The RAPP, or association of proletarian writers, was organized to exercise a peculiar censorship. Nothing considered counterrevolutionary or lukewarm could pass the scrutiny of this group. Under these conditions types alone could be drawn—a kulak must always be depicted as a bad element, a party worker as faithful and orthodox. Characters in books and plays were stereotypes, not people. Lyric poetry disappeared from the scene; numbers of poets committed suicide. Late in 1932 Stalin announced that the RAPP was disbanded. Since that time the situation under which Soviet writers have been permitted to write has been considerably modified.

As far as the newspapers were concerned, they were never free to print anything which might appear critical of the party line, but they might say anything they wished about the way the government policies were carried out.

The Soviet government maintains that no press in the world is free, but that its press is freer than most because its comments cannot be dictated by private interests owning the papers or supplying the advertising. At any rate it is apparent that the freedom of the Soviet press has its unique features.

Why did the Russian people fall into step and accept the restrictions, the privations, the severities of the Communist regime during the period of the first Five-Year Plan? They had no choice, but were obliged to do what was required of them. It should be remembered that the Russian people were accustomed to deprivation and to autocratic methods. There had never been a large class of people used to comfort and conveniences, to the exercise of private initiative, or to freedom. The Soviet government promised a better life for the masses—in the future—and some people were willing to sacrifice themselves for the sake of the welfare of their children. Others believed that a better life could be achieved rapidly, and they devoted themselves to the enterprises necessary to attain this. Again, the propaganda employed was so intensive that young people, particularly, were successfully taught that a better state of affairs could be obtained only in a Communist society. Then there was the thrill, even the necessity, of feeling one's self a part of the large group, all going in the same direction.*

When, after all sorts of pressure and vicissitudes, the first Five-Year Plan was declared completed and impressive figures showing achievement were exhibited, the people were encouraged to embark on the second Five-Year Plan, with its promises of a better supply of material comforts and its emphasis on technical skill and improvement of the general cultural level, as well as on certain aspects of heavy industry which had lagged behind during the first Five-Year Plan.

* See p. 243, *Six Soviet Plays.*

9. LIFE IN A SOCIALIST STATE

AFTER the Bolshevik revolution of 1917, life in Russia was a battle to build a new social and economic order. The battle was fought through the counter-revolutionary years, when outside nations played a part in assisting groups in Russia which were opposed to the fundamental social and economic change proposed by the Bolsheviks. It continued during the NEP period, when private enterprise was permitted and then throttled. It was carried on during the first Five-Year Plan, when the struggle with the peasantry reached its height. As the battle front shifted, the enemies of socialism were to a large extent eliminated—through what human cost, it cannot be estimated. We know that the first groups to go under in the long struggle were the most privileged—the nobility, the large landowners, the great bankers and industrialists. The educated classes—the intelligentsia—who in theory disapproved of the conditions of life in old Russia, but whose sympathies could not be extended to the violent social change advocated by the Communists, were suppressed or brought into line. The private enterprise of small merchants and traders was restricted. Thousands of peasants who held to ancient desires to possess the land for themselves, and who opposed the collectivization of agriculture, were deprived of their property and moved to distant regions, perhaps to labor on government enterprises under strict supervision.

The aim of this long and costly battle was, in the words of the chairman of the Council of People's Commissars as he reviewed achievement through 1935, the "abolition of parasites that live at the expense of the people," and the

result of the almost complete abolition of such people was
to make it possible "to place the whole income of the
country at the disposal of the toilers themselves and of
their state." This, he said, "is the basis for the rapid rise
in the standard of living of the working class and the collective farm peasantry which we are now witnessing." [1]
The battle against enemies within the state became
marked again in 1936-1937, when hundreds of men, including among them some of the most prominent leaders,
were arrested, tried, and convicted for conspiracy. Some of
the most well-known party and army leaders were accused
of conspiring with Trotsky and with Germany and Japan
to overthrow Stalin and accept foreign aid in establishing
a new government. The general atmosphere of confidence,
which by 1935, had become marked, was again shaken by
these new accusations in high places, and the international
prestige of the country was lowered.

Yet, whatever the difficulties and dangers that were kept
before the eyes of the people, life was becoming easier.
More food and clothing could be bought in the stores;
more apartments and houses were being built, so that families were not crowded in, one on top of the other, in the
cities where new factories had been put up so quickly. In
1935 a new slogan had appeared in parades and on banners: "Life has become better, Comrades. Life has become
merrier." The country seemed to be settling down
to something like "normalcy"—the new normalcy of
socialism.

The years of the second Five-Year Plan (1933-1938)
brought the final changes which in the eyes of Soviet leaders were necessary to establish socialism. Collectivization
of agriculture was the most important step in the economic field which remained to be completed. The small
farms were unproductive and "unplannable"—therefore,
in the opinion of Russian leaders, incongruous in a
planned, socialist society. It had become clear that the

peasants, who had for centuries wanted their own private little farms, would have to be shown that they could have a better living by pooling their land and cattle in the collective farms. The Communists had learned by hard experience that the peasants could not be talked into making the change for any "theoretical" reason, nor compelled by force. What was needed was good hard facts. How could they make the collective farms more productive? One way was to improve the agricultural methods: replace wooden plows with steel plows, pulled by tractors; provide the land with fertilizers and good selected seeds; send trained agronomists to advise the peasants about the best crops to plant. But there was very little farm machinery in the Soviet Union, and it would be impossible to give every collective farm enough tractors and combines to do the job. So they decided to set up service stations equipped with the machinery which would work for all the farms in the area surrounding them. These machine-tractor stations, as they were called, were first organized in 1930; and by 1938, the end of the second Five-Year Plan, they had nearly 400,000 tractors, a large proportion of them produced in the new factories of the Soviet Union.[2] On the staffs of the machine-tractor stations were agronomists and other agricultural specialists, who helped the collective farmers get the most out of their land. As a result more and more of the peasants joined together in collectives, so that by 1936 most of them belonged to these co-operative enterprises, and thus, according to the Bolshevik view, became a natural part of socialist society.

This was but one of the major changes in the way life was organized in the U.S.S.R. which meant that socialism had arrived. With these developments the constitution of the Soviet Union became outdated. It had been written in 1923 at a time when socialism was just a dim hope. It had given the workers special privileges in comparison with the peasants; it had denied a vote to groups who, in the

Communists' opinion, were most likely to oppose socialism; and in general it had been a brief outline of the
structure of the new union, with few details and no bill
of rights.

By 1935 the Soviets felt that their new society was sufficiently established so that their old constitution was not
adequate. Consequently a commission was appointed to
amend the constitution in order to provide "the further
democratization of the electoral system" and "the more
precise definition of the social-economic basis of the constitution." The commission found it necessary to make so
many changes that it wrote a whole new constitution,
which was submitted for popular discussion in 1936. During the course of these discussions, some 154,000 suggestions were sent in from groups all over the country, many
covering the same points. Of these, forty-three were embodied in the new constitution, which was finally adopted
in December 1936.

What kind of government did the new document provide? There are three most essential facts about it. First, it
is designed to guarantee the socialist economy, whereas
most other governments in the world aim to guarantee the
continuation of capitalism. It was written into the constitution that citizens are duty-bound to safeguard public
socialist property. Just what did this mean to the individual Soviet citizen? Could he own anything? Yes, he
could own anything *except* a factory or shop or farm on
which he would hire other people to work for him. He
could own his house and all his personal belongings. He
could have a vegetable garden, a cow, and chickens for his
own use. He could even own some machinery—for instance, woodworking tools with which he might make
furniture for his own use or to sell to others. But he could
not *hire* anyone to help him. In other words, the *social-
ization*—or social ownership—applied only to what are
called the basic means of production of the country.

The second special feature of the Soviet form of government is that it is a union or federation of republics. These republics superficially resemble our forty-eight states, and the national legislative body—or Supreme Council, as it is called in Russia—has two houses, like the American Senate and House of Representatives. The Council of Nationalities, as their senate is called, has twenty-five representatives from each union republic. On the other hand, delegates to the Council of Union, which corresponds to our House of Representatives, are elected on the basis of population: one delegate for every 300,000 of population. The similarity between our states and the Soviet republics ends here, however. Most of the Soviet republics are made up of distinct nationalities. For example, there are Russians, Ukrainians, Georgians, Armenians, and Uzbeks, to mention only a few. Each of these has its own republic, in which that nationality is in the majority. Of course, there is quite a mixture of peoples and races in all the republics, and in this sense the Union of Soviet Socialist Republics is, like the United States, a melting pot. But each nationality has its own homeland, too; its republic within the federation of the U.S.S.R.

Of course it is very important to the stability of the country that all these different nationalities get along together without strife or oppression of one nationality by another. Accordingly, racial and national equality has become a basic point in the government of the Soviet Union. Each republic has its own native language, and Russian is taught as the *second* language; each republic has its own constitution, which takes into account the special characteristics of its people and their needs; furthermore, each republic retains the legal right to secede.

There are other provisions in the constitution that are aimed to prevent racial difficulties. Article 123 reads as follows:

Equality of rights of citizens of the U.S.S.R., irrespective of their nationality or race, in all spheres of economic, state, cultural, social and political life, is an indefeasible law.

Any direct or indirect restriction of the rights of, or, conversely, any establishment of direct or indirect privileges for, citizens on account of their race or nationality, as well as any advocacy of racial or national exclusiveness or hatred and contempt, is punishable by law.[3]

This means that in schools and in factories you will find Orientals from central Asia working side by side with Russians or Jews or Armenians. If anyone tries to prevent a person of a different nationality from getting a job—or if anyone calls a member of another race a derogatory name —he will be arrested and fined or imprisoned.

In the early days after the revolution racial conflict was a serious problem, because under the tsars many nationalities had been treated as "inferior." Not only were the Jews segregated and forbidden to live in certain places or enter certain professions; the Oriental peoples of central Asia were actually jim-crowed; the Moslem peoples of the Caucasus were pitted against the Christian Armenians; and the Russians lorded it over non-Russians, forcing them all to speak Russian and subjecting them to what might be called a colonial regime in their own country.

During the revolution the Bolsheviks had to rally to their cause all the groups they could, and among them, of course, the former "colonial" peoples within the disintegrating Russian empire. Accordingly the abolition of all these forms of national oppression was an immediate necessity. And it is still a basic point in the bill of rights of the Soviet constitution.

This bill of rights of the constitution is its third unusual feature. It is embodied in Chapter X of the document and is titled "Fundamental Rights and Duties of Citizens." First among these, the constitution guarantees the right to a job, the right to a vacation, the right to

THE UNION OF SOVIET SOCIALIST REPUBLICS
(SOVIET UNION)

Spitzbergen

Franz Josef Land

Barents Sea

Novaya Zemlya

Kara S.

Baltic Sea

FINLAND

o Murmansk

Königsberg

Tallinn

KARELO-

LITH. Riga EST. SSR FINNISH SSR

POLAND SSR

LAT. Leningrad

Vilnius o SSR

Minsk

Petro

zavodsk

o Arkhangelsk

BELORUSSIAN

SSR

R.

MOLDAVIAN

SSR

o Kiev

MOSCOW

⑥

Kishinev

UKRAINIAN

Gorki

S.

Ob R.

Odessa

o Kharkov

⑧

③ ⑦

⑪

SSR

⑩

Rostov-on-Don

o Sverdlovsk

Black

Stalingrad

Volga R.

①

o Chelyabinsk

Sea

13

GEORGIAN

5

Omsk

Tom

SSR

14 9

o Novosib

ARMENIAN

Caspian Sea

I

SSR

Tbilisi

Yerevan

④

Barnaul

15 AZERBAIDZHAN

SSR

⑯

Baku

KAZAKH SSR

Aral Sea

L. Balkhash

IRAN

TURKMEN UZBEK

Tashkent Frunze

Ashkhabad o

Alma-Ata

SSR SSR

KIRGIZ SSR

Stalinabad

TADZHIK SSR CHINA

AFGHANISTAN

INDIA

BOUNDARY LINES

—— U.S.S.R.

—†—†— Union Republics

—·—·— Autonomous Soviet
Socialist Republics

— — — Other Countries

SCALE OF MILES

0 100 200 300 400 500

Shabad

THE 16

R.S.F.S.
UKRAIN
BELORL
UZBEK
TURKM
TADZH
GEORG
ARMEN

ARCTIC OCEAN

Bering Strait
ALASKA
Wrangel I.
East Siberian
Northland
New Siberian Islands
Sea
Bering Sea
Laptev Sea
R.
Kamchatka
⑫
S.
Yakutsk
Sea of Okhotsk
Sakhalin
Lena R.
Kurile Is.
Krasnoyarsk
Komsomolsk
L. Baikal
Amur R.
Khabarovsk
②
Chita
Irkutsk
Ulan-Ude
J-TUVA
MANCHURIA
JAPAN
Vladivostok
ONGOL PEOPLE'S REPUBLIC
Sea of Japan

N REPUBLICS – SSR	AUTONOMOUS REPUBLICS in the UNION REPUBLICS		
AZERBAIDZHAN KAZAKH KIRGIZ KARELO-FINNISH MOLDAVIAN LITHUANIAN LATVIAN ESTONIAN	R.S.F.S.R.		GEORGIAN SSR
	1 BASHKIR 2 BURYAT-MONGOL 3 CHUVASH 4 DAGESTAN 5 KABARDINIAN 6 KOMI	7 MARI 8 MORDOVIAN 9 NORTH OSETIAN 10 TATAR 11 UDMURT 12 YAKUT	13 ABKHAZ 14 ADZHAR AZERBAIDZHAN SSR 15 NAKHICHEVAN UZBEK SSR 16 KARA-KALPAK

maintenance in sickness and old age, the right to education, and equal rights for women in all spheres of life, as well as equality of treatment under the anti-discrimination provision quoted above.

These economic guarantees, as they might be called, existed in fact before they were written into the new constitution. The year 1930 was the last in which there was any considerable unemployment in the U.S.S.R.; and now young men and women find their jobs before they leave school. In fact the duty to work (Article 12) is more important, perhaps, than the right to work, for there have continued to be more jobs than workers as the tremendous program of industrial expansion under the Five-Year Plans came into operation.

Two-week vacations with pay were guaranteed to all workers, and the state built up wonderful summer resorts on the Black Sea and in the southern mountains to which some of the workers could go. Others went to small *dachas*, or cottages, near their winter homes, or on boat trips down the Volga.

The social insurance system provided money to help workers when they were sick or unable to work. This system, most of which is run by the trade unions, provides aid "from the cradle to the grave": maternity leave with pay; money grants to mothers to aid in the care of their babies; free medical care and insurance payments to make up for loss of earnings while sick; old-age pensions and pensions for the sick and injured; burial grants and aid to the family of a deceased worker. In other words, the state has undertaken the obligation to take care of its citizens when they are physically unable to work.

Of course, a vital question in this connection is, how big are the pensions and other insurance benefits? They were still very modest when the 1936 constitution was written. In general they were a percentage of the salary earned, and salaries were not high. The more efficient a man was, the larger his salary and the larger his pension when he retired. The Soviets had long before given up the idea of equal wages for everyone; now the constitution says, "He who does not work, neither shall he eat," and "From each according to his ability, to each according to his work." So the insurance system also favored those who did more and better work.

For a Soviet worker the chance to get a better job had always been closely tied up with the educational system. There was such a shortage of skilled workers, of engineers, doctors, teachers, scientists, that the government had to do its best to get the people to learn new skills and go into more advanced professions. The regular school system— the seven-year schooling which is required for all Soviet children except those in big cities, where ten years of schooling are required—came to put considerable emphasis on technical training in the sciences as well as on the standard reading, writing, and arithmetic. All education above the school level was, moreover, aimed at definite jobs. There were technical schools giving two- or three-year courses for engineers and technicians. Even the universities gave no general liberal arts courses except to students who planned to be teachers or research workers.

Graduation from school or from college, however, was not the end of education. Factory workers were required to take special training courses to improve their skills. These were given at the factories and were part of a more general program in industry which organized for the workers dramatic or literary circles and courses in music, special science, or art as part of the recreational facilities. It had become the fashion to go to school, and nearly everyone was studying something in order to get a better job. This is what the constitution meant by the right to education, and most of it was provided free of charge by the government.

Girls, as well as boys, studied in all these courses, for

they grew up expecting to take jobs just as their mothers did. There were women locomotive engineers, women doctors (in fact more than half the medical students were women), women fishermen, women lawyers, women farmers. With the exception of a few dangerous or very heavy types of work from which women were barred, girls were doing everything. For the Soviets, womanpower was as necessary as manpower to carry through their immense plans. But they also realized that women had to bring up families as well as work. This is why the constitution says that the possibility of exercising their equal rights is ensured "by state protection of the interests of mother and child, prematernity and maternity leave with full pay, and the provision of a wide network of maternity homes, nurseries, and kindergartens." At most of the big factories there are nurseries where the women leave their babies while they work. In summertime the trade unions provide for many of their members' children to go away to camps or at least to have outings in the country.

The problem of careers versus families, of course, was not completely solved. Men still expected their wives to do the housework and cook the dinner (even if lunch and sometimes breakfast could be eaten at the factory and the children ate at school); and shopping alone was a laborious job. Stores were filled with customers, and often there was a long wait in line. Groceries were never delivered. There were also very few of the modern conveniences. Iceboxes were virtually unknown; there were gas stoves only in the most modern apartments; public laundries were few and far between, though the newer buildings had laundry facilities; central heating was unusual. All the gadgets that make life easier for the American housewife were absent. Nevertheless, the vast majority of women in the Soviet Union worked, both to increase the family income and because they had been brought up with the idea that it is just as natural for a girl to get a job as for a boy.

This, however, was something very different from the effort in earlier years to diminish the strength of family ties and to wean the children away from parental influences.

By the time the new constitution was drafted, there had been such a fundamental change in social relationships that there was little fear of antisocialist influences. The people were fairly well integrated into the new system: 35 per cent were wage workers; 55 per cent were in collective farms and other kinds of co-operatives; 4 per cent were students, etc., and only 6 per cent remained as private farmers or handicraftsmen.

As this readjustment was taking place, it was paralleled by a swing back to recognizing the values in family life. A new law was introduced which made divorces more difficult to obtain and more expensive. Parental responsibility for children's care and behavior was fixed by law. While mothers were aided if they wanted to go to work, they were also encouraged, if they could afford it, to stay home while their children were little. The schools sought to work more closely with the parents, and the warmth of family life was praised as necessary to the best development of the child.

It is interesting to note that economic rights such as these come before the civil and political rights which make up the American bill of rights. This order in the constitution is not just accidental. Civil rights in Russia have not been developed as far as economic rights, and to this day the Soviet understanding of civil rights is quite different from our American understanding of them. Let us examine some of these differences. The rights embodied in the first ten amendments of our constitution, which seem most important to Americans, are: freedom of religion; freedom of speech and press; freedom of assembly and the right to petition the government; inviolability of person, home, and papers from unwarranted search and seizure; "due process of law"; habeas corpus; and trial by jury. Most of these principles are written into the Soviet constitution, the exceptions being habeas corpus and trial by jury—though the Soviet court system has in its "people's judges" something approximating the jury system. Yet the interpretation of these freedoms is not in all cases identical with ours. As freedom of religion will be discussed below in connection with the changes that took place in Russia during the war, here let us look at freedom of the press.

In the U.S.S.R. almost all newspapers are owned by public organizations of one kind or another. *Izvestia* is published by the Supreme Soviet; *Pravda* by the Communist party; *Trud* by the Central Council of Trade Unions. Many city governments have their own newspapers, as do the important economic ministries. The Soviet government uses the press as an instrument of public education rather than merely as a news outlet. The press exhorts the people to participate in current campaigns for a big harvest, for improving the schools, and so forth. Or it outlines in detail the position of the government on foreign policy. The press is also an outlet for public criticism of administration. The following are good examples of the type of criticism that can be found almost daily in the leading newspapers all over the Soviet Union:

Spring is approaching. It will soon be necessary to begin the program for improving the city. Are the construction organizations ready? Has everything been done to begin capital construction of housing on time, to pave and asphalt the streets? . . . No. . . . It cannot be said that in the City Executive Committee they do not understand how much better things would be if a large group of active citizens were drawn into the solution of these tasks. They understand, but they do not do anything to organize the active citizens, to listen to their opinions, to make use of their experience. "People are needed," they say in the Executive Committee, "but there are no suitable people." This is not true. There are people, fine people with initiative and perseverance who know how to overcome difficulties. . . . It is only necessary to give them the opportunity to participate actively in decisions on local matters and to advance the best of them boldly to important work. The mistake of the Rybinsk City Executive Committee is that it does not do this.[4]

An article criticizes the local Communists on a collective farm for avoiding hard work:

Matvei Yakovlev is not alone in avoiding dirty work. The secretary of the party organization himself, Fedor Ivanov, arranged to be the accountant in a field brigade, although a sensible youngster could do that work. Communist Elena Gadisova went to work in the chicken farm where altogether there are about fifteen hens and three or four roosters. Of the nine Communists on the collective farms only two—Vladimir Muromtsev and Nikolai Volik—have chosen for themselves the more difficult part of the work.[5]

If we look through Russian newspapers we find that there is no editorial page which does not reflect an organizational or governmental policy. Moreover, all are subject to government censorship. How then does this square with a claim to freedom of the press? The Soviets say that their press is free because the government places "at the disposal of the working people and their organizations printing presses, stocks of paper, public buildings . . . and other material requisites for the exercise of these rights." [6] In other countries, they say, where private individuals own the press, workers cannot obtain a hearing in the newspapers—they have no access to them—consequently, the press is not free. One of the leading Soviet editorial writers who was covering the San Francisco Conference was interviewed about this question. He said:

"We have no inclination to urge on anyone in America our own understanding of freedom of the press, but equally we do not want upheld as the last word of democracy such 'freedom of the press' which produces Hearst, brings papers to irresponsibility, inspires false information and the seeds of suspicion in the relations between countries, and sometimes actually provokes conflicts between them. We do not need such a 'democracy'. Let others have it. . . . What makes Americans think they have the world's most free press? The sole argument is the absence of moral and political responsibility before the people of the U.S.A. for the views set forth in the press. Practically it means that, according to the canons of formal democracy, pro-fascist reactionary forms in the U.S.A. have on the same grounds with the democratic and progressive, equal rights of circulation." [7]

In reply, most Americans would say that since all Soviet newspapers must pass the government censor, there is no freedom to write as you please in the press. In recent years there has been considerable discussion of this difference of opinion by both sides. A delegation from the American Society of Newspaper Editors visited Moscow in 1945, and their long report analyzes in detail the problem as they saw it. They summarize by saying:

The Russians cannot understand our custom of letting some writers take opposing views in the same paper, nor can they understand a paper giving both sides in political campaigns. It is equally difficult for us to understand the Soviet papers are not merely owned, but are part of the government. [8]

What about the other freedoms? Is there a fundamental difference in interpretation there too? There are no soap-box orators in the U.S.S.R., no Hyde Parks or Union Squares. There is no speechmaking against the government at election time. Public criticism, though exceedingly strenuous, is confined to criticism of administration. If we read the Soviet constitution carefully, we find that all these freedoms are guaranteed with a specific aim: "in order to strengthen the socialist system." The statement of this aim is of course a limitation as well. Anything which aims to weaken the socialist system is not guaranteed freedom. In this understanding of freedom we can find the key to the "dictatorship of the proletariat" which the Soviets are frank to admit still exists. It seems that as long as a person is working within the set framework of government policy, he can and does enjoy democratic rights and exercises a form of real control over his governmental representative. But those desiring to change the fundamental direction of the society enjoy no such freedom. When Wendell Willkie was in Russia, he reported a conversation with a young factory director on this point. When the Russian admitted there was no possibility of criticizing the basic system, Willkie challenged, "Then actually you've got no freedom." The reply is interesting for us.

He drew himself up almost belligerently and said, "Mr. Willkie, you don't understand. I've had more freedom than my father and grandfather ever had. They were peasants. They were never allowed to learn to read or write. They were slaves to the soil. When they sickened, there were no doctors or hospitals for them. I am the first man in the long chain of my ancestors who has had the opportunity to educate himself —to amount to anything. And that for me is freedom. It may not seem freedom to you, but remember, we are in the developing stage of our system. Someday we'll have political freedom, too." [9]

In view of what we find about the Soviet ideas on freedom of expression, the question for us is: who sets these fundamental policies which cannot be challenged? This is the role of the Communist party. Who are the Communists? Do they run the entire government? The answer to this is that a very large proportion of the high government officials are Communists; probably all the ministers. In the first Supreme Council 76 per cent of the members belonged to the party. The constitution gives the Communist party the right to nominate candidates for office, but in fact no candidates ran for office as Communists. They were all nominated by general meetings of farmers or workers from each district. Why are so many Communists elected, then? This is a fair question when one considers the fact that there were only some three million members of the Communist party, while ninety million people voted in the elections. The answer lies partly in the great prestige the Communist party had as the group which led the victorious revolution and the group which determined the successful policies which the country had been following. The other reason was that the individual Communist is generally supposed to work harder, take more responsibility, make himself a leader in his community and on his job. Being a Communist is not an easy nor always a pleasant thing to be in the Soviet Union. While there are some compensations in the way of better chances for promotion, there are also arduous duties. A party member is normally considered responsible for the success of his group, whether it be a shop in a factory or a unit in the army. To fail in this responsibility is a public and social disgrace. Consequently many people who agree with the Bolsheviks and wholeheartedly approve of their work are unwilling to take the risks of party membership. Those who do are very often the naturally public-spirited people who would be found in any American community and who place their personal welfare second to that of their community. The Webbs in their famous analysis of Soviet society have called this the "Vocation of Leadership." [10]

The Communists are not only public officials; they are to be found in every walk of life, and it was from their simple jobs at the lathe or the tractor, from the theater or the army, that they were elected to the Supreme Soviet. In lower governmental bodies such as city councils there is a much lower percentage of Communist party members.

But if there are so few Communists, how can they control the country and its policies? The party, as such, has never had real lawmaking powers. Its policies have always had to be embodied into law by some elective body. But in the years after the revolution the right to vote was limited to workers and peasants, and the workers were given more representation. This guaranteed a more or less favorable attitude toward Communist policies. Under the 1936 constitution, however, election procedures have been liberalized.

Every man or woman eighteen years old or over can now vote for representatives to the Supreme Council, and any-one twenty-three or over can be nominated for office. Moreover, for the first time, direct elections were introduced, whereas previously people had only elected the delegates to local legislatures, who in turn chose the delegates to the national congress.

Voting, under the new constitution, is by secret ballot. Thus the election in 1937 was the first time that the people had ever experienced elections like ours. They had never used paper ballots and curtained booths. Voting had always taken place in open meetings by show of hands. For months before election day speeches were made and articles were written explaining how to use the secret ballot. Election day became a real holiday, and more than 90 per cent of the people entitled to vote went to the polls. As is the custom throughout Europe, Sunday is election day in most of the Soviet Union; but in the republics where the Mohammedan religion is predominant and Friday is the rest day, voting for local elections is on Friday so that everyone can be free to vote.

To Americans the election of 1937 seemed like a fake because there was only one candidate for each office. How could this be? There are a number of explanations. This was the first national election by secret ballot, and the people who were nominated were the most famous people in the country—opera stars, authors, aviators, generals, the best factory workers and farmers. These people had been nominated at public meetings of workers and peasants on farms and at factories, and each district tried to get its most famous "native son" to represent it in the Supreme Council, even though he might have some other important job too.

This seems strange to us. It was possible because the Supreme Council operates differently from our Congress. It does not meet for long sessions as our Congress does. The deputies can go back to their work in between sessions. When it meets, it discusses legislation and treaties which have been worked out ahead of time by two other governmental bodies, both elected by the Supreme Council.

The first of these is the Presidium, which has a president, sixteen vice-presidents (one for each union republic), a secretary, and twenty-four members. This body meets almost continuously and issues orders to implement laws passed by the Supreme Soviet. It can even pass decrees or negotiate treaties, if necessary, when the Supreme Council is not meeting.

The other body is the Council of Ministers (called the Council of People's Commissars until after World War II), which is like the cabinet in England, with a premier, and ministers for foreign affairs, defense, education, transportation, etc. Their job is to carry out the laws and in general to administer the central government. The Soviet cabinet is much larger than that of other countries because the Soviet government not only makes laws but also operates all the factories, banks, and railroads, and plans for the whole economic life. Consequently there are some thirty-seven ministers who are in charge of various industries—a minister of the chemical industry, of iron and steel, of oil, of textile industry, etc.

There is no president for the Soviet Union. The Bolsheviks do not believe in what they call a "division of powers" in their government. The Supreme Council not only is the legislative authority but is also supreme in executive and judicial matters, because it appoints the cabinet and the supreme court. The man sometimes referred to as the Soviet president is the president of the Presidium of the Supreme Council.

In sum, under the Soviet constitution the Supreme Council, made up of the leading people of all professions, meets twice a year; it appoints the other two groups to carry on the day-by-day business of government. It discusses and votes on the most important legislation, such as the annual budget, the basic legislation on the court system, on taxation or treaties, and ratifies the other decrees enacted by the Presidium in the interim.

What governing functions do the various member republics exercise? Their governments are modeled after the central government, and they control such matters as education, social assistance, the courts, local industries. At first they retained no authority in regard to foreign affairs or the army, having relinquished this in the original treaty of union to the Soviet government in 1922. During the war, however, the constitution was amended so that the union republics may have their own ambassadors abroad and their own military units.

When the new Supreme Council first met, the second Five-Year Plan was entering its last year. This was just twenty years after the Bolsheviks had come to power, and the socialist system at last had been fully established. As 1938 was the last more or less normal prewar year—the last one for which the statistics are available—we can examine it in detail to find out just what the Soviet Union was like.

What was the country producing? How were the people living? What were they doing? First, as to the economy: it had been almost totally rebuilt and re-equipped during the two plans. The Soviets had a right to claim that in its machinery Soviet industry was among the most modern in the world. Not only was the old rebuilt, but so many new factories had come into production that Soviet industrial output in 1938 was nine times as great as in 1913. The new industries included the manufacture of automobiles and tractors and agricultural machinery, the production of aluminum and chemicals. The industries basic to any powerful modern economy had been expanded tremendously in comparison with 1928 when the Five-Year Plans were instituted: The production of electric power had risen from 5,000,000,000 to 40,000,000,000 kilowatt hours; coal from 35,000,000 to 133,000,000 tons; oil and gas from 12,000,000 to 32,000,000 tons; pig iron from 3,000,000 to 15,000,000 tons; steel from 4,000,000 to 18,000,000 tons; copper from 35,000 to 103,000 tons. The new factories were turning out 200,000 automobiles and trucks, 80,000 tractors, 54,000 metal working lathes, 54,000 tons of aluminum.[11]

If we compare these figures with those of the United States, they do not seem very large, although in many categories they took second place in world production. But in another respect the Soviet Union still fell far behind the Western countries economically. If we compare the production of iron and steel *per person* in the Soviet Union with the production *per person* in other countries, it was small. Stalin was particularly insistent on this comparison in a report he made in 1939.

In what respect are we lagging? We are still lagging economically, that is, as regards the volume of our industrial output per head of population. In 1938 we produced about 15,000,000 tons of pig iron; Great Britain produced 7,000,000 tons. It might seem that we are better off than Great Britain. But if we divide this number of tons by the number of population we shall find that the output of pig iron per head of population in 1938 was 145 kilograms in Great Britain and only 87 kilograms in the U.S.S.R. Or, further: in 1938 Great Britain produced 10,800,000 tons of steel and about 29,000,-

000,000 kilowatt-hours of electricity, whereas the U.S.S.R. produced 18,000,000 tons of steel and over 39,000,000,000 kilowatt-hours of electricity. It might seem that we are better off than Great Britain. But if we divide this number of tons and kilowatt-hours by the number of population we shall find that in 1938 in Great Britain the output of steel per head of population was 226 kilograms and of electricity 620 kilowatt-hours, whereas in the U.S.S.R. the output of steel per head of population was only 107 kilograms, and of electricity only 233 kilowatt-hours. . . .

. . . The economic power of a country's industry is not expressed by the volume of industrial output in general, irrespective of the size of population, but by the volume of industrial output taken in direct reference to the amount consumed per head of population. The larger a country's industrial output per head of population, the greater is its economic power; and, conversely, the smaller the output per head of population, the less is the economic power of the country and of its industry. Consequently, the larger a country's population, the greater is the need for articles of consumption, and hence the larger should be the industrial output of the country.

Take, for example, the output of pig iron. In order to outstrip Great Britain economically in respect to the production of pig iron, which in 1938 amounted in that country to 7,000,-000 tons, we must increase our annual output of pig iron to 25,000,000 tons. . . .[12]

This really is the test of how far the Soviets had gone toward improving the standard of living of their millions of people, who had previously been so poor. Their new heavy industries were beginning to produce machinery for making clothes and shoes, building houses, canning food. By the end of 1935 enough goods were coming out of these consumers'-goods factories so that it was no longer necessary to continue the rationing system which had been in force during the first Five-Year Plan. But still the amount of goods was modest for the huge population. In 1937 one

pair of shoes was manufactured per person, while the
United States produced 2.6 pairs per person; 16 square
meters of cotton cloth were produced as against 58 square
meters in the United States; 3 kilograms of soap in contrast to 12 in the United States. These are but a few examples. Shelves in Soviet stores were often bare, and
people rushed out to buy things whenever they heard a
new shipment had arrived.

In respect to food the picture was better. For instance,
the Soviet Union produced more sugar (beet sugar) per
person than we did (though our imports put American
consumption of sugar far ahead of Russian.) Russia had
always produced tremendous amounts of grain, and bread
remained a very important item in their diet. But now the
government bread stores had not only the famous black
bread but white bread, and fancy rolls and cakes. New
canned goods came onto the market, and Russians for the
first time in their history learned to eat canned corn, prepared cereals, and other food products long familiar to
Americans.

These changes also found new people in the new society.
The population was growing rapidly. There were about
thirty million more people in 1939 than in 1913 despite
the ravages of war, revolution, and famines. The age level
was low. Almost two thirds of the people were under thirty
and had spent their entire adult life in the new society.
The traditional muzhik no longer could be considered the
average citizen. More than half the people lived in towns
or cities; the number of wage workers had increased from
11,000,000 to 28,000,000. The peasants themselves were
changed: over 90 per cent were living and working on
collective farms, and three quarters of them had learned
to read and write. Almost all the children—some 30,000,-
000 of them—were in school; the universities had enrolled
600,000 for higher education; technical schools and courses
attached to factories had another 1,000,000 students.

These figures mean more when we compare them with 1913 or even 1928. Before the revolution there were some 8,000,000 school children and 200,000 students in universities or technical high schools; in 1928 the figures were 12,000,000 in school and 500,000 going on for further education.[13]

The map of the country had also been changed during the plans. Before 1928 the large cities were concentrated west of the Urals; but the Five-Year Plans had built new cities in Siberia and the east. In 1926 there had been only 709 cities and 125 towns in the country. But now there were 922 cities and 1,448 towns. Among these new names on the map were Magnitogorsk, Karaganda, Stalinogorsk, and Komsomolsk.

As during the westward trend in our country in the late nineteenth century, not only were people moving from the farms to the cities but they were moving eastward. Higher wages and special privileges were offered to encourage people "to go out east" where new towns were being carved out of the wilderness and on the sites of new mines. This pioneering life was tough but it was important. And the excitement of participating in the enormous projects built there caught the imagination of the new settlers, especially the youth. One of these projects was the building of Komsomolsk, the city of youth, far down the Amur near the Pacific. The Soviet novel *Red Planes Fly East* described an incident in the first years at Komsomolsk.

The district committee had been meeting for 48 hours without a break. From the window the construction site was visible. Scattered trees stood out here and there against the cleared ground. Low barracks emerged like snowdrifts. At every hundred paces camp-fires were burning under sheet iron which protected them from the wind. Wood lay piled by the fires. Clinging with a poker to the frozen snow, a watchman crawled from one to another. The low, ruddy reflection of the fires never died away above the wintry town. In the fifty degrees of frost steel instruments snapped like glass. Hands and arms went wooden. The hair in the nostrils clotted together and made breathing difficult. Hearing failed. Sight was ruined. But always in frost or snowstorm, people stood at the camp-fires warming themselves. There was something joyous, festive, almost inexpressible in those meetings around the fires. The feeling might best be expressed thus: the work was going on and all were alive, although there was a deep frost outside and inside the barracks, although supplies came in irregularly, although people had no time to fall ill and nothing to cure themselves with, and their families were far away, and there was far too much work to be done, and the work was hard. But the work went on, and everybody was alive. The realization that nothing halted the growth of the town, neither the faintheartedness of the cowards nor the loss of the most audacious, nor the deprivations and failures, was expressed in those camp-fires which never died down day or night. Because of all this, the difficulties began to seem a manifestation of personal faintheartedness, and, as though they were personal defects, nobody wanted to talk aloud of them. . . .

For the second night in succession the district committee was listening to a report on the situation in regard to the road. The ice-road along the river Amur, the only means of communication between the new town and Khabarovsk, the regional center, and the world, had been broken up by a hurricane. There was no other road. In the early spring the air was impassable for aeroplanes, the taiga was everlastingly impassable. The road along the river had broken up, yet it remained the only road, and along that road, along the ice shattered and piled on end, it was necessary to send lorries for medical supplies. And it was impossible to delay.

The Nenietz natives refused to act as guides on this lunatic journey, and certainly it was terrifying to plunge into the whistling, snowy mist which engulfed the lights of fires and cars. But there was no choice. The district committee could console itself with the reflection that a hopeless situation has its points, for one customarily emerges from it with honour.[14]

The author went on to describe the spirit of the times:

The people poured eastward. With them they brought a flood of requirements which it was beyond their power to do anything about. They needed tobacco and theatres, houses and felt boots. Matches were sold only on commission. Actors played old plays in patched costumes and without scenery, as though introducing a modernistic note, but in reality simply because of their poverty, from which there was no escape. Doctors and theatres were sent to the people in the taiga, in the hills, on the shores of the deserted sea. The doctors were followed by trainloads of medicaments, beds, instruments, while the theatres clamoured for paint and canvas.

The Nenietz hunters told stories of sledges without dogs flying over the snowy plains, and of aeroplanes which lived in the remote parts of the taiga.

Yes, aeroplanes lived in the taiga.

Yes, trainloads of equipment were sent, aeroplanes were sent, tanks were sent, and before all else man was sent.

He made his way into the taiga, populated the frontier areas, sailed over the sea and built towns.[15]

If we had met the typical Ivan Ivanovich in 1938, we would have found him tremendously interested in these new pioneering ventures. Indeed, his ambition might well have been to found a new city, build a gigantic factory, fly over the North Pole, or do any one of the dramatic things then going on in his country. He would have been confident—even cocky—about his ability to carry through his plans for the future. At the same time he would have been quite fond of what earlier had been considered "bourgeois" activities. He probably would have been learning to rhumba and would be up on the latest jazz—or dzhaz, as he called it—which he played on his phonograph. His wife would have a permanent wave and red fingernails. He might send his mother in the country some artificial pearls for her birthday. Undoubtedly he had a savings account—ten million Soviet citizens had such accounts—and received interest on it. He and his wife may have been saving up for that boat trip down the Volga, or a mountain climbing expedition in the Caucasus, for all young people were sports fans. On the job, however, he was doubtless a hard worker, trying to get ahead, trying to exceed his norm, or quota of work, on the basis of which his salary was determined. Ambassador Davies made a tour of Soviet industrial cities about that time. He was especially interested in the men he found directing the plants he visited. In Dnepropetrovsk he was shown through a steel tube manufacturing plant which employed nine thousand workers. The director was a young man of thirty-five who had learned English and had visited American factories. "He was a clean-cut, well-groomed man," writes the Ambassador, "in a well-tailored suit who might be mistaken in New York for a lawyer or businessman." In the course of their conversation Ambassador Davies asked about his life:

. . . Before I left, I asked him whether he would excuse me if I asked him a few personal questions about himself. He said, "Of course!" It developed that he was born the son of a peasant some 25 miles from Dnepropetrovsk. He was one of a family of eleven children who had lived in a typical, primitive, floorless hut of the sort commonly found in the agricultural districts of Russia. He had never worn shoes until he came to Dnepropetrovsk to go to school.

At the expense of the state, he finished his common-school education at Dnepropetrovsk and then attended the local university which had a mining, metallurgical, and technical faculty. He stated that it was a type of higher university or technical institution something like Carnegie Tech. His course was four and a half years. He graduated in the metallurgical section and obtained his diploma at the age of 23 years. I asked him how large the university was. He said it had 25,000 students at the present time. All students were given stipends by the state for clothing, living expenses, theater, etc. After finishing his course at the local university he spent some time in technical schools in Moscow and Leningrad and then he went to Germany, France, and the United States to finish off his technical education by familiarizing himself with methods of other countries. He spent seven months in the United States visiting Pittsburgh, Youngstown, Cleveland, Chicago, and Detroit in order to study American methods. He had returned to become one of the assistants in the management of the plant and at the age of thirty-five was now in charge of the entire organization.[16]

This was a young man who had made good. But his story was fairly typical of thousands of young Soviet people. They felt they were on the road to a "bigger and better" life.

The country now, under its new Constitution and with the foundation of its socialist economy firmly cemented, had not only worked out its third Five-Year Plan; it was discussing a fifteen-year plan which might bring the production of goods up nearer to American levels. The resolution on the immediate objective of the third Five-Year Plan read:

Now that the U.S.S.R. has constituted itself a socialist state, has completed in its essentials the technical reconstruction of the national economy, and is in advance of any capitalist country of Europe with respect to level of technique of production in industry and agriculture—now we can and must squarely face and carry out in actual practice the fundamental economic task of the U.S.S.R.: *to overtake and surpass the most advanced capitalist countries of Europe and the United States,* and to accomplish this task in the immediate future.

This requires a further considerable increase in the technical equipment of every branch of the national economy, and, consequently, a maximum development of machine building and heavy industry, a decided improvement in the whole organization and technology of production, accompanied by an extensive application of the latest achievements of science and invention. It further necessitates a numerical and, particularly, a qualitative increase in trained production personnel, and a thorough mastery of technique in industry, transportation and agriculture. Following Lenin's tenet that "the productivity of labor is, in the final analysis, the most important, the chief thing, for the victory of the new social system," we must ensure the utmost development of socialist emulation and the Stakhanov movement, a steady improvement of labour discipline in all factories and offices and on all collective farms, and a degree of labour productivity for workers, peasants and intellectuals that is worthy of socialist society.

At the same time national income and trade must grow sufficiently to enable the *national consumption to increase 50-100 per cent* during the years of the Third Five-Year Plan. To this end, we must, in addition to effecting a great increase in the output of the heavy and defense industries, also augment the manufacture of articles of mass consumption and foodstuffs, and make possible a corresponding increase in real wages.[17]

10. THE THREAT OF WAR

THOUGH the planners were looking forward to better times—more clothes, better shoes, more houses and apartments—they were never for a moment unmindful of the grave danger of war.

The need for defense could never be overlooked. From 1917 to 1920 civil war and intervention were at their height; until 1925, when Japan evacuated northern Sakhalin, there were foreign troops on Soviet soil. In 1927 relations with England became so strained that the danger of war seemed immediate; 1929 saw an armed clash with China over the Chinese Eastern Railway; and from 1932 on, far-eastern border incidents with the Japanese became commonplace.

To meet these recurrent threats of war, the Soviet government used all its defense weapons, diplomatic, economic, and military, beginning with the diplomatic retreat at Brest Litovsk, "yielding space to gain time," passing through the period when offers of a huge market both for goods at high prices and loans at usurious rates served in part as bribes for peaceful relations abroad, until the internal economic and military strength of the country could be built up. Co-ordinating all three methods, and shifting emphasis from one to another as circumstances dictated, the Soviet government built its program of national defense.

In discussions preceding the adoption of the first Five-Year Plan, Voroshilov, Commissar of Defense, made a report on the defense aspects of planning, the conclusions of which he summarized as follows:

1. The five-year plan for national economy should take as

its starting point the inevitability of an armed attack on the USSR and consequently the necessity, within the limits of material resources, of organizing a defense of the Soviet Union that will guarantee the victorious repulse of the united forces of our probable enemies.

2. The industrialization of the country predetermines the fighting capacity of the USSR. And for this very reason military considerations should introduce certain correctives in the concrete plans for industrial construction. In particular: a. regionalization of industry should correspond to the demands of strategic security; b. metallurgy—both ferrous and especially non-ferrous, in the very near future must guarantee the minimum requirements of defense; c. the general plan for the development of industry should provide for the investment of sufficient funds in those branches which are at present the weak spots in our economy and defense (auto-tractor production, chemical industry, etc.)

3. The development of agriculture should provide for as rapid as possible a solution of the problem of raw materials from internal sources, freeing us in that way from imports and dependence on foreign countries.

4. The creation of reserves (natural and monetary) should be undertaken on the basis of a careful consideration of defense needs.

5. The construction of the armed forces (the Red Army, the Navy and the Air Force) should proceed on the basis of the necessity of raising the technical and military power to the level of a first-class European army.

6. Along with the five-year plan, it is necessary immediately to undertake the detailed working out of the planning of the whole national economy in time of war. . . .[1]

Taking this outline as a starting point, how far did the Soviet economy meet these defense needs? For the necessary raw materials, the Soviet Union is perhaps in the most favored position of any country in the world. It has always been well endowed with natural resources. Extensive exploration work further added to its riches, and of the twenty-two strategic raw materials, the Soviet Union now produces over 50 per cent of its domestic needs in all except tungsten, tin, antimony, and nickel. Of the others, it continues to import copper, aluminum, lead, and rubber in considerable amounts.

The story of the drive for raw materials includes such colorful chapters as the opening of the Arctic regions to find deposits of nickel, tin, and phosphates; the search for rubber-bearing plants in the mountains of central Asia to supplement the work of the scientific laboratories in making synthetic rubber; and the transformation of central Asian agriculture to make that region the vast cotton field of the U.S.S.R.

In the output of basic industrial products the developments over the last decade have even more completely reversed the prerevolutionary situation. Particularly important is the expansion of geographical distribution of production within the Soviet borders. In the interests of defense, and of improving living standards of the population, industry could no longer be concentrated on the European borders. The tremendous expanses of territory supplied only scantily with transportation facilities called for the development of local resources in each district to supply local needs for fuel, food, and industrial products. This meant building industrial centers close to the sources of raw materials in order to reduce the strain on the transportation system, with bases of heavy industry in each large geographical division of the country.

The first step in this direction was the construction under the first Five-Year Plan of the great Magnitogorsk-Kuznetsk iron and steel centers in Siberia to supplement the old centers in the Don basin and the Ukraine. The next step was the development of iron and steel plants farther east—at Komsomolsk on the Amur River and at Petrovsk-Zabaikalsk just east of Lake Baikal. A parallel move for the oil industry was the establishment of a "second Baku" between the Volga and the Urals which would to some degree fill the enormous gap between the oil of the Caucasus and the oil of Sakhalin in the Pacific. In every phase of industry similar plans were laid to duplicate important industrial centers in various parts of the country. For example, the Kuibyshev hydroelectric project on the Volga was planned as a second Dneprostroi. The map of industrial construction to be undertaken under the third Five-Year Plan showed three large clusters of dots—the new plants in the Urals, those around Krasnoyarsk, and those of the far east, centered at Komsomolsk.

In agriculture we see the same processes at work in the efforts to have the level of agricultural development evened off throughout the country. The old distinctions between "producing" and "consuming" areas in large measure lost their meaning, with the introduction of truck farming and dairying around the old industrial areas. At the same time the extension of grain production to the east and north gradually reduced the necessity for heavy grain shipments within the country. Thus the redistribution of production helped to strengthen the traditional weak spot in Russian economy—the transportation system. But that system itself was being expanded radically, as we can judge from a list of the major transportation facilities which were added during the two Five-Year Plans: the Turk-Sib railway connecting central Siberia and the east with central Asia; the Baltic–White Sea canal and the Moscow–Volga canal; the double-tracking of the Trans-Siberian railway; the Khabarovsk-Komsomolsk branch line, providing a second outlet to the Pacific; the opening of the northern sea route along the Arctic coast; and the large-scale development of civil airlines, which carried 19,685,000 ton-miles in 1938 as compared with 1,925,000 ton-miles in 1933.

In this way, through the completion of the second Five-Year Plan, the national economy of the U.S.S.R. by and large met the points laid down eleven years before to prepare the country for the contingencies of modern warfare. As events developed, the Soviet Union was fortunate to have pursued such an extensive defense program all through these years. But why was the government so defense-conscious in the very years when many other countries did not recognize the threat of war?

From the early years the Bolsheviks had talked of "capitalist encirclement"; they firmly believed that the capitalist countries did not like to have a socialist country growing strong, and that they would sooner or later try to restore capitalism in Russia by force. Thus they regarded almost any foreign country as a potential enemy. As a result the Soviet government had good diplomatic relations with almost no major nation.

By the end of the first Five-Year Plan this fear of war had become much more specific. The danger spots, as the Soviets saw them, were Japan and Germany. Japan was so regarded, because of its program of expansion on the continent of Asia, from 1931, the time of the invasion of Manchuria, Russia's neighbor in the East; Germany, as soon as Hitler came to power in 1933 announcing to the world his aim to plant the German flag on the Urals and acquire *Lebensraum* in the rich Ukraine and Caucasus. In an interview with Roy Howard in 1936 Stalin said:

STALIN. "In my opinion there are two seats of war danger. The first is in the Far East, in the zone of Japan. I have in mind the numerous statements made by Japanese military men containing threats against other powers. The second seat is in the zone of Germany. It is hard to say which is the most menacing, but both exist and are active. Compared with these two principal seats of war danger the Italo-Ethiopian war is an episode. At present the Far Eastern seat of danger reveals the greatest activity. However, the center of this danger may shift to Europe. This is indicated, for example, by the interview which Herr Hitler recently gave to a French newspaper. In this interview Hitler seems to have tried to say peaceful things, but he sprinkled his 'peacefulness' so plentifully with threats against both France and the Soviet Union that nothing remained of his 'peacefulness.' You see, even when Herr Hitler wants to speak of peace he cannot avoid uttering threats. This is symptomatic." [2]

While building up its own defenses, the Soviet government tried to improve its relations with other countries which were endangered by Germany and Japan. During this period Maxim Litvinov, Commissar of Foreign Affairs, coined the phrase "peace is indivisible," maintaining that in modern times when war breaks out anywhere, it is likely to spread and engulf the whole world. To prevent war, he advocated organization of all peace-loving nations so as to isolate the would-be aggressor. To this end the U.S.S.R. made neutrality or nonaggression pacts with as many of its neighbors as it could, and mutual assistance pacts with France, Czechoslovakia, and Outer Mongolia. It became a member of the League of Nations in 1934, and tried—though vainly—to get the nations at Geneva to work together to halt the tide of aggression: first to stop the Italian invasion of Ethiopia; then to force the Germans and Italians to cease aiding Franco's rebellion against the democratic government of Spain; then to aid China when Japan renewed its attack, driving south from Manchuria along the entire coast of Asia; and finally to stop Hitler in the mounting crisis in Europe that culminated with the Munich agreement. On the eve of the Munich Conference, Litvinov addressed himself to the League of Nations with a final plea to resist aggression:

At a moment when the mines are being laid to blow up the organization on which were fixed the great hopes of our generation, and which stamped a definite character on the international relations of our epoch; at a moment when, by no accidental coincidence, decisions are being taken outside the League which recall to us the international transactions of pre-war days, and which are bound to overturn all present conceptions of international morality and treaty obligations; at a moment when there is being drawn up a further list of sacrifices to the god of aggression, and a line is being drawn under the annals of all post-war international history, with the sole conclusion that nothing succeeds like aggression—at such a moment, every state must define its role and its responsibility before its contemporaries and before history. That is why I must plainly declare here that the Soviet Government bears no responsibility whatsoever for the events now taking place, and for the fatal consequences which may inexorably ensue.

After long doubts and hesitations, the Soviet Union joined the League in order to add the strength of a people of a hundred and seventy millions to the forces of peace. In the present hour of bitter disillusionment, the Soviet Union is far from regretting this decision, if only because there would undoubtedly have otherwise been attempts to attribute the alleged impotence and collapse of the League to its absence.

To avoid a problematic war to-day and receive in return a certain and large-scale war tomorrow—moreover, at the price of assuaging the appetites of insatiable aggressors and of the destruction or mutilation of sovereign States—is not to act in the spirit of the Covenant of the League of Nations. To grant bonuses for sabre-rattling and recourse to arms for the solution of international problems—in other words, to reward and encourage aggressive super-imperialism—is not to act in the spirit of the Briand-Kellogg Pact.

The Soviet Government takes pride in the fact that it has no part in such a policy, and has invariably pursued the principles of the two pacts I have mentioned, which were approved by nearly every nation in the world. Nor has it any intention of abandoning them for the future, being convinced that in present conditions it is impossible otherwise to safeguard a genuine peace and genuine international justice. It calls upon other Governments likewise to return to this path.[3]

The Soviet people were acutely aware of these developments. During the Spanish Civil War there were mass meetings throughout the country raising funds to buy food and other relief goods for the Spanish republicans.

Later many Spanish children were brought to the Soviet Union, and the Russian people came to know them first hand. In 1938 there again were meetings all over the country, on farms and in factories, protesting Japan's attack on the Soviet eastern border at Changkufeng, voicing the patriotism of the Soviet people and their anger at Japan, their traditional enemy in the Pacific.

Never for a moment was defense forgotten. There had always been compulsory military service in the U.S.S.R., beginning at the age of nineteen. In fact, universal military service for men was included in the 1936 constitution as one of the common obligations of citizens. Each year wide publicity was accorded to practice maneuvers. There for the first time the world saw large units of troops dropped by parachute along with all their equipment. Glider trains were tried out. The civilian defense organization, *Osoaviakhim*, received more and more public attention. First aid, air-raid protection, anti-gas precautions, parachute jumping, sharpshooting were taught to millions of Soviet citizens.

After Munich the Soviets felt that the struggle for peace had failed and that there could be no "peace in our time." To Moscow perhaps more than anywhere else war seemed imminent. Litvinov made another attempt to bring together the anti-Axis powers, but to no avail, and once more the Soviets turned inward to insure their own defense. Following the failure of Anglo-French-Soviet negotiations for a mutual defense arrangement, in the summer of 1939 the Soviets signed a nonaggression pact with Germany.

Americans ask how could the Soviet people, so long schooled in antifascism, accept a pact with the Nazis? The fact is that they did not. During the pact's existence no attempt was made by the Soviet government to "explain away" nazism. While the press no longer carried denunciations of fascism, it did, through quoting foreign news items, keep before the Soviet people the worst aspects of nazism while at the same time stressing the fact that the pact did not injure Soviet interests and did, while it lasted, keep war outside the Soviet borders. One American observer has explained this phenomenon as follows:

In general it may be assumed that the Soviet people didn't like the Soviet-Nazi pact but that they understood the need for it. For they had been told of the negotiations with Britain and France. They had known in detail of Munich and the sellout of Czechoslovakia. Stalin's assertion in his speech of March, 1939, that the Soviets would not be a cat's paw to pull other people's chestnuts out of the fire was constantly repeated. The Soviet leaders were seen to take energetic steps for the defense of the country. It was, all in all, a well-maneuvered race against time.[4]

They concentrated on developing a security belt on their western frontier. They occupied the eastern part of Poland in 1939 after the collapse of Polish resistance to the Nazis, and subsequently enlarged the Ukraine and White Russian republics to include those areas of Poland inhabited, in the majority, by Ukrainians and Byelorussians. After the war with Finland in the winter of 1940 they obtained naval bases well out into the Baltic and pushed their western frontier farther from Leningrad, second city of the U.S.S.R. In 1940 Rumania was asked to relinquish control over Bessarabia, which had been seized from Russia after World War I. And finally the three small Baltic states, Estonia, Latvia, and Lithuania, which had obtained their independence from Russia during the revolution, were reabsorbed. Thus the border of the country was moved farther west to meet the advancing Germans.

It is clear that in some respects the country was on a war footing for years before the Nazis attacked. But in 1940 further steps were taken to make sure production would be great enough in case of war. We have seen how for some years all sorts of financial incentives had been developed to urge workers to increase their output: differential wages, incentive bonuses; special privileges for Stakhanov workers—those workers who "used their heads as well as their hands"—who tried to work out more efficient ways of doing their jobs so that they could produce more in a given time. But that was not enough. The biggest problem was to keep workers on the job. As we know, it is the common experience of all countries that when jobs are easy to get and there is no unemployment, people are likely to go from one job to another, always looking for better conditions. This is called labor turnover and is especially bad for the efficiency of mass production industries. To stop this the Soviets made it illegal for workers to leave their jobs without a permit. At the same time fines and punishments were instituted for lateness and absence from work without legitimate cause.

The working day was also lengthened. In 1933 the Soviet Union had been the first country in the world to achieve the seven-hour day as a maximum for any occupation. But now in view of the serious international situation the working day was again lengthened to eight hours, and the seven-day week (six work days and one rest day, Sunday) replaced the six-day week.

To speed up job training for young people, new vocational schools were established at the end of 1940 under the Labor Reserves Administration. The law made it possible to recruit a million youths for the schools; but this did not prove necessary, as there were more than enough applications to fill the new schools.

Although the Soviet Union had managed to stay out of the big war for two years after Hitler invaded Poland, it nevertheless had few illusions about the danger of its position. The Finnish war had been won at great cost, and the Soviet government was doing all in its power to increase

the defensive might of the country. It was isolated completely from Great Britain and the United States by the
British blockade and the American embargo established
at the time of the move against Finland. With Europe it
had many trade agreements, but few goods were delivered.

The chairman of the State Planning Commission, re-
porting on the National Plan for 1941, said:

In respect to the output of the defense industry, the government was guided by a simple truth, namely, if you want to be
prepared for any "surprises," if you do not want our people to
be caught unawares, keep your powder dry and do not stint
means on the production of aircraft, tanks, armaments, warships and shells.[5]

Thus the country made itself ready for the blow which
was to fall before many months had passed.

11. WAR AND THE FUTURE

ON June 22, 1941, the Germans suddenly crossed the new Soviet frontiers all along the front; bombing the great cities of Odessa, Kiev, Minsk. It had been apparent to the world that this was likely to happen. The German conquest of the Balkans had been accompanied by some public friction with the Soviets, and British Intelligence had good reason to warn Moscow in the spring of 1941 that the blow might be struck at any moment. However, the Nazi attack had the great initial advantage of tactical surprise, and it hurled the Red Army back rapidly in the opening months of the war. In the first six months—until December 5—its 170 divisions smashed forward to the very gates of Moscow and Leningrad, and in the south as far as Rostov. Fighting with the Germans were the Finns, the Italians, the Hungarians, the Rumanians, Spanish fascists, and quisling units from the occupied countries. Behind this army stood the manpower, the raw materials, and the industry of the whole of Europe—a population and economic strength considerably in excess of that of the U.S.S.R.

This initial blitz, which the world watched with horror and fear, was stopped dead in its tracks before Moscow, and the first Soviet counterattack was launched by the Russians in the winter of 1941.

The first six months, the most crucial as it turned out, set the pattern that was to be followed. On June 22, the very day of the German invasion, Churchill had declared, "The Russian danger is, therefore, our danger and the danger of the United States, just as the cause of any Rus-

235

sian fighting for his hearth and home is the cause of free men and free people in every quarter of the globe." [1]

By the time of the Soviet counterattack the British and Russians had achieved a military alliance; the United States had extended lend-lease to include Russia (though the first considerable shipments could not reach the U.S.S.R. until late in 1942); and the Soviets had endorsed the Atlantic Charter.

Inside the Soviet Union total mobilization was being carried out. Stalin's grim speech of July 3 set the tone:

Above all, it is essential that our people, the Soviet people, should understand the full immensity of the danger that threatens our country and abandon all complacency, all heedlessness, all those moods of peaceful constructive work which were so natural before the war but which are fatal today when war has fundamentally changed everything.

The enemy is cruel and implacable. . . .

. . . There must be no room in our ranks for whimperers and cowards, for panic-mongers and deserters. . . .

We must organize all-around assistance to the Red Army. . . .

In case of a forced retreat of Red Army units, all rolling stock must be evacuated. . . .

Collective farmers must drive off all their cattle. . . .

In areas occupied by the enemy, guerrilla units, mounted and foot, must be formed. . . .

In the occupied regions conditions must be made unbearable for the enemy. . . .[2]

Stalin foresaw that large sections of the country might be overrun by the enemy, and preparations were made for that contingency. Mobilization was universal—all men between sixteen and sixty-four and women between sixteen and forty-five could be recruited for war industries. Girls and boys, men and women not in war industry could be drafted for farm work. Even the children, millions of them, spent their summers helping on the farms.

In industry all limits on overtime were abandoned and an eleven-hour day was not uncommon. All production of consumers' goods—clothes, shoes, and so forth—was diverted to military purposes. For the major part of European Russia martial law was invoked; people could be drafted for building fortifications, for providing transport, and for other duties necessary to the army.

The army became tremendous; at the outbreak of war it was made up of young men from eighteen to twenty-two serving their period of military service; immediately the twenty-three to thirty-six age groups were called up. In addition volunteer citizens' armies participated in the battles for the great cities, Leningrad, Odessa, Sevastopol. Every man from sixteen to fifty not in the army was compelled to take a special military training course.

We have all heard of the heroism of the Russian people in famous sieges such as that of Leningrad, where during the twenty-nine months when the city was cut off from the rest of the country more than a million people died of starvation. Stalingrad, however, has come to mean the greatest triumph, for there out of the rubble of the completely devastated city came the victory that proved the decisive turning point of the war.

The spirit that won these battles lives again in these excerpts from diaries of Soviet school children, which give us some idea of that terrible winter in Leningrad:

In one essay a girl wrote: "One day we were sitting silently round the *burzhuika* warming our numb fingers. The bell had rung several minutes before. We were waiting for our teacher of literature. Instead of him, Yakov Mikhailovich arrived and announced, 'There will be no classes today. We must all go and take to pieces a wooden house because our wood supply is at an end, and we must get more wood in.' Well, it couldn't be helped. It was terribly cold outside. A piercing wind was blowing, freezing our faces and stopping the blood in our veins."

And here is more, from another essay by the same girl: "The

winter came, fierce and merciless. The water-pipes froze, and there was no electric light, and the tramcars stopped running. To get to school in time I had to get up very early every morning, for I live out in the suburbs. It was particularly difficult to get to school after a blizzard when all roads and paths are covered with snowdrifts. But I firmly decided to complete my school year. . . . One day, after standing in a bread queue for six hours (I had to miss school that day, for I had received no bread for two days), I caught a cold and fell ill. Never had I felt more miserable than during those days. Not for physical reasons, but because I desperately needed the moral support of my schoolmates, their encouraging jokes. . . ." [3]

Another of the epics of the battle against the Nazis was the defense of Sevastopol, Russia's historic naval base in the Crimea. A Soviet correspondent who was there describes the spirit of the last stand of the marines left to cover the final withdrawal:

. . . During those last hours the men of Sevastopol surprised themselves in courage defying description; they were fantastic and magnificent in their fearlessness. They had no illusions about their peril and faced death calmly.

Gathering around him the Marines of Captain Alexander's Thirty-fifth Battery on Malakhov Kurgan, the political commissar spoke as follows: "I know that every one of you would rather fight one hundred desperate battles on the sea than to be dive-bombed once ashore. But the Germans have forced us to fight ashore. Eighty-two years ago a Russian admiral ordered his men to sink their vessels in this Sevastopol Bay. These orders were obeyed and their guns were brought ashore to defend the city as these our guns are doing today. Twenty-four years ago Lenin ordered our ships to be sunk at Novorossiisk. These orders were obeyed. Last year Stalin ordered us to blow up the Dnieper Dam and we did. Now we have to die. We have to die for those who one day will return to Sevastopol. We have to die for those who will one day build another Dnieper Dam. We have to die for those who will go on fighting at sea."

The men removed their caps and stood silent for a short time. Then they swore their oath to Stalin and their Fatherland to conquer or die. They returned to their guns wearing under Red Army blouses their striped sailor jerseys—"for luck" and twisted around their forage caps hat-bands bearing the names of their former ships.[4]

The guerrillas behind the Nazi lines played a great part in the final rout of the Nazis. Guerrilla fighters were a great tradition in Russia. They had harassed and beaten Napoleon's great army; they had been the heroes of the revolution and civil war. Now they rode again. This time they had good preparation, for collective farms were good training grounds for partisan bands. Working together for the harvest had taught them teamwork; military training had been well developed on the farms; and arms were supplied those who served as the guerrillas. Often the operations of these bands behind the German lines were actually co-ordinated with those of the regular army.

The battle of production had its heroes as well. By looking at a map, one realizes that the areas occupied by the Germans were the old industrial areas. Although new industries had been developed in the east, some 60 per cent of the country's production lay in the area of combat. The plan was to evacuate as much of as many of the factories as possible, and destroy all the rest that might fall into German hands. Thus they destroyed their greatest dam— on the Dnieper. And, finally, they would operate for war purposes any plants that had to be left near the front lines. As we have seen, prewar plans had laid down the foundations for duplicate plants in the east. As the Nazis advanced, the Soviets were able to ship 200,000 carloads of industrial equipment east—whole factories with their workers and their raw materials. The factories sent east by railroad were integrated with these duplicate plants. For instance, a new factory in the Urals at Tankograd was made up of part of the Putilov plant evacuated from Leningrad, part from the Kharkov agriculture machinery plant, and part from the Stalingrad tractor plant. The saga of such a trip east is told in the Soviet novel *The Ordeal*.

On the lines to the east there was a tremendous concentration of rolling stock. The country had undertaken to evacuate not only people but materials, food supplies, industrial equipment, museums, art galleries, libraries, theatres, from all zones subject to air raids. Freight and passenger trains from the west were held up while troops and military equipment raced through to their destination. The front needed men and munitions.

Life on the trains carrying the workers from Dubenko's factory east was typical of conditions on other evacuation trains. The workers had left all their possessions behind. The women lived in boxcars and in the evenings gathered in quiet groups and spoke wistfully of the belongings, large and small, that they had had to leave at home. The life they had but lately lived and had taken so easily for granted seemed supremely desirable to them now, and past worries very trivial. There was a fire in an iron stove in the middle of the boxcar, and at mealtimes the top of it was covered with pots. The women took turns cooking their meals. In order to maintain their proper turn, they placed their pots and teakettles in orderly lines on the floor. The men—there were not many of them— traveled on the flatcars, in the tentlike shelters made of thin boards and covered with tarpaper. . . .

He saw train upon train loaded with evacuated industrial plants. Machine tools from Kremenchug, Zaporozhye, Dnepropetrovsk and Gamalei. Grinding machines lay on flatcars exposed to the weather. Movable parts had been greased and wrapped in paper before loading, but the journey had been a long one, and the paper had been torn by the wind and the grease washed off by the rain and sleet, and the machines had rusted badly. Pigs of aluminum, magnesium, and other nonferrous metals were piled up among the machinery. Stalin had ordered that not an ounce of nonferrous metal was to be left to the enemy, and the order had been strictly carried out.

Already Dubenko's train had reached points where the evacuated machines and tools of other factories were being unloaded. The machines were lowered down the railway embankment; then, to the accompaniment of shouts of exhortation and warning from the workers, were moved to sheds which had been hastily built from logs, planks, and pine branches. Forests were being cut down, roads broken through the deep snowdrifts, and timber hauled to the construction sites. If the engineer in Dubenko was shocked by some of the methods and makeshifts, the patriot in him was proud. What did it matter, after all, so long as the work went forward? Forest clearings glowed with the fires of autogenous welders, and the workers warmed themselves and cooked their meals over bonfires. New transmission lines were being set up, bringing electric power nearer and animating every undertaking. Here in the rear, people were fighting with the stubbornness and self-sacrifice of the soldiers at the front.[5]

The four years of war served as a test of the new socialist system—the most grueling test to which a country could be subjected. At the height of the German advance, in the winter of 1942, the Nazis completely occupied six of the Soviet republics and part of two more. This area of some 700,000 square miles normally had a population of sixty or seventy millions. A similar area of the United States occupied by the enemy would extend from the east coast to the Mississippi River, and would include all the states north of Tennessee and West Virginia. It would swallow up our greatest industrial centers, most of our biggest cities, and the rich agricultural states of the middle west.

How did the system stand up? We know it won through to victory; but did the war change it? Many changes took place in the pressure of war that seem to have resulted from a new-found confidence in the fundamental unity of the Soviet people. Contradictory as it may seem, one sign of this inner unity was a new emphasis on the many separate nationalities which make up the country. In the army, units from the various republics were established, though most of the army remained mixed. In war propaganda a kind of nationalism was emphasized through recalling historic heroes—Bogdan Khmelnitsky for the Ukrainians, for instance. Suvorov and Kutuzov, the great generals of Russian history, became honored again in the names given the high military awards. This trend back to history was not entirely a wartime phenomena. In the years just before the war the outsanding figures of Russian history—Peter the Great, Ivan the Terrible, to mention but two—were studied and praised for their role in making Russia great. Each republic was finding its national heroes and glorifying their tradition—the same heroes who had been ignored or debunked in the early years after the revolution. This new nationalism, which was emerging before the war, became during the war an inspiration to all the varied nationalities which served in the Red Army. In this lay its peculiarity. Each nation had its heroes— heroes who had in some cases gained their fame in fighting the Russians or other members of the Soviet family of nations; yet now they were respected by all the Soviet peoples. It was a little like George Washington's becoming a hero for the British as well as the Americans, or Lincoln's being praised by the South as well as the North.

As we have seen above, this growing sense of national importance also resulted in a constitutional amendment giving the republics the right to establish diplomatic representation abroad and to maintain military units.

Another strictly wartime evolution toward unity was the return of the church to favor. We have seen how the Russian Orthodox church, which had been an integral part of the tsarist state apparatus and had consequently fought, as an organization, against the revolution, was bitterly resisted by the Bolsheviks in return. Although the successive Soviet constitutions retained a clause guaranteeing freedom of conscience, the Soviets were unflinch-

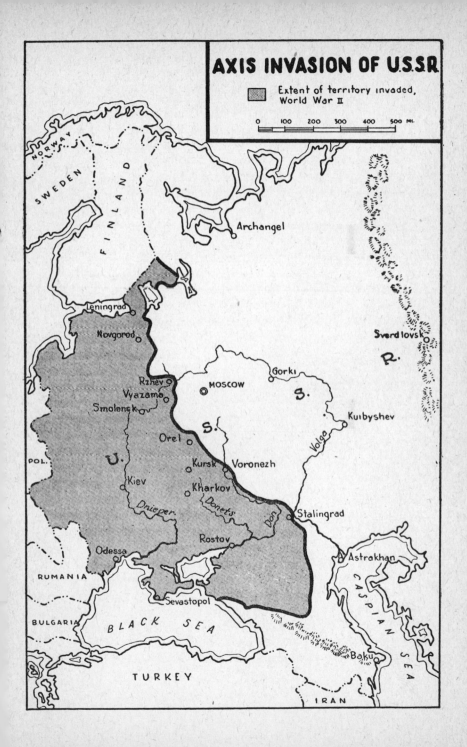

AXIS INVASION OF U.S.S.R.

Extent of territory invaded, World War II

0   100   200   300   400   500 MI.

NORWAY

SWEDEN

FINLAND

Archangel

Leningrad

Novgorod

Sverdlovsk

Rzhev

Vyazama

Smolensk

Gorki

MOSCOW

S.

Kuibyshev

Orel

Volga

R.

U.

Kursk

Voronezh

S.

S.

Kiev

Kharkov

Dnieper

Donets

Don

Stalingrad

POL.

Rostov

Odessa

Astrakhan

RUMANIA

Sevastopol

BLACK   SEA

CASPIAN   SEA

BULGARIA

Baku

TURKEY

IRAN

ingly determined to break the grip of the church on their people. They separated the church from the state, disfranchised the clergy, deprived the church of all its lands and wealth, conducted extensive antireligious propaganda, and encouraged social pressures against religion.

This fight against religion in general, and in particular against the Russian Orthodox church, became more intense at times of crisis, as for instance during the period of the purges in the mid-1930's. But, curious as it may seem, in the greatest crisis of all, that of war, the trend was reversed. The first move came from the church: it declared its support of the people against the invaders. It sent gifts to the front, and though previously forbidden by law to participate in community social work, it became a source of comfort and aid to the families of servicemen. In return the government gave public recognition to the church's position. Permission was granted in 1943, to reestablish the Holy Synod, and the patriarchate was filled again. Not only the Russian Orthodox church found its way to government favor again. Mohammedans, too, held for the first time an election for the head of the Moslems in the U.S.S.R. The Protestants and other Christian sects likewise became more active. To regulate the legal status of the various churches two government committees were appointed; schools for training for the ministry were reopened; printing facilities were put at the disposal of the churches. Organized religion, and not just the Russian Orthodox, at last had found a place in Soviet life.

This, of course, did not mean an end to agnosticism and scientific education directed against certain religious beliefs. It did, however, mean that religion was legalized and given a chance to serve its followers without social restrictions.

The aftermath of the war is something especially difficult for us to visualize. Almost the whole of European Russia as far as Moscow and Stalingrad—historic cities, rich farmland, and tremendous factories—was utterly and completely devastated. Much of it was barren wasteland. Not only had the Russians "scorched the earth" behind them as they withdrew in retreat; not only was there the destruction of battle itself; but the Germans in their retreat had destroyed everything, literally everything that time permitted, as they withdrew.

An American general who was among the first Americans to travel through large sections of the Ukraine reported that the Nazis had even burned the chicken coops. He told of a highway along which the Russians had taken the pains to plant rows of trees (and trees do not grow easily on the plains of the Ukraine) where the Germans had methodically cut down every tree along the road—for no purpose other than destruction.

We know, too, that it was not only trees they sought to destroy, but people—the Slav people. Russia's greatest loss was its human loss. It is estimated that some twenty million men, women, and children were killed, more than half of them civilians. Some perished in Nazi murder camps; some died in slavery (two million were liberated by the advancing Allied Armies); and thousands were murdered wantonly during the occupation. In addition to the dead there are the wounded. Soviet medical science had an enviable record during the war, returning more than 70 per cent of the wounded to combat, while only about 5 per cent remained incapacitated. Even this fraction, however, means that several hundred thousand are permanent invalids. The Soviets did everything possible to bring these men and women back into a productive life, and job training was provided at hospitals and sanatoria. Factories were required to make provisions for re-employing the men who were no longer able to carry on full jobs. Special departments for assisting them were organized in the larger plants, in addition to the invalid co-operatives which had always existed and were now expanded.

Wounded servicemen were just one of the groups of war casualties that had to be cared for. Another large group were the children: war orphans who had lost one or both parents, many of whom themselves suffered wounds and maltreatment, all suffering the terrible shock of their personal experiences. As many of these children as possible were placed in foster homes. Thousands of others were cared for in children's homes far from the battlefields, where they were nursed back to health and given the loving care necessary to help them forget the harrowing sights they had seen.

As we have seen before, the Soviets feel a special responsibility about children and have always, even in hard times, given them the best care and food, for in them lies the hope of the future. After the war they again have to give them special attention. There are those who for three years went to school under the Nazis and were taught the hateful Nazi doctrines of race prejudice. There are those whose fathers were Nazis and who must now find their place in the community that hates the memory of their fathers.

Many of these same problems exist as well among the adults; those who were forced to work under the Nazis must make their peace with their neighbors who somehow withstood the pressures. The returning "slaves" from Germany must try to find their families and rebuild their lives.

As for the material damage, no number of dollars can express to us the price the Russians had to pay for the war. In the Ukraine alone it was estimated that half of the means of production were gone—half of all machinery, tools, factory buildings, agricultural equipment, livestock, farm buildings, railroads and their rolling stock and locomotives, river ships and port facilities. To this we must add the homes and personal possessions of the forty-two million Ukrainian citizens.

Reconstruction began in December 1941 when the first counterattack before Moscow won back small areas from the Nazis. From then until V-E day reconstruction was part of the Soviet war effort, because the liberated areas immediately became the rear areas for the advancing Red Army. Chaos and famine could not be permitted to develop. Consequently rehabilitation was planned along with the military plan for retaking an area. Behind the front, administrative personnel was assembled to move in with the troops, and efforts were made to learn through guerrilla sources the extent of damage to be expected. Medical and public health officials went in with the troops; the army at first supplied food, but soon civilian authorities took over. The first objective was to get the community back into operation as a productive group—producing its own needs such as bread, building materials, fuel and electricity—and, if possible, to get it to produce for the front as well. Along with this went the immediate restoration of the social services—the hospitals and schools especially. The Nazis made a particular effort to destroy all such public buildings as schools, museums, theaters, hospitals—anything that was used to serve the community. To restore these was a first concern of the returning Russians.

On a national scale the priorities in reconstruction were agriculture, railroads, local industry for construction work, and housing. Even before the end of the war there was some reconversion of industry to produce tractors and other essential agricultural machinery. In August 1943 the first detailed reconstruction decree was issued, and this dealt primarily with farms. More than 600,000 head of livestock were driven from the east back to the devastated farms; seeds were furnished and machine-tractor stations reorganized with the object of alleviating famine conditions. Within the framework of the planned economy and with government ownership of most of the economy, reconstruction as well as reconversion to peacetime production did not require special governmental organization. The administrative machinery developed during the Five-Year Plans could with little change be used for the overwhelming and urgent job of making it possible for people to live in the battle-torn areas.

Did the task of reconstruction mean that the Soviet Union had suffered such losses during the war that it was very weak by the time victory was won? No. This is one of the important things we learn when we consider how the Soviets got to Berlin. They won the war largely by their own strength. Our lend-lease aid did not even begin to reach them in significant amounts until after the battle of Stalingrad. While it was immensely helpful—perhaps decisive—in giving the Russians the extra margin of superiority over the Germans, it was Russian-made equipment that formed the bulk of Red Army supplies. At the end of the war the Red Army was larger than at the beginning of the war; its equipment was more effective, its supplies more adequate. The secret lay in the Urals, and there we find that the Soviet Union was actually strengthened during the war. In the war years industrial output increased 3.6 times in the Urals, 2.8 times in Siberia, and 3.4 times in the Volga area.[6] At Sverdlovsk production in 1944 was 7 times as great as in 1940; at Nizhni Tagil and Kamenski Uralsk 8.5 times. The amount of new electric power brought into operation in 1944 equaled the total new capacity added by the first Five-Year Plan.[7] These are a few examples we can find explaining the new sources of industrial strength in the U.S.S.R.

But the setback to Russia's economic development was tremendous. If we read the astronomical figures in the Soviet government's official report on war damages,[8] we can understand it: 31,850 industrial enterprises, in which 4,000,000 workers had been employed, were demolished; 65,000 kilometers of railway track were destroyed, and with them 4,100 railway stations, 40,000 hospitals, and 84,000 schools and colleges; 7,000,000 horses, 17,000,000 cattle, 20,000,000 hogs, and 27,000,000 sheep were driven off to Germany. In effect the Soviet Union lost a decade of its growth. This became clear when in March 1946 the fourth Five-Year Plan was adopted by the Supreme Soviet. The third plan had been scheduled to end in 1942 but was cut short by war. The new plan, covering the years 1946 to 1950, sets goals only slightly above those scheduled for 1941. Take oil, for instance, the heart's blood of modern industry: the prewar level of production will not be reached until 1949; or steel—the 1950 plan of 25,400,000 tons is only 3,000,000 tons above the 1941 plan. In agriculture, livestock losses were so tremendous that they will not nearly reach the prewar level in 1950, and consequently output of meat will be less than half the figure for prewar years. It may take a generation to restore housing even to its inadequate level of 1941.

Of the things that people eat and wear, production will still be painfully low by 1950. In that year Soviet industry will turn out little more than one pair of shoes per person, three pairs of stockings, less than one yard of woolen cloth, and about twenty-five yards of cotton cloth per person— for clothing, bedding, and all other purposes. For millions who were left with nothing but rags to wear and burned out cellars to live in, this small production is more than ordinarily difficult to face.

There seems to be little the Russians can do to speed up the recovery. They cannot produce cloth without first building the mills; they cannot build mills until they cut timber, mine cement or make bricks, and build the railways to haul these supplies to the site of the mill; then they must make the textile machinery. The utter destruction of Russia's main industrial areas forces the new plan again to concentrate on building factories instead of making cloth. Thus we find the rebuilding of the giant Dneprostroi dam one of the first postwar undertakings. We can get some idea of the scope of the new plan from the following random quotations from the law.

. . . The principal aims of the Five-Year Plan for the Rehabilitation and development of the National Economy of the U.S.S.R. in 1946-1950 are to rehabilitate the devastated regions of the country, to recover the prewar level in industry and agriculture, and then considerably to surpass that level.

For this purpose it is necessary:

1. To give priority to the restoration and development of heavy industry and railway transport, without which the rapid and effective recovery and development of the entire national economy of the U.S.S.R. would be impossible.

2. To promote agriculture and the industries producing consumer goods in order to raise the material well-being of the people of the Soviet Union and to secure an abundance of the principal items of consumer goods in the country.

3. To promote technical progress in all branches of the national economy of the U.S.S.R., as a condition for a powerful increase of production and a rise in the productivity of labor, which will necessitate not only catching up with but surpassing scientific achievement outside the U.S.S.R. in the near future. . . .

In the five-year period, 45 blast furnaces with a total output of 12,800,000 tons, 165 open hearth furnaces, 15 converters and 90 electric furnaces with a total output of 16,200,000 tons of steel, 104 rolling mills with a total output of 11,700,000 tons, and 63 coke batteries with a total output of 19,100,000 tons shall be rehabilitated or newly built and put into operation. New iron ore mines with an annual output of 35,400,000 tons shall be opened. . . .

In the five years from 1946 to 1950, the following new pits are to be sunk and put into operation: in the Moscow coalfield, 66 pits with a total capacity of 18,800,000 tons; in the Kuznetsk Basin, 30 pits with a total of 18,000,000 tons; in Karaganda, 17 pits and open-cut mines with a total capacity of 6,500,000 tons; in the Urals, 49 pits and open-cut mines with a total capacity of 19,000,000 tons; and in Central Asia, nine pits with a total capacity of 3,200,000 tons. The Pechora coalfield, a new source of supply for the northern section of the European U.S.S.R. and Leningrad, shall be extended. In this region new pits with a total capacity of 7,700,000 tons shall be started. . . .

The production of high octane aviation gasoline shall be developed, and the quality of gasoline for motors, kerosene for tractors, oil for Diesel engines and lubricating oils improved. The quantity of oil products obtained from petroleum must be increased by reducing losses and introducing catalytic and other up-to-date methods of producing gasoline and industrial oils. In the five-year period four oil refining installations shall be built. Three oil refineries shall be rehabilitated to supply oil products to the agricultural and industrial regions of the South. . . .

The rebuilding and building of power stations must be conducted at such speed that the increase in power-producing capacity shall keep ahead of the restoration and development of other branches of industry. . . .

Six hydro-electric stations, including the Lenin Power Station on the Dnepr, are to be rehabilitated, the building of 30 hydro-electric stations completed, the first sections of eight hydro-electric stations built and put into operation, and work on five big new hydro-electric stations begun. The surveying and drafting in preparation for the building of new power stations on the Dnepr and the Syr-Darya are to continue. . . .

By 1950 this industry [machine-building] shall have doubled its output as compared with pre-war. Priority shall be given to the rehabilitation and development of the manufacture of equipment for the iron and steel, power, coal and oil industries, the manufacture of electrical machines, railway rolling stock, motor vehicles, tractors, agricultural machinery, equipment of the building industry, equipment for geological survey work, special and complex machine-tools, foundry equipment, and equipment and instruments for the chemical industry. . . .

The mass production of agricultural machinery—tractor ploughs, seed drills, cultivators, disc and colter tillers, combines and other harvesters, grain cleaners, machines for gathering industrial crops, and grass seed, mowing machines, fodder preparation and processing machines, sheep shearing and milking machines, separators, refrigerators and other dairy equipment, water-supply equipment for stock farms, collective farm flour mills and apparatus for combatting farm pests—shall be rehabilitated and developed. Nine plants for the production of agricultural machines shall be restored. The building of five plants for the production of agricultural machines and one for the production of harvester combines shall be completed and put into operation. . . .

The production of textile machines shall be increased to four times the pre-war level. The production of new technically improved machinery—high-speed roving frames and warping machines—shall be inaugurated. . . .

The production of excavators, the latest building and road-making machinery, hoisting and transport equipment, loading and unloading machinery and various types of equipment for mechanizing laborious operations shall be undertaken. . . .

The mass production of new types of microscopes, apparatus for spectral analysis, cinema projectors and cine-cameras, cameras and binoculars shall be undertaken and developed in accordance with the latest advances in the sphere of optics. The mass production of improved and cheap motorcycles, bicycles, shot guns, radio receivers, clocks, matches and gramophones shall be resumed and developed. The production of modern television receivers shall be organized. The large-scale production of refrigerators shall be organized. . . .

By 1950 the production of synthetic rubber shall be doubled, of automobile tires trebled, and of rubber footwear increased 1.3 times compared with pre-war; in the synthetic rubber industry the use of raw material other than food crops shall be extensively developed and by 1950 the share of rubber produced from non-food raw materials shall be 38 per cent of the total. By 1950 the output of regenerated rubber shall be increased to 56,000 tons. The production of natural rubber in the U.S.S.R. shall be organized on a large scale. . . .

The pre-fabrication of dwelling-houses and of standard component parts made of wood, gypsum, asbo-cement and other materials shall be started as a new industry. . . .

The assortment and finish of fabrics, garments, knitted goods and footwear must be definitely improved; the production of improved dress fabrics and suiting shall be increased, as well as that of mercerized, napped, jacquard and extra-fast printed fabrics. The capacity of spinning-mills shall be increased in the five-year period by 2,860,000 spindles, of the artificial silk industry by 102,000 tons, of the boot and shoe industry by 100,000,000 pairs, and of the stocking industry by 345,000,000 pairs of socks and stockings. . . .

The most important task of agriculture in 1946-1950 is the general improvement of crop yields and an increase in the gross harvest of agricultural produce to be effected by considerably improving farm methods and applying the latest achievements in agricultural science. . . .

In the five-year period 950 machine and tractor stations shall be rebuilt and every machine and tractor station shall be provided with subsidiary buildings and workshops for running repairs. . . .

New and perfected machines shall be designed and supplied to the farms. . . .

The training of sufficient agronomists, engineers, livestock experts, veterinary surgeons, land surveyors and other specialists for the farms shall be ensured, as well as the training of skilled workers in the commoner trade for the machine and tractor stations, collective and state farms.

There shall be a further development in the use of electricity in the collective farms, machine and tractor stations and state farms. Small hydro-electric stations shall be widely built in the rural areas, and where there are no water-power resources stations driven by locomobiles, or gas-generator engines working on local fuel shall be built. . . .

One thousand five hundred railway stations, round-houses with accommodation for 1,300 locomotives, and 128 car-repair shops and centers shall be restored or newly built. New lines are to be built in the five-year period to a total of 7,230 km., including the Stalinsk—Magnitogorsk trunk line. Secondary tracks to a total length of 12,500 km. shall be built or restored. Lines totalling 5,325 km. shall be electrified, and automatic block-signalling systems installed on 10,400 km. of track. . . .

The conversion of the Northern Sea Route into a normally working sea lane shall be completed by 1950. . . .

With the growth of the productivity of labor, the average annual earnings per worker by hand and brain engaged in the national industries of the U.S.S.R. shall increase by 1950 to 6,000 rubles, which is considerably above the 1940 level. . . .

The progressive piece-rate system of the payment of workers, as well as the system of bonuses for engineers and technicians for fulfillment and overfulfillment of output programs, shall be perfected, the proportion of bonuses to wages and salaries being systematically increased. . . .

With a view of supplying adequate numbers of skilled workers for the major branches of the national economy and improving the technical training of industrial personnel, the annual graduation of young skilled workers by the factory, trade and railway schools shall be increased to 1,200,000 pupils, and the state labor reserve training system shall in the five-year period provide 4,500,000 young skilled workers.

The practice of training skilled workers on the job in the common trades shall be widely extended by means of individual and group training and courses of instruction, so that 7,700,000 new workers are given technical training, and the skilled qualifications of 13,900,000 workers enhanced in the five years. . . .

The state expenditure on the cultural and social services in town and country . . . shall be raised to 106 billion rubles in 1950, or to 2.6 times the expenditure in 1940. . . .

By 1950 the number of primary, seven-year and secondary schools shall be raised to 190,000 and of their pupils to a total of 31,800,000, universal compulsory education being extended to all children from the age of seven both in town and country.

By 1950 the number of students in higher educational institutions shall be raised to 674,000 and of students of specialized secondary schools to 1,280,000. . . .

The number of cinema installations shall be increased to 46,700 in 1950 as against 28,000 in 1940. . . .

The number of children accommodated in kindergartens in 1950 shall be increased to 2,260,000, or double the number in 1940. . . .

The plan of rehabilitation and new construction of state-owned houses for the five-year period is endorsed at 72,400,000 sq. m. of living space, including 65,000,000 sq. m. to be built by the ministries and departments and 7,400,000 sq. m. by the local soviets. In addition, provision shall be made in the five years for the rebuilding and further construction of individually owned houses, at the expense of the individual owners themselves and with the aid of government loans, to a total of 12,000,000 sq. m. of living space. With a view of improving living conditions, creating permanent cadres of workers in industry·and averting a high labor turn-over, business organizations shall undertake the building of one-family and two-family houses provided with garden and vegetable plots, for sale on the installment plan to workers, clerks, technicians and engineers. . . .

The production and sale of consumer goods shall be increased in 1950 to the following dimensions: aluminum, enamelled, porcelain and chinaware utensils, 260,000,000; samovars, 200,000; tumblers, 160,000,000; furniture (reckoned in fixed prices), 1,200,000,000 rubles; sewing machines, 450,-000; clocks and watches, 7,400,000; gramophones, 1,000,000; radio sets, 925,000; motor cycles, 135,000, and bicycles, 1,050,000.

Beginning in 1946 the retail sale of lumber, iron, nails, bricks, window glass, paints and varnishes, and other building and repair materials, shall be organized.[9]

These pitifully small figures for consumers' goods are the key to what life in postwar U.S.S.R. will be like. There are only two short cuts to plenty not taken into account in these plans. Both are contingent on the state of the world. One is to eliminate all Soviet expenditure on armaments, which, while not indicated in the law establishing the plan, undoubtedly uses up a sizable proportion of current output in the heavy industries. The other is to expand Soviet foreign trade enormously to exchange the things the U.S.S.R. can produce more quickly and plentifully for the things it will take it years to make. In a peaceful and trading world, the lot of the Soviet people would be much better.

Unfortunately for them, as for us, the course of events since the end of the war has not led to improved relations between the U.S.S.R. and this country. The compelling needs of war forced co-operation between all the Allies, despite their differences of viewpoint. When the pressure of a common enemy was removed, all the old frictions and suspicions again returned.

This short history has not dealt with Russia's foreign relations down through the centuries. But in the twentieth century, diplomacy and wars are no longer the sole concern of diplomats and mercenaries. They affect so directly the life and standard of living of the individual Russian and American that it would be academic to speak of the future without some word on this subject so crucial to all of us all over the world.

The Soviets early in the war proclaimed the necessity for Allied unity to build the peace. They signed twenty-year military defense alliances with Great Britain, France, Yugoslavia, Poland, and Czechoslovakia. They participated actively in the organization of the United Nations. But even at the San Francisco Conference, establishing the U.N., ugly arguments came out into the open between the great powers—arguments on procedures as well as on questions of substance. If Americans find it difficult to understand the Soviet behavior at the many Allied conferences which have been meeting in rapid succession since the end of the war, many Soviet citizens in their turn seem to be puzzled and troubled by America's policy. Until both peoples can progress toward understanding what the other is driving at, it will be difficult to reconcile their foreign policies. Perhaps the best way to get an idea of Russia's basic postwar aims is to quote in part the answer given by a leading Soviet journalist to the question "What does Russia Want?"

To begin with, we want peace—a genuine, durable, sincere peace. The Soviet state is young. It is only 28 years old. But in this brief space of time, it has been subjected to several attacks. In their relations with the Soviet Union some Governments have pursued a policy of isolation, blockade and political blackmail. The main burden of the second World War fell upon the shoulders of our country and caused us tremendous losses and privations. Nearly 7,000,000 people in the Soviet Union perished in the battle with the Germans, and in consequence of German occupation and deportation to German slavery.

We want peace. This is not merely our desire. It is a vital necessity. . . .

We want to restore our devastated economy to raise the living standards of our people and enrich our country. . . .

We harbor no designs on the lands of other nations. We do not rave about "Lebensraum" nor do we believe that we are superior to all other nations and hence predestined to dominate them. We desire friendly relations with all peaceable peoples. We would like to maintain economic and cultural relations with them.

American technique played no small part in helping us to carry out our five-year plans. American talent and ability were invested in the Dnieper hydroelectric station and other great enterprises of Socialist industry. We remember this and appreciate it. We remember with satisfaction the assistance rendered to us by our Allies during the war with German fascism. The services we rendered to all freedom-loving nations during the war were inestimable. . . .

We want to have loyal friends throughout the world. Primarily, we want to have trustworthy neighbors. We do not live on the moon. We live on the earth—a rather sinful earth at times. Hitherto history and geography have not endowed us with good neighbors. Up to the second World War, preparations to attack us were conducted on our very threshold. . . .

Agents of governments inimical to the Soviet Union operated everywhere hand in hand with agents of international monopoly trusts who would be unreconciled to the independent existence of the Soviet Union's national economy. Today after the victory of the Red Army and the liberation of the peoples in Eastern Europe our country has for the first time established good neighborly relations with the peoples of Poland, Yugoslavia, Bulgaria, Rumania and other states. These states are now truly independent and genuinely democratic.

That is why the Soviet people view with some anxiety any attempts made from without to impose on these nations persons of such dubious reputation as Anders in Poland and Maniu in Rumania. That the Soviet people are building up amicable relations with the neighbors is the best guarantee of the peace of Europe. . . .

We realize that those European politicians—not only German Fascists but British reactionaries as well—who have always sought to sow the seeds of enmity toward the Soviet Union do not relish the prospect of our being on good terms with our neighbors. . . . We note with regret that this English "malady" has infected some American politicians as well.

What United States interests are threatened by friendship between the Soviet Union and democratic Poland, democratic Bulgaria and other countries? We realize that we live in a world that respects strong men and strong nations, a world in which the lot of weak men and weak nations is an unenviable one. We know that we are strong. . . .

Hostile cries leveled against us do not throw us into panic. . . . We rebuff slander and make no claim to unwonted delicacy when it comes to exposing lies. . . . We like to call a spade a spade. When, for example, we hear the rat-tat of machine guns somewhere in Indonesia, we cannot be expected to believe that we are hearing dulcet music. . . .

The best way to deal with us is to be realistic and businesslike as one should be dealing with a great country which is conscious of its own worth and that of others as well.

It is just because we know our own worth that we cannot be intimidated. . . . We are not one whit scared by would-be terrifying war dances executed by the same journalists, that new "atom trot" that has taken the place of the fox trot. But neither do we underestimate the danger it presents to peace.

It is because we desire peace that we are optimists. . . . The World War showed that democratic governments can find a common language against aggression. They found it during war. There are no grounds for assuming they cannot find it in time of peace.

The United Nations is far from perfect, but nevertheless it is the instrument with which to fight the enemies of democracy and malevolent aggressors. We want to see that organization grow strong and become a real force. That is why we are opposed to any careless handling of it. It goes without saying that any conspiracy against the Soviet Union threatens the prestige and the very existence of the U.N. . . .

There are some who would like to "interior decorate" all Europe according either to American or British taste. . . . We do not seek to force others to adopt the Soviet style of arranging their home. We prefer to let our neighbors settle their affairs in their own way. But in our own home, we wish to live in peace and quiet, without squabbles and quarreling across the fence. We want to look freely out into the world through our own windows, and like any householder, we want to have the key to our doors in our own pockets. That, as I see it, is basically, what we want.[10]

This article exposes clearly enough the historical legacy of suspicion which motivates much that the Soviet diplomats do. Americans, too, have their deep-seated suspicions and prejudices about Russia. They do not readily follow all the arguments put forward here by Zaslavsky. Unfortunately, history does not completely refute the fears of either side. Only a determined effort to resolve the frictions and to reject the possibility of war can save both our civilization and theirs.

A great American, who in many ways represented what we like to think of as the "typical American," visited the Soviet Union during the war. It was Wendell Willkie, and he said:

I had gone determined to find an answer for myself to the actual problems posed for our generation of Americans by the simple fact that the Soviet Union, whether we like it or not, exists.

Some of the answers I believe I found, at least to my own satisfaction. I can sum up the three most important in a few sentences.

First, Russia is an effective society. It works. It has survival value. The record of Soviet resistance to Hitler has been proof enough of this to most of us, but I must admit in all frankness that I was not prepared to believe before I went to Russia what I now know about its strength as a going organization of men and women.

Second, Russia is our ally in this war. The Russians, more sorely tested by Hitler's might even than the British, have met the test magnificently. Their hatred of Fascism and the Nazi system is real and deep and bitter. And this hatred makes them determined to eliminate Hitler and exterminate the Nazi blight from Europe and the world.

Third, we must work with Russia after the war. At least it seems to me that there can be no continued peace unless we learn to do so.[11]

SOURCES AND REFERENCES

CHAPTER I

[1] Patrick, George Z., *Popular Poetry in Soviet Russia*, University of California Press, 1929, p. 47.

[2] Turgenev, Ivan, *Dream Tales and Prose Poems*, translated from the Russian by Constance Garnett, William Heinemann, London, 1916, p. 242.

[3] Gorky, Maxim, *In the World*, translated by Mrs. Gertude M. Foakes, the Century Company, New York, 1919, p. 64-65 and 72.

[4] Gogol, Nikolai, *Taras Bulba and Other Tales*, Everyman's Library, E. P. Dutton, New York, pp. 19-20.

CHAPTER II

[1] Wiener, Leo, *Anthology of Russian Literature*, G. P. Putnam's Sons, New York, Vol. I, p. 84.

[2] *Ibid.*, Vol. I, pp. 66-67.

[3] *Ibid.*, Vol. I, p. 67.

[4] *Ibid.*, Vol. I, p. 118.

[5] *Ibid.*, Vol. I, p. 125.

[6] *Ibid.*, Vol. I, pp. 173-174.

[7] *Ibid.*, Vol. I, pp. 132-133.

[8] *Ibid.*, Vol. I, p. 134.

[9] *Ibid.*, Vol. I, pp. 186-187.

[10] Pares, Bernard, *History of Russia*, Jonathan Cape, London, 1926, p. 160.

CHAPTER III

[1] Turgenev, Ivan, *Smoke*, translated from the Russian by Isabel F. Hapgood, Charles Scribner's Sons, New York, 1907, p. 95.

[2] Turgenev, Ivan, *Liza*, translated by W. R. S. Ralston, Everyman's Library, New York, pp. 17-18.

[3] Quotations taken from the acting version of Gogol's *Inspector General*, arranged by John Anderson, Samuel French Co., Ltd., London, 1931.

[4] Seltzer, Thomas, editor, *Best Russian Short Stories*, the Modern Library, New York, p. 55.

[5] Gogol, Nikolai, *Dead Souls*, translated by Constance Garnett, Chatto and Windus, London, 1922, and Alfred A. Knopf, New York, pp. 11-12.

[6] Pushkin, Alexander, *The Captain's Daughter*, translated by Natalie Duddington, J. M. Dent & Sons, London, 1928, p. 110.

[7] *Ibid.*, p. 192.

[8] Robinson, G. T., *Rural Russia Under the Old Regime*, Longmans, Green, New York, 1932, p. 33.

[9] Patrick, George Z., *Popular Poetry in Soviet Russia,* p. 7.

[10] *Ibid.,* p. 4.

[11] Dostoievsky, Feodor, *The House of the Dead,* translated from the Russian by Constance Garnett, William Heinemann, London, 1915, pp. 352-353

[12] Turgenev, Ivan, *A Sportsman's Sketches,* translated from the Russian by Constance Garnett, William Heinemann, London, 1917 ed., Vol. I, pp. 38-39.

[13] Dostoievsky, Feodor, *Letters and Reminiscences,* translated from the Russian by S. S. Koteliansky and J. Middleton Murry, Chatto and Windus, London, 1928, and Alfred A. Knopf, New York, pp. 5-6.

CHAPTER IV

[1] *Select Tales of Chekhov* translated by Constance Garnett, Chatto & Windus, London, 1927, pp. 129-130.

[2] Chekhov, Anton, *The Kiss and Other Stories,* translated by R. E. C. Long, Frederick A. Stokes Co., New York, 1915, pp. 315-316.

[3] Gorky, Maxim, *My University Days,* Boni and Liveright, New York, 1923, pp. 179-181.

[4] Tolstoy, Leo, *Anna Karenina,* translated by Rochelle S. Townsend, Everyman's Library, E. P. Dutton, New York, Vol. I, pp. 245-247.

[5] Patrick, George Z., *Popular Poetry in Soviet Russia,* p. 10.

[6] *The Plays of Anton Chekhov,* translated by Constance Garnett, Modern Library, New York, p. 90.

[7] *The Stories of Anton Chekhov,* edited by Robert Linscott, the Modern Library, New York, 1932, p. 103.

[8] *Ibid.,* p. 106.

[9] *Ibid.,* pp. 108-109.

[10] Gorky, Maxim, *In the World,* pp. 349-350 and 369-371.

[11] Gorky, Maxim, *My Childhood,* the Century Company, New York, 1915, pp. 267-268.

[12] Turgenev, Ivan, *Virgin Soil,* translated from the Russian by Constance Garnett, William Heinemann, London, 1920, Vol. I, pp. 181-182.

[13] Turgenev, Ivan, *Fathers and Children,* translated from the Russian by Isabel F. Hapgood, Charles Scribner's Sons, New York, 1903, pp. 38-39.

[14] Chekhov, Anton, *The Schoolmistress and Other Stories,* translated by Constance Garnett, Macmillan, New York, 1921, p. 166.

[15] *Select Tales of Chekhov,* p. 171.

[16] Chekhov, Anton, *The Schoolmistress and Other Stories,* p. 9.

[17] *Select Tales of Chekhov,* p. 190.

[18] Gorky, Maxim, *My University Days,* pp. 171-172.

[19] Robinson, G. T., *Rural Russia Under the Old Regime,* p. 207.

[20] *Little Lenin Library,* International Publishers, New York, 1930, Vol. IV, pp. 56-57.

[21] *Collected Works of V. I. Lenin,* International Publishers, New York, 1929, Vol. IV, pp. 20-21.

CHAPTER V

[1] Reed, John, *Ten Days That Shook the World*, the Modern Library, New York, pp. 11-16.
[2] Patrick, George Z., *Popular Poetry in Soviet Russia*, pp. 18-20.
[3] *Ibid.*, p. 95.
[4] *Russian Poetry*, chosen and translated by Babette Deutsch and Avraham Yarmolinsky, International Publishers, New York, 1927, pp. 176-185.

CHAPTER VI

[1] Furmanov, Dmitry, *Chapayev*, International Publishers, New York, p. 128.
[2] Graves, William S., *America's Siberian Adventure*, Jonathan Cape & Harrison Smith, New York, 1931, pp. 277-278.
[3] *The Bullitt Mission to Russia*, B. W. Heubsch, New York, 1919, p. 7.
[4] *Ibid.*, p. 21.
[5] Furmanov, Dmitry, *op. cit.*, pp. 188-190.
[6] *Ibid.*, pp. 205-206.
[7] Patrick, George Z., *Popular Poetry in Soviet Russia*, p. 24.
[8] *Ibid.*, p. 25.
[9] *Ibid.*, p. 74.
[10] *Russian Poetry*, chosen and translated by Babette Deutsch and Avraham Yarmolinsky, p. 223.
[11] Patrick, George Z., *op. cit.*, p. 49.
[12] *Ibid.*, p. 122.
[13] Chamberlin, William Henry, *The Russian Revolution*, the Macmillan Company, New York, 1935, Vol. II, pp. 66-67.

CHAPTER VII

[1] Ognynov, N., *The Diary of a Communist Schoolboy*, translated from the Russian by Alexander Werth, Harcourt Brace and Company, New York, 1928, pp. 12-14.
[2] *Ibid.*, p. 17.
[3] Duranty, Walter, in *New York Times*, November 1927.
[4] Duranty, Walter, *Duranty Reports Russia*, published by The Viking Press, New York, copyright 1934, p. 49. (Originally appeared in the *New York Times*.)
[5] Duranty, Walter, in *New York Times*, March 1929.
[6] *The Bullitt Mission to Russia*, pp. 123-124.
[7] Fischer, Louis, *The Soviets in World Affairs*, Jonathan Cape, London, 1930, Vol. II, pp. 692-693.
[8] Zostchenko, Mikhail, *Russia Laughs*, translated from the Russian by Helena Clayton, Lothrop, Lee, and Shepard Company, Boston, 1935, pp. 197-198.

CHAPTER VIII

[1] Data from Chamberlin, William Henry, *Russia's Iron Age*, Little, Brown, Boston, 1934, p. 74.

[2] Duranty, Walter, in *New York Times,* dispatch dated Oct. 10, 1929.

[3] Duranty, Walter, in *New York Times,* dispatch dated Nov. 24, 1932.

[4] Data from Ladejinsky, W., *Collectivization of Agriculture in the Soviet Union,* Academy of Political Science, New York, 1934, p. 211.

[5] From *Summary of the Fulfilment of the First Five-Year Plan,* State Planning Commission U.S.S.R., Moscow, 1933, p. 146.

[6] *Ibid.,* p. 21.

[7] *Ibid.,* p. 201.

[8] From *New York Herald-Tribune,* July 26, 1931.

[9] Duranty, Walter, in *New York Times,* Oct. 16, 1931.

[10] Duranty, Walter, in *New York Times,* Dec. 2, 1931.

[11] From *Summary of the Fulfilment of the First Five-Year Plan,* p. 196.

[12] *Ibid.,* p. 184.

[13] *Ibid.,* p. 236.

[14] *Ibid.,* p. 200.

[15] Data from Duranty, Walter, special article in the *New York Times,* Aug. 28, 1932.

[16] From *New York Herald-Tribune,* July 26, 1931.

[17] From *Summary of the Fulfilment of the First Five-Year Plan,* p. 160.

[18] Duranty, Walter, in the *New York Times,* Mar. 15, 1929.

[19] Data from *Summary of the Fulfilment of the First Five-Year Plan,* p. 209.

[20] *Ibid.,* p. 237.

[21] *Ibid.,* p. 214.

[22] *Ibid.,* pp. 237-238.

CHAPTER IX

[1] Molotov, V. N., *The Plan of Construction and Peace,* International Publishers, New York, p. 24.

[2] *The Land of Socialism Today and Tomorrow* (Report of the 18th Congress of the Communist Party of the Soviet Union, March 1939), Foreign Languages Publishing House, Moscow, 1939, p. 25.

[3] *Constitution of the Union of Soviet Socialist Republics,* American Russian Institute, New York, 1940.

[4] *Izvestia,* March 27, 1946.

[5] *Pravda,* April 5, 1943.

[6] *Constitution of the U.S.S.R., op. cit.,* Article 125.

[7] *New York Herald Tribune,* June 14, 1945.

[8] "Complete Report of the ASNE World Freedom of Information Committee," *Editor and Publisher,* June 18, 1945, p. 22.

[9] Wendell L. Willkie, *One World,* Simon and Schuster, New York, 1943, pp. 28-29.

[10] Webb, Sidney and Beatrice, *Soviet Communism, a New Civilization?*, Longmans, Green and Co., New York, 1935, Vol. I, Chap. V.

[11] *American Review on the Soviet Union*, June 1941, p. 48.

[12] *The Land of Socialism Today and Tomorrow, op. cit.*, p. 21.

[13] *American Review, op. cit.*, p. 49.

[14] Pavlenko, P., *Red Planes Fly East*, International Publishers, New York, 1938, pp. 193-195.

[15] *Ibid.*, p. 203.

[16] Davies, Joseph E., *Mission to Moscow*, Simon and Schuster, New York, 1941, pp. 570-571.

[17] *The Land of Socialism Today and Tomorrow, op. cit.*, p. 418.

CHAPTER X

[1] Voroshilov, K. E., *Stati i Rechi*, Moscow, 1937, p. 210.

[2] Interview given by J. Stalin to Roy W. Howard, March 1, 1936, *The Soviet Union and the Cause of Peace*, International Publishers, New York, 1936, p. 35-36.

[3] Litvinov, M., *Against Aggression* (Speech of September 21, 1938 to the League of Nations Assembly), International Publishers, New York, 1939, p. 127-131.

[4] Harper, Samuel N., *The Russia I Believe In*, University of Chicago Press, Chicago, 1943, p. 278.

[5] Voznesensky, N., *The Growing Prosperity of the Soviet Union* (Report of the Chairman of the State Planning Commission, February 18, 1941), Workers Library Publishers, New York, 1941, p. 7.

CHAPTER XI

[1] *New York Herald Tribune*, June 23, 1941.

[2] *Soviet War Documents*, Embassy of the U.S.S.R., Washington, D. C., 1943, pp. 5-6.

[3] Werth, Alexander, *Leningrad*, Alfred A. Knopf, New York, 1944, p. 87.

[4] Voyetekhov, Boris, *The Last Days of Sevastopol*, Alfred A. Knopf, New York, 1943, pp. 214-215.

[5] Perventsev, Arkady, *The Ordeal*, Harper and Brothers, New York, 1944, pp. 162-164, 170-171.

[6] *The Great Stalin Five-Year Plan*, Embassy of the U.S.S.R., Washington, D. C., June 1946, p. 3.

[7] "Russian Reconstruction," *The Economist*, March 24, 1945.

[8] "Statement of Extraordinary State Committee," *Information Bulletin*, Embassy of the U.S.S.R., Washington, D. C., October 11, 1945.

[9] *The Great Stalin Five-Year Plan, op. cit., passim.*

[10] "A Russian States Russia's Case," by David Zaslavsky, *New York Times Magazine*, April 14, 1946.

[11] *One World, op. cit.*, p. 23.

OTHER BOOKS TO READ ABOUT RUSSIA

GENERAL

Cressey, George B. *The Basis of Soviet Strength.* McGraw-Hill: New York, 1945. 287 pp. $3.00.
The most up-to-date authoritative survey of industry, agriculture, climate, regional characteristics and nationalities.

Encyclopedia Americana, Volume 27: Union of Soviet Socialist Republics.
To be published by Cornell University Press. Encyclopedia Americana: New York, 1946. 169 pp. Contains a new and comprehensive section of some 170,000 words on the U.S.S.R., under the headings Geography, Political Science, Social Sciences, Social Institutions, and Humanities. The twenty-eight articles in this section constitute a practical handbook on the Soviet Union.

Mandel, William. *A Guide to the Soviet Union.* The Dial Press: New York, 1946. 511 pp. $5.00.
An over-all survey of all aspects of Soviet development, including material on the war and postwar plans.

Webb, Beatrice and Sydney. *Soviet Communism: A New Civilization.* Longmans, Green: New York, 1935. 2 vols., 1,174 pp. $7.50.
Written before the 1936 constitution, this work still remains the most thorough and detailed analysis of the Soviet Union.

Williams, Albert R. *The Russians: The Land, the People and Why They Fight.* Harcourt, Brace: New York, 1943. 248 pp. $2.00.
A very readable book, giving much detailed information on wartime developments, and the first attempt at a general reference book on the Soviet Union since the author's *The Soviets,* published in 1937. For those with limited

reading time this book will serve as a good introduction
to the subject.

ARTS

Chen, Jack. *Soviet Art and Artists.* Pilot Press, Transatlantic
Arts: New York, 1944. 106 pp., ill. $1.85.
A brief but full account of the many schools of painting
in the Soviet Union and the best exponents of Russian art.

Houghton, Norris. *Moscow Rehearsals.* Harcourt, Brace: New
York, 1936. 291 pp. $2.75.
The author, an American producer, analyzes in detail the
aesthetic organization of the Soviet theater in an attempt
to understand the technique of its creative efforts. Invaluable for the student of the stage.

Kaun, Alexander. *Soviet Poets and Poetry.* University of California Press: Los Angeles, 1943. 208 pp. $2.50.
An essay dealing with the various literary movements and
their theories, liberally illustrated by translations of the
leading poets.

London, Kurt. *Seven Soviet Arts.* Yale University Press: New
Haven, 1937. 365 pp. $4.00.
A careful account of the organization of the arts in the
Soviet Union and the relationship between the govern-
ments and culture.

Simmons, Ernest J. *An Outline of Modern Russian Literature
(1880-1940).* Cornell University Press: Ithaca, New York,
1943. 93 pp. $.90.
A brief guide to the principal writers and works of modern Russian literature.

Struve, Gleb. *Twenty-five Years of Soviet Russian Literature
(1918-1943).* George Routledge: London, 1946. 347 pp.
$5.75.
A survey and critical appraisal of the major writings published in the Soviet Union.

ECONOMY

Baykov, Alexander. *The Development of the Soviet Economic
System: An Essay on the Experience of Planning in the*

U.S.S.R. Cambridge University Press: London, 1946. 514 pp. $6.50. (Distributed in the United States by the Macmillan Company.)
A historical review and description of the present-day economic system in the Soviet Union. A book for study of the subject.

Dobb, Maurice. *Soviet Planning and Labor in Peace and War.* International Publishers: New York, 1943. 124 pp. $1.00.
A careful explanation of the Soviet economic system by a British economist.

EDUCATION

King, Beatrice. *Changing Man: The Education System of the U.S.S.R.* Viking Press: New York, 1937. 319 pp. $2.75.
A comprehensive study of the Soviet educational system and administration. Discusses preschool education and primary and secondary school systems in detail, with curricula, etc.

FOREIGN POLICY AND FOREIGN RELATIONS

Baykov, Alexander. *Soviet Foreign Trade.* Princeton University Press: Princeton, 1946. 126 pp. $2.00.
A study of the operation of the Soviet foreign trade monopoly, including statistical data.

Dulles, Foster Rhea. *The Road to Teheran: The Story of Russia and America.* Princeton University Press: Princeton, 1944. 279 pp. $2.50.
The relations between the people of the United States and the people of Russia from the early days of American independence to those of the common association of the two nations in the world struggle against Nazi Germany.

Yakhontoff, Victor A. *U.S.S.R. Foreign Policy.* Coward-McCann: New York, 1945. 311 pp. $3.50.
A review of the Soviet Union's foreign policy since its beginning, based on official documents.

GOVERNMENT

Harper, Samuel N. *The Government of the Soviet Union.* Van Nostrand: New York, 1938. 204 pp. $1.75. Revised edition now being prepared.
A textbook for American universities. Contains sections on the historical development of government in Russia and the U.S.S.R.; structure of government; determination of policy; the state and the individual; the Soviet Union and the world.

HISTORY

Duranty, Walter. *Duranty Reports Russia.* Viking Press: New York, 1934. 401 pp. $2.75.
A compilation of his news reports. Good especially for the early years of the Soviet Union.

Duranty, Walter. *U.S.S.R.: The Story of Soviet Russia.* Lippincott: Philadelphia, 1944. 293 pp. $3.00.
An informal history by one who lived many years in the Soviet Union.

History of the Communist Party of the Soviet Union. International Publishers: New York, 1939. 364 pp. $1.00.
Official Communist party publication. Covers the period from 1883 to 1937, with special reference to the history of the Communist party.

Martin, John Stuart, Ed. *A Picture History of Russia.* Crown Publishers: New York, 1945. 376 pp. $3.75.
An account of the Russian people from earliest times to the present with 1,200 illustrations obtained from archives and museums, with chronology and index.

Pares, Bernard. *A History of Russia.* Alfred A. Knopf: New York, 1944. 575 pp. $4.75.
The most complete and detailed history of Russia available in English.

LAND AND THE PEOPLE

Buck, Pearl S. *Talk about Russia with Masha Scott.* John Day: New York, 1945. 128 pp. $1.75.

The human story of life in the Soviet Union as told by
Masha Scott, the Russian wife of an American correspondent.

Lamont, Corliss. *The People of the Soviet Union.* Harcourt,
Brace: New York, 1946. 229 pp. $3.00.
A vivid and factual description of the almost two hundred
million peoples of the Soviet Union and of the unique
Soviet policy concerning minorities.

Strong, A. L. *Peoples of the U.S.S.R.* Macmillan: New York,
1944. 245 pp. $2.50.
The story of the sixteen Soviet republics, vividly told by
one who has traveled in most of them.

RELIGION

Casey, Robert P. *Religion in Russia.* Harper and Bros.: New
York, 1946. 198 pp. $2.00.
An objective account of the history and prospects of reli-
gion in Russia.

SCIENCE AND PUBLIC HEALTH

National Council of American-Soviet Friendship. *Science in
Soviet Russia.* Jacques Cattell Press: Lancaster, Pa., 1944.
97 pp. $1.50.
Papers presented by prominent American scientists at the
science panel of the Congress of American-Soviet Friendship, 1943, dealing with Soviet science and technology and
with public health and wartime medicine in the U.S.S.R.

Sigerist, Henry E. *Socialized Medicine in the Soviet Union.*
W. W. Norton: New York, 1937. 378 pp. $3.50.
A full account of the public health system.

BIOGRAPHY

The Letters of Lenin. Translated and edited by Elizabeth Hill
and Doris Mudie. Harcourt, Brace: New York, 1937. 500
pp. $4.00.
Covering the period 1895-1922, these letters give a lively
account of Lenin's eventful life in exile and in power.

Pope, Arthur U. *Maxim Litvinoff*. L. B. Fischer: New York, 1943. 544 pp. $3.50.
An account of the work of the Soviet Union's leading diplomat in prewar years.

A SELECTED LIST OF SOVIET LITERATURE

Cournos, John, Ed. *A Treasury of Russian Life and Humor*. Coward-McCann: New York, 1943. 670 pp. $4.50.
Dana, H. W. L. *Seven Soviet Plays*. Macmillan: New York, 1946. 520 pp. $3.00.
Includes the most popular war plays.
Gorky, Maxim. *Seven Plays of Maxim Gorky*. Yale University Press: New Haven, 1945. 396 pp. $3.75.
Guerney, Bernard G. *A Treasury of Russian Literature*. Vanguard Press: New York, 1943. 1048 pp. $4.50.
Reavey, George, and Slonim, Marc, Eds. *Soviet Literature: An Anthology*. Covici-Friede: New York, 1934. 426 pp. $2.50.

MAPS

American Russian Institute. *Wall Map of the U.S.S.R.* American Russian Institute: New York, 1943. 28″ x 44″ in color. $.50.
Highly recommended for classroom use because it contains the most important place names and chief industrial areas of the Soviet Union, with boundaries as of June 1941.
Goodall, George, Ed. *Soviet Russia in Maps*. Denoyer-Geppert: Chicago, 1942. 32 pp. $1.00.
A very fine collection of economic and political maps, based on *The Great Soviet World Atlas*.
Grosvenor, Gilbert, Ed. *Map of the Union of Soviet Socialist Republics*. National Geographic Magazine: Washington, D. C. 1944. $.50.
Most detailed place-names map available in English with international boundaries according to Russian treaties and claims as of October 1, 1944.

ACKNOWLEDGMENTS

THIS book was first published ten years ago in a shorter edition by the American Council of the Institute of Pacific Relations as a part of its *Peoples of the Pacific Series*. In response to a demand, particularly from teachers and librarians, for a new edition covering the war and postwar periods, it has now been revised and expanded by Harriet L. Moore.

I wish here to express my gratitude not only to Miss Moore but to the many individuals and organizations which have helped in the preparation of the early edition as well as the revised one. I am particularly indebted to the Honolulu Institute of Pacific Relations, the Kamehameha and Punahou Schools and the Department of Public Instruction of Honolulu, which sponsored the *Peoples of the Pacific Series* and gave me continued support and assistance throughout the period of its preparation.

For particular help in the preparation of this book, I also gratefully acknowledge the invaluable assistance given by Kathleen Barnes of the staff of the American Council of the Institute of Pacific Relations. I wish, likewise, to express my appreciation to Dr. G. T. Robinson of Columbia University, who read and criticized the manuscript, and to Mr. Joseph Barnes of the staff of the *New York Herald Tribune*, who made stimulating criticisms while the work was in progress.

I also wish here to thank the following publishers who have permitted me to quote from their publications:

D. Appleton-Century Company, New York; Jonathan Cape, Ltd., London; Chatto and Windus, London; Duckworth and Company, London; E. P. Dutton and Company, Inc., New York; Samuel French, New York; Harper and Brothers, New York; Harcourt, Brace and Company, New York; William Heinemann, Ltd., London; International Publishers Company, New York; Alfred A. Knopf, New York; Liveright Publishing Company, New York; Longmans Green and Company, New York; Lothrop, Lee and Shepard Company, Boston; The Macmillan Company, New York; The Modern Library, New York; *The New York Herald Tribune*, New York; *The New York Times*, New York; G. P. Putnam's Sons, New York; Simon and Schuster, New York; Charles Scribner's Sons, New York; Peter Smith, New York; University of California Press, Berkeley; University of Chicago Press, Chicago; The Viking Press, Inc., New York.

HELEN GAY PRATT

INDEX